Transatlantic Homeland Security

Europe and the United States have reacted differently to the emergence of catastrophic terrorism and occasionally squabbled over how to deal with this new threat. Yet an effective response to a transnational problem has to be international. The premise of *Transatlantic Homeland Security* is that the ultimate effectiveness of efforts to prevent and protect against large-scale terrorism will be contingent on the ability of the US and its European partners to overcome their differences and cooperate closely.

This book explains the concept of homeland security and the international requirements of success within areas such as:

- efforts against nuclear and biological terrorism
- protection of critical infrastructure
- defence against cyber-terrorism
- border and transportation security
- law enforcement efforts.

Moreover, it discusses how to integrate intelligence in the homeland security effort while protecting civil liberties and the right to privacy.

Transatlantic Homeland Security attempts to provide conceptual and practical guidance to analysts, policymakers, and practitioners at a crucial time when homeland security efforts should move beyond a still dominantly domestic focus. This book is essential reading for those with professional and research interests in security policy, counterterrorism, and international relations.

Anja Dalgaard-Nielsen is Senior Fellow at the Danish Institute for International Studies and Non-Resident Fellow at the Center for Transatlantic Relations at the Paul H. Nitze School of Advanced International Studies (SAIS), Johns Hopkins University. **Daniel S. Hamilton** is Richard von Weizsaecker Professor and Director of the Center for Transatlantic Relations at the Paul H. Nitze School of Advanced International Studies (SAIS), Johns Hopkins University; and Executive Director of the American Consortium on EU Studies (ACES).

Transatlantic Homeland Security

Protecting society in the age of catastrophic terrorism

Edited by
Anja Dalgaard-Nielsen and
Daniel S. Hamilton

Routledge
Taylor & Francis Group

LONDON AND NEW YORK

First published 2006
by Routledge
2 Park Square, Milton Park, Abingdon, Oxon OX14 4RN

Simultaneously published in the USA and Canada
by Routledge
270 Madison Ave, New York, NY 10016

Routledge is an imprint of the Taylor & Francis Group

© 2006 Selection and editorial matter, Anja Dalgaard-Nielsen and
Daniel S. Hamilton; individual chapters, the contributors

Typeset in Garamond by Wearset Ltd, Boldon, Tyne and Wear
Printed and bound in Great Britain by MPG Books Ltd, Bodmin

British Library Cataloguing in Publication Data
A catalogue record for this book is available from the British Library

Library of Congress Cataloging in Publication Data
A catalog record for this book has been requested

ISBN 0–415–36032–3

Contents

Notes on contributors

Morten Bremer Maerli is a researcher at the Norwegian Institute of International Affairs. He works on nuclear non-proliferation and prevention of nuclear terrorism. Dr. Bremer Maerli is a physicist by training, and has had both practical and research experience in the fields of nuclear safety and security. From 1995 to 1999 he worked at the Norwegian Radiation Protection Authority, with control and protection of nuclear materials as his prime responsibility. Through his work he has gained regional knowledge and extensive experience of the practices concerning the handling, storing and security of nuclear materials in Northwest Russia. He has served as a technical consultant to the Norwegian Ministry of Foreign Affairs, for example at the Conference on Disarmament, at the 2000 Review Conference, and also on the 2002 Preparatory Committee of the Treaty on the Non-Proliferation of Nuclear Weapons. During the 1999/2000 academic year, Bremer Maerli was a Fulbright Science Fellow at the Center for International Security (CISAC) at Stanford University. The subsequent year he was a Visiting Research Scholar at Sandia National Laboratories, California. Dr. Bremer Maerli is a member of the Norwegian Pugwash Committee and of the International Network of Engineers and Scientists Against Proliferation (INESAP).

Esther Brimmer is Deputy Director and Director of Research at the Center for Transatlantic Relations at the Paul H. Nitze School of Advanced International Studies (SAIS) at The Johns Hopkins University. Dr. Brimmer has served in the United States government and in international affairs think tanks. From 1999 to 2001 she was a Member of the Office of Policy Planning at the US Department of State, working on the European Union, Western Europe, the UN, and multilateral security issues. She also served on the United States delegation to the United Nations Commission on Human Rights in spring 2000. From 1995 to 1999 she managed projects as a Senior Associate at the Carnegie Commission on Preventing Deadly Conflict. From 1993 to 1995 she served as a Special Assistant to the Under Secretary of State for Political Affairs working on UN, peacekeeping, human rights and political–military issues. Her publications include *The United States, the European Union and International Human Rights Issues*. Dr. Brimmer received her PhD and MA in international relations from the University of Oxford, and her BA in international relations from Pomona College in Claremont, California. She is a member of the Council on Foreign Relations and Women in International Security.

Anja Dalgaard-Nielsen is a Senior Fellow at the Danish Institute for International Studies (DIIS), Non-Resident Fellow at the Center for Transatlantic Relations at the Paul H. Nitze School of Advanced International Studies (SAIS), Johns Hopkins University, and lecturer at Denmark's International Study Program, University of Copenhagen. Dr. Dalgaard-Nielsen has previously worked as Washington Analyst and Coordinator for the Aspen Institute Berlin. She holds a PhD and MA from the Paul H. Nitze School of Advanced International Studies (SAIS), Johns Hopkins University, a BA/MA in Political Science from the University of Aarhus, and has done graduate work at the Ruprecht-Karls Universität, Heidelberg, and Universitá di Bologna. She has published on topics including counterterrorism, homeland security, European security and defense policy, and German security policy, and is a frequent commentator in the Danish printed and electronic media.

Daniel S. Hamilton is Richard von Weizsaecker Professor and Director of the Center for Transatlantic Relations at the Paul H. Nitze School of Advanced International Studies (SAIS), Johns Hopkins University, and Executive Director of the American Consortium on EU Studies (ACES). He is the publisher of the bimonthly magazine *Transatlantic: Europe, America & the World*, and Principal Advisor to the Congressional Caucus on the European Union. Dr. Hamilton was the co-leader of *Atlantic Storm*, a table-top bio-terrorism exercise mimicking a transatlantic summit of presidents and prime ministers from Europe and North America who must respond to a bio-terrorist attack. He is the US Chair of the Euro-Atlantic Strategy Group for the 46-nation Partnership for Peace Defense Academies Consortium, and is a board member of various transatlantic NGOs and foundations. He has served as Deputy Assistant Secretary of State for European Affairs, Associate Director of the Policy Planning Staff for Secretaries of State Madeleine Albright and Warren Christopher, Policy Advisor to Assistant Secretary of State for European Affairs Richard Holbrooke, Senior Policy Advisor to Ambassador Holbrooke and the US Embassy in Germany, US Special Coordinator for Northern Europe, and US Special Coordinator for Southeast European Stabilization. Dr. Hamilton has a PhD and MA from the Johns Hopkins School of Advanced International Studies. He received his BSFS from Georgetown University's School of Foreign Service. He has authored or edited many published works, including *The New Frontiers of Europe* (2005); *Transatlantic Transformations: Equipping NATO for the 21st Century* (2004); *Part-*

ners in Prosperity: The Changing Landscape of the Transatlantic Economy (2004); and *Conflict and Cooperation in Transatlantic Relations* (2004)

Brian M. Jenkins is Senior Advisor to the President of the RAND Corporation, and one of the world's leading authorities on terrorism. He founded the RAND Corporation's terrorism research program 30 years ago, has written frequently on terrorism, and has served as an advisor to the federal government and the private sector on the subject. Brian Jenkins is a former Army captain who served with the Special Forces in Vietnam, and also a former Deputy Chairman of Kroll Associates. He served as a captain in the Green Berets in the Dominican Republic and later in Vietnam (1966–1970). In 1996, Mr Jenkins was appointed by President Bill Clinton to be a member of the White House Commission on Aviation Safety and Security. He also served as an advisor to the National Commission on Terrorism (1999–2000) and in 2000 was appointed as a member of the US Comptroller General's Advisory Board. Mr Jenkins is also a special advisor to the International Chamber of Commerce (ICC) and a member of the board of directors of the ICC's Commercial Crime Services. He has authored and co-authored numerous books, including *International Terrorism: A New Mode of Conflict*; *Terrorism and Personal Protection*; *Aviation Terrorism and Security*; and *The Fall of South Vietnam*.

Rey Koslowski is Associate Professor of Political Science at Rutgers University – Newark. At Rutgers, he also serves as Political Science Graduate Program Director and Director of the Center for Global Change and Governance Research Program on Border Control and Homeland Security. He recently held a fellowship at the Woodrow Wilson International Center for Scholars, where he worked on a project entitled "International Migration, Border Control and Homeland Security in the Information Age." Rey Koslowski has also held fellowships at the Center of International Studies at Princeton University, and the Center for German and European Studies at Georgetown University's School of Foreign Service. He is the author of *Migrants and Citizens: Demographic Change in the European States System* (Cornell University Press, 2000); co-editor (with David Kyle) of *Global Human Smuggling: Comparative Perspectives* (Johns Hopkins University Press, 2001), and editor of *International Migration and the Globalization of Domestic Politics* (Routledge, forthcoming). His articles have appeared in *International Organization, International Studies Quarterly, The Journal of Common Market Studies, The Journal of European Public Policy, The Journal of Ethnic and Migration Studies, The Cambridge Journal of International Studies*, and *The Brown Journal of World Affairs*.

James A. Lewis is a Senior Fellow and Director of the Technology and Public Policy program at the Center for Strategic and International Studies. Before coming to CSIS, Lewis was a career diplomat who worked on national security issues. Dr. Lewis's diplomatic experience includes the

Cambodia Peace Process, and the Five Power Talks on Arms Transfer Restraint. Lewis led the US delegation to the Wassenaar Arrangement Experts Group for advanced civil and military technology. He was assigned as a political advisor to the US Central Command for Operation Desert Shield and Operation Just Cause, and to the Central American Task Force. Dr. Lewis was responsible for drafting the 1999 and 2000 regulations that liberalized US encryption controls. His publications include *Strengthening Law Enforcement Capabilities for Counter-Terrorism* (December 2001); *Assessing the Risk of Cyber Terrorism, Cyber War and Other Cyber Threats* (December 2002), and *Cyber Security: Turning National Solutions into International Cooperation* (May 2003), and *Globalization and National Security* (November 2004). Forthcoming works include *Aux Armes, Citoyens: Cyber Security and Regulation in the United States*. His current research involves digital identity; innovation and national security; and China's information technology industry. He received his PhD from the University of Chicago in 1984.

Bradley T. Smith, a molecular biologist and policy analyst, is a Fellow at the Center for Biosecurity of UPMC, and an Assistant Professor at the University of Pittsburgh School of Medicine. Dr. Smith joined the Center for Biosecurity at its founding on 1 November 2003. Prior to this, he was a Fellow at the Johns Hopkins University Center for Civilian Biodefense Strategies and an Assistant Scientist at the Johns Hopkins Bloomberg School of Public Health. Dr. Smith's efforts at the Center for Biosecurity focus on promoting a strategic biodefense R&D program for the United States, facilitating an effective interface between the biomedical research and national security communities, as well as strengthening collaborative international bio-terrorism preparedness efforts. Dr. Smith was the Project Director for *Atlantic Storm*, a table-top bioterrorism exercise mimicking a transatlantic summit of presidents and prime ministers from Europe and North America who must respond to a bio-terrorist attack. Dr. Smith is an Associate Editor of *Biosecurity and Bioterrorism: The Journal of Biodefense Strategy, Science, and Practice*. Dr. Smith has extensive hands-on laboratory experience with bacteria and with the tools of molecular biology that are used in genetic engineering. After graduating *magna cum laude* from Williams College with highest honors in Biology, Dr. Smith joined the Biology Department at the Massachusetts Institute of Technology. At MIT, he worked with Professors Graham Walker and Alan Grossman to study mechanisms of DNA repair, DNA mutagenesis, and DNA damage tolerance in the bacteria *Escherichia coli* and *Bacillus subtilis*. In 2001, Dr. Smith graduated from MIT with a PhD in Biology. Dr. Smith has published a series of papers and reviews on biodefense as well as on bacterial DNA repair. He is a member of the American Society for Microbiology, the American Society for the Advancement of Science, Sigma Xi, and Phi Beta Kappa.

Jonathan M. Winer, a partner in the law firm of Alston & Bird in Washington, DC, is the former US Deputy Assistant Secretary of State for International Law Enforcement. During the Clinton Administration, Mr Winer was one of the architects of US international policy and strategies in financial services regulation and enforcement. He led US negotiations on these and related issues with the European Union, G8, and UN, and bilaterally with many countries. Previously, Winer served for ten years as Chief Counsel and principal legislative assistant to Senator John F. Kerry, where he conducted a series of Congressional investigations, including the US Senate's investigation of the Bank of Credit and Commerce International. Jonathan serves as a Member of the Council on Foreign Relations Task Force on Terrorist Financing, and the Steering Committee of the Transnational Threats Initiative of the Center for Strategic and International Studies (CSIS). Recent publications include "The finance of illicit resource extraction," in *Natural Resources and Violent Conflict* (The World Bank, 2003) and "Applying anti-money laundering standards to conflict commodities," in *Economic Agendas in Civil Wars* (UN International Academy of Peace, June 2003).

Foreword

Homeland security – the new security challenge

Effective approaches to the major political challenges of our era require transatlantic cooperation.

Global challenges like trade liberalization, poverty reduction, and non-proliferation of weapons of mass destruction (WMD) can best be handled through cooperation between Europe and the US. The same is true when it comes to homeland security in the age of catastrophic terrorism. Homeland security is a transatlantic concern, since it is clear that we are facing a common threat in Europe and the United States.

The tragic background is known to all. Almost 3,000 people lost their lives on 11 September 2001. The horrific terror attacks on New York and Washington DC changed international and national politics. It changed the way we look at our own security. Subsequent differences between Europeans and Americans in the perception of the challenge have been lessened by events on this side of the Atlantic Ocean, most notably the attacks in Istanbul in November 2003, and in Madrid on 11 March 2004.

There are no safe havens. There can be no separate peace with terrorists.

We in Europe have participated in the international campaign against terror. For many years now, we have been actively engaged "out of area" in the traditional NATO sense. Through development assistance and the combat against poverty, we are attacking root causes of terrorism. But we also have to prepare ourselves at home. While continuing our daily lives, we have to prepare for the worst. That is the challenge of homeland security.

Within a surprisingly short time span after September 11 the countries of the European Union (EU) agreed on a number of quite remarkable steps to counter terrorism through enhanced cooperation on police, intelligence, air safety, controls on financial transactions, civil emergency protection and health security. After 11 March 2004, EU member states solemnly promised to act in solidarity if one of the member states were to suffer a terror attack, or a natural or manmade disaster. In addition, an EU counterterrorism coordinator was appointed.

Thus, important steps have already been taken. But more can be done. Terrorism and extremism have to be countered by forward defense. The challenge of homeland security will therefore also have implications for our armed forces in terms of increased participation in international operations. We should build up European capacities, including airlift and measures against non-conventional threats, and improve our ability to respond by training and streamlining procedures.

However military forces must also contribute to solving domestic anti-terror tasks related to "total defense," which is the way homeland security involving all relevant agencies has traditionally been labeled in the Scandinavian countries.

In sum, improved homeland security in Europe requires close cooperation and coordination between many sectors: military, police, intelligence services, civil emergency workers, fire fighters, and health services. Optimal cooperation and coordination between the various regional, national and international actors and institutions is needed.

National and European measures are important, but in the field of countering terrorism we are dealing with a global problem. The free and democratic nations of the world are facing a common threat. A strong transatlantic relationship is key to handling the big challenges of our modern world, among them homeland security. We share the same fundamental values of democracy, freedom, human rights, and open markets. That is a natural basis for stronger and closer cooperation within homeland security. We need optimal cooperation and coordination between the relevant regional, national and international actors and institutions, and a seamless web between them across the Atlantic Ocean.

I welcome and encourage contacts between Danish and European homeland security institutions, the US Department of Homeland Security, and other relevant US agencies. We have different geographical and institutional conditions as points of departure. Despite these differences, we can learn from each other and will all benefit from enhanced mutual cooperation.

I am confident that this anthology, covering the key areas of homeland security, can help enhance transatlantic cooperation in this field.

Anders Fogh Rasmussen
Prime Minister of Denmark

Preface

The United States and Europe have reacted differently to the emergence of catastrophic terrorism, and occasionally squabbled over how to deal with this new threat. Yet the ultimate effectiveness of efforts to prevent and protect against catastrophic terrorism will be contingent on the ability of the US and its European partners to overcome their differences and cooperate closely. The basic premise of this book is that homeland security requires transatlantic cooperation.

Chapter 1 explains the concept of homeland security and its various components while outlining the different approaches of the US and Europe respectively. Chapters 2 through 6 concentrate on the individual mission areas of homeland security, including efforts against biological and nuclear terrorism, protection of critical infrastructure, defense against cyberterrorism, border and transportation security, and law enforcement efforts. The authors explain the key issues and problems of each area, as well as the divergent threat perceptions and approaches on the two sides of the Atlantic. Chapters 7 and 8 take a broader perspective and discuss how to integrate intelligence in the homeland security effort, and how to protect civil liberties and the right to privacy in an era where security has become a top political priority. The authors show how the US and Europe can learn from each other in most of these areas, despite different traditions and approaches. Chapter 9 sums up the conclusions of the various chapters, and suggests how the two sides of the Atlantic might move forward to improve homeland security in the transatlantic area.

Acknowledgments

We would like to thank our authors for their contributions and the good spirit that energized our collaboration. Although the book is intended to form a whole, each chapter is solely the view of its author(s). Differences of interpretation or opinion remain, and are not homogenized into a consensus. The authors met on various occasions to compare perspectives, but not to form a single opinion. Each author writes in his or her personal capacity; the views expressed are those of the authors and not their institutions. We would also like to thank the German Marshall Fund of the United States, the Defence and Security Studies project of the Danish Institute for International Studies (which is funded by a grant from the Danish Ministry of Defence), and the POBB Program of the Ministry of Foreign Affairs of the Government of the Netherlands for their encouragement and support of our efforts in this field. Thanks also go to our colleagues at the Center for Transatlantic Relations, and the Danish Institute for International Relations. Special thanks go to Sofie Schroeder and Line Selmer Friborg.

Anja Dalgaard-Nielsen
Daniel S. Hamilton

Abbreviations

ACLU	American Civil Liberties Union
ALA	American Libraries Association
ATF	US Treasury Bureau of Alcohol, Tobacco and Firearms
BFV	Bundesamt für Verfassungsschutz – Office for the Protection of the Constitution
BKA	Bundeskriminalamt – Federal Criminal Police Office
BRC	Biological Resource Center
BTS	Border and Transportation Security
BWC	Biological and Toxin Weapons Convention
CAPPS	Computer Assisted Passenger Profiling System
CBP	Customs and Border Protection
CBRN	Chemical, Biological, Radiological and Nuclear
CCS	Civil Contingencies Secretariat
CDC	Centers for Disease Control
CEPOL	European Police College
CERT	Computer Emergency Response Team
CFR-CDF	Collection of Fundamental Rights – Collection Droits Fondamentaux
CFSP	Common Foreign and Security Policy
CIA	Central Intelligence Agency
CIS	Customs Information System
CISAC	Center for International Security and Cooperation
COE	Council of Europe
CSI	Container Security Initiative
CTC	Counter Terrorist Center
CTR	Cooperative Threat Reduction
DEA	Drug Enforcement Administration
DG	Directorate-General
DGSE	Direction Générale de la Sécurité Extérieure
DHS	Department of Homeland Security
DIIS	Danish Institute for International Studies
DOD	Department of Defense
DST	Direction de la Surveillance du Territoire

EADRCC	Euro-Atlantic Disaster Response Coordination Centre
EAPC	Euro-Atlantic Partnership Council
ECDC	European Centre for Disease Prevention and Control
ECHR	European Convention on Human Rights
EEC	European Economic Community
EJN	European Judicial Network
ELO	European Liaison Officer
ENISA	European Network and Information Security Agency
ETS	Council of Europe Treaty Series
EU	European Union
EWRS	Early Warning and Response System
FATF	Financial Action Task Force
FBI	Federal Bureau of Investigation
FIDE	Fichier d'identification des dossiers d'enquêtes douanières
FLETC	Federal Law Enforcement Training Center
FSF	Financial Stability Forum
FTO	Foreign Terrorist Organization
GAO	Government Accounting Office
GRECO	Group of States against Corruption
HEU	Highly Enriched Uranium
IAEA	International Atomic Energy Agency
IC	Integrated Circuit
ICAO	International Civil Aviation Organization
ICC	International Criminal Court
ICE	Immigration and Customs Enforcement
ICGEB	International Center for Genetic Engineering and Biotechnology
ICRC	International Committee of the Red Cross
ID	Identity Card
ILEA	International Law Enforcement Academy
IMO	International Maritime Organization
INS	Immigration and Naturalization Service
IOSCO	International Organization of Securities Commissions
IP	Internet Protocol
IPPAS	International Physical Protection Advisory Service
IRA	Irish Republican Army
IRS	Internal Revenue Service
IT	Information Technology
JHA	Justice and Home Affairs
JTTF	Joint Terrorism Task Force
LEU	Low Enriched Uranium
MEP	Member of the European Parliament
MI5	Military Intelligence-5
MI6	Military Intelligence-6
MLAT	Mutual Legal Assistance in Criminal Matters Treaty

MOU	Memorandum of Understanding
MPC&A	Nuclear Material Protection, Control and Accounting
NAFTA	North American Free Trade Agreement
NATO	North Atlantic Treaty Organization
NCCT	Non-Cooperative Country or Territory
NCIS	National Criminal Intelligence Service
NCS	National Crime Squad
NGO	Non-Governmental Organization
NIH	National Institutes of Health
NPT	Non-Proliferation Treaty
NSABB	National Science Advisory Board for Biosecurity
NUPI	Norwegian Institute of International Affairs
OAS	Organization of American States
OECD	Organization for Economic Cooperation and Development
OFAC	Office of Foreign Assets Control
OIG	Office of the Inspector General
OSCE	Organization for Security and Cooperation in Europe
OTA	Office of Technology Assessment
PAC	Programme of Action against Corruption
PDD	Presidential Decision Directive
PNR	Passenger Name Record
PSI	Proliferation Security Initiative
RF	Radio Frequency
RFID	Radio Frequency Identification
SARS	Severe Acute Respiratory Syndrome
SECI	Southeast European Cooperation Initiative
SIS	Schengen Information System
SIS	Secret Intelligence Service
SISDE	Servizio per le Informazioni e la Sicurezza Democratica
SISMI	Servizio per le Informazioni e la Sicurezza Militare
SitCen	Joint Situation Center
SORT	Strategic Offensive Reductions Treaty
TECS	Treasury Enforcement Communication System
TIGR	Institute for Genomic Research
TSA	Transportation and Security Administration
T-TIC	Terrorist Threat Integration Center
UN	United Nations
USCIS	US Citizenship and Immigration Services
US-VISIT	US Visitor and Immigrant Status Indicator Technology
VWP	Visa Waiver Program
WCO	World Customs Organization
WHO	World Health Organization
WMD	Weapons of Mass Destruction
WME	Weapons of Mass Effect
WTO	World Trade Organization

1   Transatlantic homeland security

Why, what, and how?

Anja Dalgaard-Nielsen

How do we prevent another September 11? How do we protect open, democratic, interdependent societies with long, porous borderlines, millions of foreign visitors, and large volumes of goods, services and capital flowing in and out every year? Where do we concentrate our efforts when everything is a potential target, and numerous objects ranging from aircraft to germs can be used as weapons? How do we deal with elusive enemies who may operate anonymously within our own societies and enjoy the tactical advantage of choosing the time and place of a strike?

These were the burning questions that leapt to the top of the US political agenda in the wake of the terrorist attacks on New York and Washington DC on 11 September 2001. Exactly two-and-a-half years later the urgency of these questions was brought home to European policymakers as well, when concerted terrorist attacks against commuter trains in Madrid caused the greatest number of deaths (due to terrorism) in Europe since the bombing of Pan Am 103 over Lockerbie in 1988.

If anything, the emergence of catastrophic terrorism should have reminded the US and Europe of their common values and shared vulnerabilities. But despite the vast outpouring of European public solidarity with the United States in the wake of September 11, differences over the appropriateness of a military response to international terrorism, the legitimacy of preemptive strikes, and the Bush Administration's approach to Iraq roiled relations within Europe and between Europe and the United States.

While these disagreements received much attention, another transatlantic divergence went largely unnoticed: the difference in how the US and the countries of the European Union reacted to terrorism on the home front.

Following the September 11 attacks, a new policy area – homeland security – comprising intelligence, justice and law enforcement, border and transportation security, infrastructure protection, counter-CBRN[1] measures, detection, early warning, anti-terrorism research, and emergency preparedness and response took shape within the US. The initial EU response, in contrast, was concentrated in the area of justice and law enforcement. Vulnerability reduction and protection against catastrophic terrorism were granted relatively low priority.

Whereas transatlantic cooperation in the area of intelligence and law enforcement has moved forward, there is a lack of coordination of various initiatives to enhance border and transportation security, and to protect critical infrastructure and civil populations against new catastrophic threats. In other words, there has been no systematic transatlantic effort to advance coordinated or complementary homeland security initiatives.

The premise of this book is that the ultimate effectiveness of efforts to improve domestic security on each side of the Atlantic will be contingent on the ability of the US and its European partners to overcome their differences and cooperate closely. This opening chapter provides a brief introduction to the concept of homeland security, outlines the different domestic responses to September 11 in the US and Europe respectively, and makes the case for a common homeland security effort.

What is homeland security?

Homeland security is defined in the US *National Strategy for Homeland Security* as "a concerted national effort to prevent terrorist attacks within the US, reduce America's vulnerability to terrorism, and minimize the damage and recover from attacks that do occur."[2]

Homeland security is an amorphous and complex policy field. As elaborated in the following sections, it involves a host of different actors on either side of the Atlantic and covers a variety of sectors and professions. It pertains to foreign as well as homegrown threats to the civil population, government institutions, and critical infrastructure of a given society, and spans initiatives and measures in numerous different policy areas.

Homeland security does not make for a comprehensive strategy against terrorism – far from it. Such a strategy would comprise many preventive efforts as well as international action, which lie beyond homeland security. Among the elements of a comprehensive strategy would be efforts against radicalization, both within and outside Western societies; intelligence and law enforcement efforts targeting terrorist leaders, sponsors and operatives abroad; diplomatic and military pressure on state sponsors; counter-proliferation policies; public diplomacy etc. A comprehensive strategy would draw on the whole gamut of national policy instruments, spanning diplomatic, judicial, economic, cultural, and military means.[3]

Homeland security is about adding an extra layer of protection against large-scale terrorism when other instruments fail, as they will from time to time. It is but one element in a grand strategy against terrorism, yet an important one in an era where increasingly ruthless attacks on increasingly complex and interdependent societies can cause massive destruction.

At the same time, however, homeland security is more than simply an element of a grand strategy against terrorism. Many of the measures to protect critical infrastructure and enhance the resilience of civil society are equally useful against other risks and problems, such as accidents, natural disasters or epidemics. Increasingly, and rightly so, homeland security is seen through an all-hazard lens on both sides of the Atlantic and thus as a means to enhance the safety and security of modern society in general, not just vis-à-vis terrorism.[4]

America's domestic response to September 11

The US was not unacquainted with terrorism when the September 11 hijackers caused the most deadly terrorist incident in history. In 1993 a failed attack on the World Trade Center caused six deaths and injured more than a thousand, and in 1995 a massive car bomb reduced the federal offices in Oklahoma City to rubble.

Though a limited expert community had been debating the issue of societal vulnerabilities and asymmetrical threats for about a decade at the time of the attacks, and even though during the Cold War US territory could have been obliterated in a matter of seconds by Soviet nuclear weapons, the popular illusion of a secure homeland was only discarded on September 11. The magnitude of these attacks, combined with the anthrax letters that terrorized the US East Coast in the months that followed, forced policymakers to look at the problem of terrorism and societal vulnerabilities as an immediate rather than a distant or theoretical concern. Threat scenarios which in earlier times had been passed off as science fiction suddenly appeared quite real and urgent. The question of how to prevent another September 11 – or an even worse event entailing the use of weapons of mass destruction – was placed at the top of the national agenda.[5]

The immediate response was a torrent of stop-gap measures aimed at plugging the most glaring gaps in airport and border security. Different agencies and different levels of government each acted within their respective fields of competence, giving the overall response a rather inchoate character. A White House Office of Homeland Security was established to provide central guidance, and in the summer of 2002 the first attempt at formulating an overall plan – the *National Strategy for Homeland Security* – was released.[6]

The Strategy called for upgraded and tightly integrated efforts in six so-called critical mission areas – intelligence and warning, border and transportation security, domestic counter-terrorism and law enforcement, protection of critical infrastructure, protection against CBRN threats, and emergency preparedness and response (see Table 1.1).[7]

A variety of preventive and protective measures within the six mission areas are currently in implementation and, taken together, might be conceived as a multi-layered domestic shield.

One of the first focus areas was to make the protection of US borders more coherent and effective by integrating US Customs, the border enforcement functions of the Immigration and Naturalization Service, the Border Patrol, and the Department of Agriculture's quarantine functions. New rules for the issuing of visas, the eventual introduction of biometric

Table 1.1 Homeland security: mission, mission areas, actors.

Mission	Mission areas	Actors*
Prevent terrorist attacks	Intelligence and warning	FBI CIA
Reduce vulnerability	Border and transportation security	DoD State
Minimize damage and recover from attacks	Domestic counter-terrorism	Treasury Justice Transportation
	Protecting critical infrastructure	Agriculture Energy FEMA
	Defending against CBRN terrorism	Health and Human Services (HHS) Environmental Protection
	Emergency preparedness and response	Agency Commerce
		State and local government Private sector The public

Note
* The table displays the key actors in homeland security prior to the establishment of the Department of Homeland Security in January 2003. This reorganization entailed a reduction in the number of agencies involved.

identifiers on travel documents, heightened standards for port security, increased resources for the Coast Guard, and physical inspection of more of the containers crossing US borders were intended to help prevent dangerous persons and dangerous materials from entering the country.

Inside the borders stronger law enforcement measures, more effective intelligence sharing, and enhanced analytic capabilities have all been part of a considerable effort to increase the chance of interdicting terrorist attacks.

A National Counterterrorism Center was established to fuse terrorism information from various US agencies into a comprehensive picture. Meanwhile, the Federal Bureau of Investigation (FBI) and the Central Intelligence Agency (CIA) both entered into major recruitment drives to enhance their collection and analytical capabilities, and existing restrictions on information sharing between the two agencies were relaxed. Moreover, the USA Patriot Act (Uniting and Strengthening America by Providing Appropriate Tools Required to Intercept and Obstruct Terrorism) – endorsed at record speed by Congress within six weeks of the attacks – granted greater authority to the FBI to focus on domestic intelligence gathering. Federal powers to obtain search warrants, conduct electronic surveillance, and detain persons suspected of connection to terrorism were also expanded.[8]

On the protective side, the *National Strategy* called for hardening and physical protection of particularly vulnerable or attractive targets such as nuclear and chemical plants, symbolic buildings and monuments, or important government installations. Critical physical and cyber infrastructure is currently being charted in order to devise better ways of protecting it. Since the ownership of much of this infrastructure is in private hands, the *National Strategy for Homeland Security* called for new strategies for public–private cooperation – an effort which, according to critics, has proceeded slowly.[9]

Transportation security, in particular air transportation security, received special attention, including the introduction of federally employed screeners in all major airports, new explosives detection devices, and a beefed-up air marshal program.

Finally, as the last line of defense, the training, equipment, and interoperability of first responders was to be upgraded, and the public educated about how to react in case of different forms of attack. The "Ready" campaign, launched in March 2003, was a first attempt to raise public awareness about how to prepare for and react in case of different types of terrorist attacks.[10]

In sum, the National Strategy for Homeland Security called for a broad-based effort to prevent, protect from, respond to, and recover from terrorism – an effort involving multiple actors, covering numerous societal sectors and professions, and many levels of government.

Reorganizing for homeland security

To promote coordination of the many actors and focus areas listed in Table 1.1, a new Department of Homeland Security was established in January 2003 (Figure 1.1). The Department is now the designated homeland security lead agency, which means it is to coordinate national efforts and to serve as the point of contact for state and local government as well as the private sector. By March 2003 bureaus and offices previously scattered between 22 different federal agencies had been transferred into the new Department, creating a bureaucracy of 190,000 employees and total annual budget of more than $40 billion.[11]

Despite this consolidation and reorganization, homeland security functions span broadly and remain beyond the control of any single federal agency. The Department of Defense, the Department of Justice, the Department of Health and Human Services, as well as the CIA and FBI all remain major players, making cross-governmental coordination crucial to an effective effort.

Though the new US Department of Homeland Security replicates some of the functions of European interior ministries, in a US context it is a new and unique entity. Moreover, in contrast to European institutions like, for example, the Directorate-General for Justice, Freedom and Security, the purview of the Department of Homeland Security spans "hard" instruments

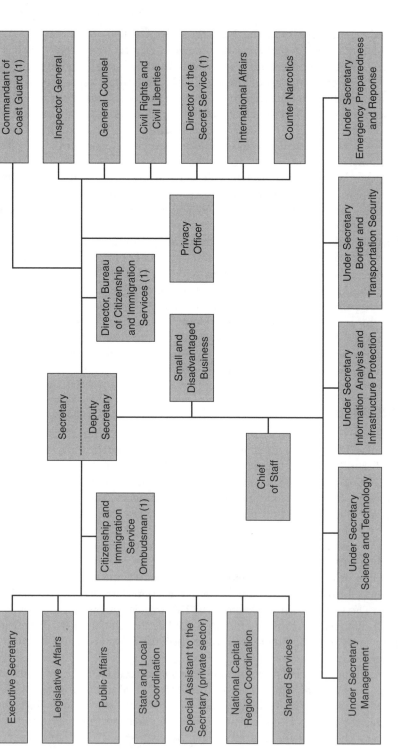

Figure 1.1 The US Department of Homeland Security (source: US Government(www.dhs.gov/interweb/assetlibrary/DHS_Org_Chart.ppt)).

Note (1): Effective March 1, 2003

like the enforcement capabilities of the Coast Guard and border control agencies, and "soft" instruments like research, public education and civil protection. This gives the Department, at least in principle if not yet in practice the possibility to take an overall view on homeland security and prioritize and coordinate the various instruments for maximum effect.

As pointed out by numerous reports and studies, current US homeland security efforts leave much to be wished for in terms of focus, effectiveness, efficiency, and coordination. Indeed, more than two years after its creation, the US Department of Homeland Security had barely started establishing performance criteria and measures of success within individual programs, and the allocation of resources to state and local government is still not based on rigorous risk assessment about likelihood, vulnerabilities, and consequences of attacks in different areas.[12] The new Secretary of Homeland Security has announced his intention to improve on these deficiencies, but might be up against powerful political interests in some areas. So far, legislators from sparsely populated and rural communities have, for example, been able to block a strictly risk-based formula for distributing homeland security funds to local communities – a formula which would clearly entail that big US cities would receive proportionally more than they currently do.[13]

However, even if the current approach to homeland security arguably needs to be readjusted to become effective, and though American policymakers and analysts argue among themselves as to how to provide homeland security, what tasks to prioritize, how to distribute funds, how to organize for homeland security, etc., the attacks of September 11 prompted a bipartisan consensus around the need for a comprehensive effort to deal with vulnerabilities on the home front. The quantity of political, financial, academic, and scientific resources dedicated to securing the US homeland has increased significantly over the past years.[14]

Europe's response: counter-terrorism

On the European side of the Atlantic, the attacks of September 11 elicited a somewhat different and less dramatic reaction. Whereas the US government opted for a defense in multiple layers and significant bureaucratic restructuring, European governments mostly chose to continue existing policies of relying on intelligence and law-enforcement agencies to deal with the threat from terrorism.

Countries like France and the UK already had decades of experience with separatist or politically motivated violence, and special legislation and law enforcement instruments in place to counter it – instruments further sharpened in the wake of the attacks on the US. Legislation expanding the powers of intelligence agencies, police authorities, and prosecutor's offices were also introduced in other EU countries and passed by national parliaments at extraordinary speed. Additional funding was provided for these agencies, and a number of countries that before September 11 did not have special anti-terrorism legislation – Denmark, for example – enacted such laws.[15]

Individual European countries also strengthened their protective capabilities to different extents. Some increased the funding for emergency preparedness agencies, established bio-terrorism research centers, and verified or increased national stockpiles of vaccines. However, in contrast to the situation in the US, responsibility for the various protective initiatives remained scattered among different cabinet level ministries and services such as health, energy, commerce, transportation, and research. The inter-ministerial bodies and committees charged with coordinating the overall national efforts against terrorism remained dominated by the traditional counter-terrorism ministries – justice, interior, and defense.[16]

At the EU level, the attacks on the US added impetus to a nascent cooperation in the field of internal security. Informal counter-terrorism cooperation between the big EU countries had already started in the 1970s with the so-called Trevi Group. The Schengen Agreement and the Justice and Home Affairs cooperation introduced with the 1991 Maastricht Treaty provided a more formalized framework for legal cooperation.[17]

Within a few months of September 11 the European Council of EU member states agreed on a common European definition of terrorism, harmonization of penalties against terrorist crimes, a common arrest warrant, and provisions for the freezing or seizure of terrorist assets.[18] Moreover, a common European list of organizations and persons linked to terrorist activities was established, a new agency – Eurojust – composed of high-level magistrates and prosecutors was created to assist in investigating cross-border crimes, and a counter-terrorism unit was established within Europol, the European Police Office in the Hague. To improve and harmonize control of the external border, a European Border Management Agency was established in the spring of 2005, and it was agreed to introduce biometric identifiers in passports issued by EU countries from mid-2006.[19]

Taken together, these initiatives represented a significant expansion of EU cooperation against terrorism. However, a number of the measures agreed upon during the last months of 2001 had not yet been implemented by all member states at the time of the Madrid attacks on 11 March 2004.[20] This tardiness pinpoints a key challenge in European counter-terrorism and homeland security cooperation: despite the free movement across non-guarded internal EU borders, intelligence, law-enforcement, and prosecution remain jealously guarded national prerogatives. The result is an asymmetry between EU-wide risks and challenges, and the geographically limited response options of national agencies. Since threat perceptions vary across the EU countries, common action frequently reflects the lowest common denominator – a fact which has prompted interior ministers from the biggest five EU countries to form an avant-garde group for reinforced counter-terrorism cooperation in the area of intelligence sharing and data exchange.[21]

European Union efforts to reduce societal vulnerabilities and strengthen civil protection were given lower priority than law enforcement and prosecution, while suffering from the same asymmetry between the scope of the challenge on the one hand and national response options on the other.

The relatively low priority given to protection was reflected in the EU's anti-terrorism action plan of September 2001. The first five of seven priorities identified in the plan related to creating or strengthening instruments and cooperation within the spheres of intelligence, police, and justice. Only one – air transport security – was of a protective nature. The final priority related to strengthening the integration of counter-terrorism efforts with the Union's Common Foreign and Security Policy (CFSP).[22]

Eventually, towards the end of 2002, the Council approved a program to improve the Union's ability to support member state efforts in the area of civil protection with special emphasis on chemical, biological, radiological and nuclear (CBRN) threats. However, since the task of civil protection remained the preserve of EU member states, rather than the European Commission, the program had no legal implications and the Union provided no funding to promote its implementation.[23]

Moreover, in the wake of March 11 a so-called solidarity clause was adopted, committing EU member states to aid each other in the case of a terrorist attack. European leaders also declared their resolve to reinforce transportation security and the protection of EU-wide critical infrastructure. Initial documents charting some of the issues and challenges have been drafted, but actual initiatives or binding regulations have yet to emerge.[24] Currently, policies, procedures, standards, and equipment vary widely across member states, and attempts at harmonization and coordination are hampered by the fact that civil protection remains an area of member state competence, while responsibility for other relevant homeland security policy areas is divided between member states and several different EU Directorate-Generals (DG), such as DG Environment, DG Transportation, and DG Science and Technology.[25]

The *EU Plan of Action on Combating Terrorism* lists the various EU initiatives and provides an overview over the actors involved.[26] Table 1.2 indicates the scope of the challenge of effectively coordinating counter-terrorism and homeland security in the EU. The left hand column exemplifies the number of agencies involved at the member state level in a smaller country, by listing the actors involved in Danish efforts to improve homeland security. The right hand column lists the actors involved at the EU level.

In the wake of the Madrid attacks, a new position of anti-terrorism coordinator was created within the Council Secretariat.[27] However, in contrast to the US Secretary of Homeland Security, the EU coordinator has a very limited staff and no line authority over relevant EU or member state agencies. The EU coordinator also does not dispose of discretionary funds to promote harmonization of policies, procedures, standards, and equipment between different member states. The anti-terrorism coordinator's ability to upgrade Europe's

Table 1.2 Actors in national and EU homeland security efforts

Actors in Danish homeland security	Actors in EU homeland security
Interior and Health	Council
Justice	Commission
Transportation	DG Justice and Home Affairs
DEMA (Danish Emergency	DG Environment
Management Agency)	DG Energy and Transportation
Environment	DG Health and Consumer Protection
Knowledge, Technology, and Education	DG Research, Development, Technology
Commerce	and Innovation
FE (Danish Defence Intelligence Service)	Europol
PET (Danish Security Intelligence	Eurojust
Service)	Police Chief's Task Force
Defense	European Judicial network
	Customs Cooperation Working Group
Counties and municipalities,	Visa Working Party
private sector, population	European Border Agency
	Strategic Committee on Immigration,
	Frontiers and Asylum
	National governments
	National agencies
	Local governments
	Private sector, population

defenses will therefore depend on the political skills of the officeholder. His or her ability to persuade the various actors listed in Table 1.2 above to prioritize security and coordinate with other relevant actors will be crucial.

In sum, the European reaction to the emergence of catastrophic terrorism was concentrated mainly within the areas of intelligence, justice, and law enforcement. At the EU level, member states broke new ground in the area of judicial and legal cooperation. Vulnerability reduction and civil protection, however, remained of relatively low priority. The post-March 11 endorsement of an EU solidarity clause and the appointment of an anti-terrorism coordinator indicate a dawning interest in the protective side of homeland security, but concrete common and binding action remain limited due to diverging threat assessments, jealously guarded national competencies and, arguably, the lack of a strong coordinating center to prioritize and drive the EU effort and the numerous actors and agencies involved.

Does Europe need homeland security?

In November 2003 Istanbul was shaken by four suicide blasts, presumably carried out by a group affiliated with al-Qaeda. International terrorism had struck a second NATO member.[28] On 11 March 2004 it struck in Europe proper, killing almost 200 civilians on packed commuter trains in Madrid. The same year a Dutch filmmaker was killed, apparently due to his criticism of the status and treatment of women in Islam. The statements of the murderer clearly indicated that the act was inspired by Osama bin Laden's message of violent jihad against the "enemies of Islam."[29]

These attacks underlined what had already been indicated by intelligence, arrests, and information emerging during court proceedings: that Europe was not only a logistical base for cells planning and supporting jihad against the US, but also a target.

To date intelligence and police agencies have managed to foil several attacks, seizing bomb-making material, weapons, floor plans of suspected targets, propaganda material, poison recipes, and poison-making equipment at raids on safe houses and hideouts in major European cities. Courts across Europe have handed down prison sentences in connection with planned attacks on targets ranging from places of worship to transatlantic airliners and subway systems in major European cities, US military bases, and museums and tourist attractions on the continent. One of the attacks was presumably to involve use of the poison ricin. The planning and preparation for most of the attacks involved the territories of several European countries, and many of the key figures behind the plots were, like the plotters of September 11, widely traveled and operated in a transnational manner. In sum, there is no doubt that cells and groups sympathizing with al-Qaeda constitute a threat to Europe, and that many implicated groups and individuals operate across EU borders.[30]

Moreover, Europe shares many of America's vulnerabilities with its long, porous external borderline, open societies, population and asset concentrations, a plethora of potential soft targets, and dependence on critical infrastructure, which in turn depends on networked information technology (IT) systems.[31]

The US approach to homeland security is far from unproblematic, and European counterterrorism efforts are all but negligible, as indicated by the many successfully foiled plots. However, whereas Europe's earlier experiences with terrorism may offer valuable lessons for the US, in many ways al-Qaeda-inspired catastrophic terrorism is of a new quality. National intelligence services and police forces may suffice in dealing with the old form of limited terrorist violence as experienced by Europe in the 1970s and 1980s. September 11 and the foiled plots against European targets, however, indicate how terrorists operate across borders to a greater extent than earlier, and no longer appear to observe self-imposed limits as to the number of civilian casualties they are willing to inflict. Some believe that the continued democratization of technology and proliferation of weapons of mass destruction mean it is only a question of time before groups inspired by al-Qaeda's violent message will use WMDs in their attacks, since the technical barrier seems to be the only restraint holding them back.[32]

Obviously, from a human, political, and economic perspective it is preferable to disrupt plots in the planning phase instead of trying to stop an attack at a later stage through protective measures. Effective intelligence and law-enforcement measures remain crucial.[33] But it is quite unlikely that every attack can be interdicted, unless we resign ourselves to being secure in an Orwellian world of surveillance and control. Thus, arguably, a systematic European effort to reduce vulnerabilities and improve civil protection is a necessary complement to current efforts against the new terrorism. Just as it makes little sense for individual states in the US to pursue separate plans, procure different equipment, and adhere to different standards for protecting critical infrastructure and dangerous materials, it makes little sense for EU member states to try to go it alone in a borderless, interdependent Europe.

A common transatlantic homeland and a common homeland security strategy?

From a formal or strictly judicial point of view, there is obviously no transatlantic homeland. Nation states retain sovereignty in a number of key homeland security areas such as intelligence, police, health, defense, and civil protection. Yet, as illustrated with the September 11 plot, Europe's vulnerability is America's vulnerability and vice versa. Europe served as logistical base for a number of the September 11 attackers, and in turn felt the impact of the attacks directly as Europeans died in the collapsing World Trade Center in New York, European airlines suffered economically, and the global economy deteriorated. Thus, from a functional point of view the notion of a transatlantic homeland makes sense.

As a result of September 11, transatlantic cooperation in the areas of justice and law enforcement has broken new ground, as elaborated elsewhere in this book, but major international initiatives for vulnerability reduction and protection have, in contrast, been scarce.[34]

As argued, homeland security was given relatively low priority in the EU cooperation, and no strong lead agency emerged to push for European (not to speak of transatlantic) homeland security cooperation. On the US side, the Department of Homeland Security focused mainly on the domestic situation. Efforts and funding have been directed at improving security at US airports, creating strategic national stockpiles of medical supplies, developing CBRN countermeasures in cooperation with the US scientific community, charting national critical infrastructure, and replacing aging cutters in the Coast Guard's deepwater fleet.[35]

The *National Strategy for Homeland Security* identified a number of international tasks, such as improving security in international transportation systems and commerce, expanding protection of transnational critical infrastructure, and improving capabilities to assist and support other nations in the wake of a terrorist attack.[36] International agreements about maritime and sea container security have been reached.[37] Moreover, the EU–US Policy

Dialogue on Border and Transport Security represents a potentially important forum for developing common policies, and the Department of Homeland Security has announced its intention to send an attaché to the European Union in Brussels.[38]

Yet, as detailed in Chapters 2 through 6 of this book, more common efforts are needed to establish a credible and effective defense against bioterrorism, to cope with the proliferation of CBRN materials, to secure cyberspace and protect critical international infrastructure, to forge effective approaches to border and transportation security, and to prosecute terrorist crimes in an effective manner, without sacrificing civil liberties. Ideally, common efforts should enable Europeans and Americans to compensate for the asymmetry between a transnational threat and nationally limited response options by pooling resources, drawing on best practice, sharing information and coordinating closely. To that end, it is crucial that policymakers, analysts, and practitioners in the fields of emergency preparedness, infrastructure protection, border security, and health become more aware of the international requirements of effective homeland security.

Obviously total elimination of the terrorist risk is impossible, and ultimately it is up to each society to determine what resources it is willing to devote to vulnerability reduction and civil protection. Moreover, national as well as enhanced common transatlantic efforts should be accompanied by hard thinking about where we are going, how we intend to get there, and how we measure progress toward that end goal, lest homeland security develops into a black hole of spending.[39] Still, when the consequences of a terrorist attack can easily spill over borders there ought to be a common interest in coordination and harmonization in areas where lagging or uneven efforts on either side of the Atlantic render every European and American less secure, and where national efforts cannot be effective or efficient unless coordinated with the policies of neighbors and partners.

Ultimately, many solutions will have to be global, not just transatlantic. Yet, common or complementary transatlantic efforts would seem to offer natural starting points for wider cooperation, since Europe and the US remain politically, economically, and culturally closer than any other two parts of the world, and often form the core of any effective global coalition. Europe and the US could function as an international homeland security avant garde, charting new ground for others to follow.[40]

Conclusion

As illustrated by current efforts on both sides of the Atlantic, it represents a formidable challenge to formulate homeland security strategies, prioritize the multitude of potential tasks, and make the large number of stakeholders pull in the same direction. Inevitably, the efforts to protect against large-scale terrorism will involve a substantial measure of learning by doing, and most policy initiatives and bureaucratic constructions will probably have to be readjusted along the way. Some of the programs which today pass for homeland security will probably turn out to add little to our security, and others that we have not yet thought about may turn out to be crucial.

Forging a common transatlantic effort would entail further challenges. Divergent threat perceptions and different willingness to accept risk, as well as issues of national sovereignty and different national cultures and administrative traditions, pose considerable obstacles. Decades of transatlantic squabbles over military strategy, trade, and economic issues indicate the kind of differences that would complicate a common effort. Yet there is also much to be gained by cooperating. Close coordination, pooling of assets, and best-practice exchange hold out the promise of fostering more effective and efficient homeland security on both sides of the Atlantic. Today, as in the past, Europe's security is America's security and vice versa.

As witnessed by summits and high-level meetings over the past year, there is a beginning recognition of the importance of transatlantic homeland security.[41] With this book we attempt to provide conceptual and practical guidance in the efforts to move homeland security beyond a still dominantly domestic focus.

Notes

1 Chemical, Biological, Radiological, and Nuclear.
2 *National Strategy for Homeland Security*, Washington DC: Office of Homeland Security, July 2002, p. 2.
3 A. K. Cronin and J. M. Ludes (eds), *Attacking Terrorism. Elements of a Grand Strategy*, Washington DC: Georgetown University Press, 2004, p. 24; C. Graham, "Can foreign aid help stop terrorism?" *The Brookings Review*, 20, (3), 2002, 28; *Second Report of the Monitoring Group pursuant to resolution 1363 (2001) and as extended by resolutions 1390 (2002) on Sanctions against al-Qaida, the Taliban and their associates and associated entities*, United Nations, December 2003, pp. 2, 26, 34, available online at www.un.org/Docs/sc/committees/1267/1267mg.htm.
4 The Advisory Panel to Assess Domestic Response Capabilities for Terrorism Involving Weapons of Mass Destruction, *Fifth Annual Report*, 15 December 2003.
5 For examples of studies into domestic security before the September 11 attack, see *Assessing the Threat*. Advisory Panel to Assess Domestic Response Capabilities for Terrorism Involving Weapons of Mass Destruction. First Annual Report, Washington DC, December 1999; *Critical Foundations. Protecting America's Infrastructures*. Report of the President's Commission on Critical Infrastructure Protection, Washington DC, October 1997; *Towards a National Strategy for Combating Terrorism*. Advisory Panel to Assess Domestic Response Capabilities for Terrorism Involving Weapons of Mass Destruction. Second Annual Report, Washington DC, December 2000.
6 *National Strategy for Homeland Security*, Washington DC: Office of Homeland Security, July 2002.
7 *National Strategy for Homeland Security*, Washington DC: Office of Homeland Security, July 2002, pp. vii–x and p. 3. See also D. McIntyre, *A Quick Look at the Proposed Department of Homeland Security*, Anser Summary and Analysis, Anser Institute for Homeland Security, November 2002.

8 H. F. Tepker, "The USA Patriot Act," *Extensions*, Fall 2002; Lee Tien, *Foreign Intelligence Surveillance Act*, Electronic Frontier Foundation, 27 September 2001; Jim McGee, "An intelligence giant in the making; anti-terrorism law likely to bring domestic apparatus of unprecedented scope," *Washington Post*, 4 November 2001.

9 G. Wodele and W. New, "Bush signs new homeland security directive," *GovExec.com*, 17 December 2003.

10 Yet surveys indicate that a vast majority of Americans remain uncertain of how to react in case of attacks involving weapons or materials of mass destruction. A. J. Dory, "American civil security: the US public and homeland security," *The Washington Quarterly*, 27/1, Winter 2003–04, p. 48.

11 *Homeland Security Funding Primer: Where We've Been, Where We're Headed*, Terrorism Prevention Project, Center for Arms Control and Non-Proliferation, 1 May 2003, p. 4; J. E. Lake and B. Nûnez-Neto, *Homeland Security Department: FY2006 Appropriations*, CRS Report for Congress, 14 April 2005.

12 The House Select Committee on Homeland Security, *An Analysis of First Responder Grant Funding*, Washington DC, April 2004, available online at www.homelandsecurity.house.gov/files/First%20Responder%20Report.pdf; US General Accounting Office, *Combating Terrorism. Evaluation of Selected Characteristics in National Strategies Related to Terrorism*, Washington DC, 3 February 2004, GAO–04–40ST; C. Strohm, "Report gives DHS mixed grades after one year," *GovExec.com*, 5 March 2004.

13 J. Mintz, "Security spending initiates dispute," *Washington Post*, 13 April 2005; Remarks for Secretary Michael Chertoff US Department of Homeland Security George Washington University Homeland Security Policy Institute, 16 March 2005, available online, at www.dhs.gov.

14 S. Flynn, *America the Vulnerable*, New York: Harper Collins Publishers, 2004; House Budget Committee Hearing on National and Homeland Security: Meeting our Needs, Committee on the Budget, Washington DC, 16 February 2005, available online at www.budget.house.gov/hearing/jnstmnt021605.htm.

15 O. Lepsius, "The relationship between security and civil liberties in the Federal Republic of Germany after September 11," in Daniel S. Hamilton (ed), *Fighting Terror: How September 11 is Transforming German–American Relations*, Washington, DC: American Institute for Contemporary German Studies, 2002, p. 85; E. van de Linde, K. O'Brien, G. Lindstrom, S. de Spiegeleire, and H. de Vries, *Quick Scan of Post 9/11 National Counterterrorism Policy-making and Implementation in Selected European Countries* Leiden: RAND Europe, 2002, pp. 4–6; J. Shapiro and B. Suzan, "The French experience of counterterrorism," *Survival*, 45(1), 2003, 75–77.

16 "Deutschland wappnet sich gegen Pockenviren," *Financial Times Deutschland*, 14 February 2003; J. Eldridge, "Weapons of mass destruction: controlling the hype," *Homeland Security and Resilience Monitor*, 2(3), 2003, 11; "France ill-equipped for bio-terror attacks – report," *Reuters*, 9 July 2003; J. Holmgren and J. Softa, *Functional Security. A Comparative Analysis of the Nordic States' Political Agenda in the Fields of Critical Infrastructure, IT Security, NBC Issues and Terrorism*, Stockholm: The Swedish Institute of International Affairs, 2002, pp. 15, 35, 41; H. Müller, "Terrorism, proliferation: a European threat assessment," *Chaillot Paper*, No. 58, March 2003, Paris: Institute for Security Studies, European Union.

17 M. Anderson and J. Arp, *Changing Perceptions of Security and Their Implications for EU Justice and Home Affairs Cooperation*, CEPS Policy Brief No. 26, October 2002, pp. 3–4; M. den Boer, *9/11 and the Europeanization of Anti-Terrorism Policy: A Critical Assessment*, Notre Europe, Policy Papers No 6, September 2003, p. 5;

A. Townsend, *Guarding Europe*, Centre for European Reform, Working Paper, May 2003, p. 39.

18 European Union Council Decision 2002/475/JI; Council Document 14867/1/ 01REV 1.

19 Declaration by the Heads of State or Government of the European Union and the President of the Commission, Brussels, 19 October 2001, SN 4296/2/01; "Eurojust – Helping the EU's legal systems to combat cross-border crime," Justice and Home Affairs, Brussels, December 14, available online at: www. europa.eu.int/comm/justice_home/news/laecken_council/en/eurojust_en.htm.

20 By March 2004, Germany, Greece, and Italy had yet to implement the common arrest warrant. By May 2005, the warrant had finally been implemented in all member states. Moreover, national authorities had remained very reluctant to use Eurojust and common investigative teams to support and facilitate cross-border cooperation in investigating terrorist crimes out of fear that sensitive information might be leaked through the involvement of more actors in investigation and prosecution.

21 "The EU's role in counter-terrorism," *IISS Strategic Comment*, 11(2), March 2005.

22 Conclusion and Plan of Action of the Extraordinary European Council Meeting on 21 September 2001, SN 140/01, pp. 1–3; Council Document 12608/02.

23 Council Decision of 23 October 2001, available online at: www.europa.eu.int/ comm/environment/civil/pdfdocs/mecanisme_da.pdf.

24 Commission of the European Communities, Communication from the Commission to the Council and the European Parliament. Preparedness and consequence management in the fight against terrorism, Brussels, COM(2004) 701 final; Commission of the European Communities, Communication from the Commission to the Council and the European Parliament. Critical Infrastructure Protection in the fight against terrorism, Brussels, COM(2004) 702 final.

25 G. Lindstrom, "Protecting the European homeland. The CBR dimension, European Union Institute for Security Studies, *Chaillot Paper*, no 69, 2004.

26 European Council, EU Plan of Action on Combating Terrorism – Update, Brussels, 2004, 14330/1/4.

27 European Council, Declaration on Combating Terrorism, Brussels, 25 March 2004.

28 J. C. Helicke, "Turkey links deadly bombings to al-Qaida," *Washington Post*, 1 December 2003.

29 P. Nesser, *The Slaying of the Dutch Filmmaker – Religiously Motivated Violence or Islamist Terrorism in the Name of Global Jihad?* Norwegian Defence Research Establishment, FFI/Rapport-2005/00376.

30 "Killer jailed over poison plot," *BBC News*, 13 April 2005; P. Nesser, Jihad in Europe, Thesis submitted for the cand. polit. degree, Department of Political Science, University of Oslo & Norwegian Defense Research Establishment, 15 January 2004; C. C. Smith, "6 French-Algerians get prison for US Embassy plot," *International Herald Tribune*, 17 March 2005; "Terror suspect admits plane plot," *BBC News*, 28 February 2005; "Trials give terror battle insights," *BBC News*, 13 April 2005. See also Non-confidential Report on the Terrorism Situation and Trends in Europe, EU TE-SAT 14280/2/02, pp. 19–27.

31 T. Homer-Dixon, "The rise of complex terrorism," *Foreign Policy*, January/February 2002, 53; B. M. Jenkins, *Countering al Qaeda*, Santa Monica: Rand, 2002, p. 28.

32 The prospects of biological or nuclear terrorism are discussed in Chapters 2 and 3 of this book. See also *Second Report of the Monitoring Group pursuant to resolution 1363 (2001) and as extended by resolutions 1390 (2002) on Sanctions against al-Qaida, the Taliban and their associates and associated entities*, United Nations,

December 2003, p. 38, available online at: www.un.org/Docs/sc/committees/ 1267/MG_2nd_1455_report_template.htm.

33 The attacks of September 11 cost almost 3,000 lives. The immediate economic costs amounted to an estimated $16.2 billion in destroyed property and $11 billion in rescue and clean-up. Moreover, lower Manhatten lost about 30 percent of its office space and an estimated 200,000 jobs were destroyed. P. Lenain, M. Bonturi and V. Koen, *The Economic Consequences of Terrorism*, OECD, Economics Department Working Papers No. 334, July, 2002, p. 6.

34 The EU and US have concluded agreements on extradition and legal cooperation between the EU and the US. The agreement on legal cooperation implies increased exchange of information between police authorities and the possibility to establish common investigation teams. The extradition agreement simplifies the procedures and widens the possibilities for handovers, although only on the condition that the suspect is not sentenced to death in the US. D. Dubois, "The attacks of 11 September: EU–US cooperation against terrorism in the field of justice and Home affairs," *European Foreign Affairs Review*, 7, 2002, 327–329; *European Union Factsheet, Extradition and Mutual Legal Assistance*, Brussels, June, 2003; Center for Transatlantic Relations, *Shoulder to Shoulder: Views From Governments and Civil Society on Cooperative Security*, Washington, DC, 1:2, June 2003, p. 1.

35 *Homeland Security Funding Primer: Where We've Been, Where We're Headed*, Terrorism Prevention Project, Center for Arms Control and Non-Proliferation, 1 May 2003.

36 *National Strategy for Homeland Security*, Washington DC: Office of Homeland Security, July 2002, pp. 60–61.

37 General Secretariat of the Council of the European Union, *European Union Factsheet, Container Security*, June, 2003; "EU and US reach customs agreement on container security," available online at www.euractiv.com.

38 "US, EU discuss transportation, border security," April 26, Brussels, USINFO.STATE.GOV, available online at: www.usinfo.state.gov.

39 For attempts to think systematically through several of the key elements listed above, see R. David, "Homeland security: building a national strategy", *Journal of Homeland Security*, July 2002. Online, available at: www.homelandsecurity. org/journal/Articles/davidnatstrategy06282002.htm; D. Gouré, "Homeland security," in A. K. Cronin and J. M. Ludes (eds), *Attacking Terrorism. Elements of a Grand Strategy*, Washington DC: Georgetown University Press, 2004.

40 D. Hamilton, *Renewing Transatlantic Partnership: Why and How?* Testimony to the House Committee on International Relations, 11 June 2003.

41 C. Arcos, *The Role of the Department of Homeland Security Overseas*, Heritage Lectures, No. 840, June, 2004; EU–US Declaration on Combating Terrorism, Dromoland Castle, 26 June 2004.

2   The challenge of bio-terrorism

Daniel S. Hamilton and Bradley T. Smith

Bio-terrorism poses a unique, strategic threat to the transatlantic community. A bio-terrorist attack in Europe or North America is arguably more likely than and could be as consequential as a nuclear attack, but requires a different set of national and international responses. Current systems to manage national and international epidemics of infectious disease have been consistently stretched to their limits by SARS and other natural outbreaks, and are wholly inadequate for the unique challenges of bio-terrorism. Europeans and Americans alike are ill-prepared either to prevent bio-terrorist attacks or to mitigate their consequences. Building societal resilience to the threat of bio-terrorism requires political leaders and security experts to recognize that epidemics unleashed intentionally by a thinking enemy are significantly different from other security threats, and demand coordinated and complementary US and European efforts in prevention, preparedness and response.

This chapter begins by describing the unique challenges of bio-terrorism. It assesses the difficulties of response, distinguishing between bio-safety, non-proliferation, and bio-defense, and assesses current transatlantic and global efforts. It then suggests ways forward in each of these three areas.

Bio-terrorism: a unique strategic threat

There are essentially two types of bio-weapon agents. The first are pathogens – disease-causing microorganisms such as bacteria and viruses (e.g. the causative agents of anthrax, smallpox, plague). The second are toxins – non-living molecules that are produced by a plant, animal, or microorganism, but that do not replicate in the body (e.g. ricin, botulinum toxin).[1] Pathogenic microorganisms have the potential to be far more dangerous than toxins because many microbes cause contagious disease that can result in devastating epidemics (e.g. smallpox).

There are a number of reasons to consider pathogenic bio-terrorism, and the epidemics it may cause, as a unique strategic threat to the transatlantic community. Pathogenic bio-agents can be extremely lethal and are hard to detect. They are cheap, they are accessible, and they are easy to transport.

They can reproduce, and they have the potential to be made more powerful and diverse as bioscience rides the tides of globalization.

Only biological weapons rank with nuclear weapons in their lethality. The US Congressional Office of Technology Assessment (OTA) has estimated that an attack, under ideal conditions, with 100 kg of aerosolized *Bacillus anthracis* spores (i.e. the causative agent of anthrax) over an urban area could cause as many as three million casualties, rivaling the lethality of a thermonuclear weapon.[2]

It has been estimated that the 2 g of powder contained in the anonymous letter sent to Senator Thomas Daschle in October of 2001 contained over two trillion *Bacillus anthracis* spores.[3] Given the best medical estimates of the lethal dose of inhaled spores, these 2 g could contain thousands or even millions of lethal doses – assuming perfect distribution to each person and no medical intervention.[4] This is an extraordinary amount of lethal potential, considering that 2 g of this powder can fit in the palm of one's hand. A biological weapon could be far less concentrated than this and still have a devastating effect. Significantly, most of the people who became ill with inhalational anthrax (and four of the five who died) in October 2001 did not actually open a letter – their exposures were from indirect means

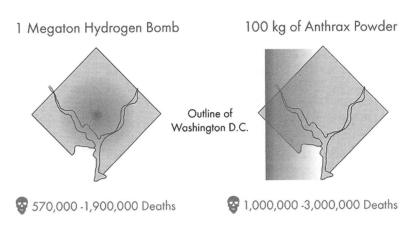

1 Megaton Hydrogen Bomb   100 kg of Anthrax Powder

Outline of
Washington D.C.

570,000 -1,900,000 Deaths   1,000,000 -3,000,000 Deaths

Figure 2.1 The lethality of biological weapons mirrors that of nuclear weapons (source: US Congress, Office of Technology Assessment, *Proliferation of Weapons of Mass Destruction: Assessing the Risks*, OTA-ISC-559 (Washington, DC: US Government Printing Office, August 1993).

Note
Analyses by the US Congressional Office of Technology Assessment determined that the estimated number of deaths that could result from the detonation of a 1 megaton hydrogen bomb in a major US city would be similar to the deaths that would occur from an outdoor, line-source aerosol release of 100 kg of anthrax powder under ideal meteorological conditions. In this study, only biological weapons matched the lethal potential of nuclear weapons – not chemical weapons or conventional explosives. An indoor release of a biological weapon has the potential to be an even more efficient attack than on outdoor release; resulting in more lethality per kilogram – or even gram – of material.

(i.e. dust from mail sorting machines, or cross-contamination of their mail with one of the anthrax letters), and they did not receive prompt medical care.

Pathogenic organisms are cheap and accessible. Many are present naturally in the environment. Natural outbreaks of anthrax, plague, Ebola, and other dangerous pathogens occur in humans and animals throughout the world almost continuously.[5] In addition, there are thousands of biomedical laboratories, hospitals, biotechnology firms and universities worldwide, containing stocks of pathogens and the tools of molecular biology and bio-manufacturing required to engineer and produce wet or dry preparations of biological agents.[6] The knowledge and equipment required to grow pathogens, modify them, and turn them into weapons is essentially a matter of public information, available on the Internet. To test the feasibility of assembling a covert bio-terror lab, the US Government successfully built a "proof-of-concept" covert production facility in an abandoned building in Nevada for less than $1 million using a handful of personnel and commercially available equipment, illustrating that a large industrial infrastructure is not required for production of bio-weapons.[7] Additionally, many of the techniques required to "engineer" pathogens to render them potentially more dangerous are everyday skills of biologists throughout the world, and are used for entirely beneficent purposes.

Pathogens can reproduce. Unlike fissile materials, infectious microorganisms reproduce rapidly under the right conditions. For example, a small "seed culture" or even just one *Bacillus anthracis* bacterial cell could be cultivated under optimal growth conditions to trillions of organisms in a matter of days. For this reason, biological agents stored in a laboratory cannot be inventoried in the way fissile materials can. The theft of even minute quantities of a pathogen can pose a security threat. Moreover, trade in microbial cultures is poorly regulated within and among most nations, although this is beginning to change.[8]

Although skeptics charge that biological weapons are hard to produce – that weaponized *Bacillus anthracis*, for instance, is too hard to mill or too difficult to disperse – the technologies needed to build aerosolizable weapons are readily available and are being used every day for perfectly legitimate purposes such as pharmaceutical applications and agriculture. The science of aerosols has advanced greatly since the end of the offensive US bio-weapons program in the late 1960s. The delivery of medicines via inhalers has spawned significant research into how to aerosolize drugs, proteins, and organisms.[9] There is an entire industry focused on the aerosol dissemination of biological agents over large areas for control of pests in agricultural settings. One of the prime agents used for this agricultural application is *Bacillus thuringiensis*, a close relative of *Bacillus anthracis*. A recent study of the spraying of *Bacillus thuringiensis* near the city of Victoria in Canada found that such spraying results in significant amounts of biological agent being produced in a form and particle size-range that is easily inhaled into human lungs, where inhalational infections would begin.[10]

Biological weapons are diverse, and thus offer terrorists and military planners considerable flexibility. US experts were surprised to learn of some of the agents that Iraq and the former Soviet Union had chosen to produce and weaponize.[11] At least 30 known pathogens have the physical and biological characteristics needed for mass casualty – producing biological weapons. Most national biological warfare programs have focused on ten to 15 agents.[12] Even this shorter list of biological weapons, however, offers a range of possibilities, from the lethal *Bacillus anthracis* to incapacitating agents such as *Coxiella burnetii* (which causes Q fever) and Venezuelan equine encephalitis virus. Pathogens that cause contagious diseases that have been developed as biological weapons include smallpox virus and *Yersinia pestis* (the cause of plague). This list of agents, however, reflects only known threats. The continual emergence of new infectious diseases (e.g. Ebola hemorrhagic fever, SARS) and the accelerating power of biotechnology and genetic engineering mean that unexpected or novel pathogens may also emerge as threats.

Stunning progress in biotechnology, advanced food processing and pharmaceuticals promise untold benefits for humankind. The deciphering of microbial genomes as well as the human genome has been a massive multiplier of the power of individual scientists and small groups to accelerate beneficent research. But this knowledge is dual-use. The same information can be used by a thinking enemy – whether a state, a group, or even an individual – to create antibiotic resistance, to avoid the human immune system, or even to engineer virulent new pathogenic organisms.[13] As the power of biology expands throughout the twenty-first century, the spectrum of possible threats will grow. Well-understood "twentieth century" bio-weapons such as *Bacillus anthracis* and smallpox virus are likely to be joined by these engineered, twenty-first century bio-threat agents.[14]

Bio-weapons are portable and reloadable.[15] They can be built and deployed by individuals or small groups using small-scale, dual-use equipment, with no discernable "signature" that an offensive program is underway. For example, in spite of the industrial scale of the former Soviet bio-weapons program, Western intelligence had not been able collect enough evidence of its existence to convince political leaders to take action until defectors came to the West in the 1990s. While fissile materials give off ionizing radiation that can be picked up by instruments at a distance, biological pathogens and toxins have no comparable signatures that can be detected at a distance with currently available technologies.[16] A terrorist could smuggle a few grams of a dry powder preparation of a bio-weapon in a sealed plastic vial through a security checkpoint with little risk of detection.[17] Bio-terror weapons can be deployed through unusual routes (such as the mail or low-tech sprayers) that make them hard to identify, treat and contain. Because bio-weapons are relatively easy to deploy, they are also relatively easy to reload – a thinking enemy could carry out covert "sneak" attacks on multiple cities or regions simultaneously or in quick succession. This "reload" potential could significantly enhance the lethality of possible attacks, confound possible countermeasures and response efforts, and further heighten fear and uncertainty among publics.[18]

A biological weapon is unlikely to come with a specific "return address," as does a ballistic missile or even a truck bomb. While there is the potential for microbial forensics experts to use "genetic fingerprints" to link bio-weapons back to a lab or geographical region, this is very challenging. The required forensic technologies are just beginning to be developed.[19] Even after almost three years and one of the most intensive investigations in the history of the FBI, there have been no arrests in the 2001 anthrax letters case. The extreme difficulty in tracing a covert biological attack to any person or nation compromises what is perhaps the most effective tool nations have to deter attacks with weapons of mass destruction – the capacity for rapid attribution and retaliation. Deterrence theories rooted in the nuclear stand-off of the Cold War are unlikely to apply to bio-weapons in an age of catastrophic terrorism.

A further distinguishing quality of bio-terrorism is its delayed effect. Those attacked with bio-weapons may not even know they have been attacked. The most likely result of a covert bio-terrorist attack is an epidemic that is not recognized until days after the actual attack takes place, when ill people begin to appear at hospitals, clinics and doctors' offices. Even then, proper diagnosis is likely to be challenging and time-consuming, since the earliest symptoms of such diseases may be non-specific and "flu-like." And such an attack is unlikely to produce an obvious "ground zero" that draws fire fighters, police, and ambulances – or immediately galvanizes political leaders and their national security apparatus. Moreover, the explosive increase in flows of people, goods and ideas around the globe that has occurred in the last few decades would amplify the effects of delayed identification of the attack. What were once local curses now have global range. In 1918, it took six weeks for pandemic flu to circle the globe. Now someone who gets sick in Africa can be in Los Angeles the next day. In the SARS outbreak of 2003, one of the earliest patients traveled from Singapore to New York to Frankfurt before his symptoms became apparent.[20] Numerous exercises and simulations have demonstrated current US vulnerability to clandestine attacks with biological weapons, and these exercises have only brushed the surface of what would be involved in an international response to a bio-terror attack.[21]

Finally, this threat is both real and growing. The United States was attacked with anthrax in 2001. Radicals based in London and Lyon managed to manufacture and test toxins like ricin and botulism, presumably for attacks across Europe, before being arrested by the authorities. A dozen countries are estimated to either possess or be seeking an offensive bio-weapon capacity – including all those named by the US Department of State as sponsors of terrorism.[22] A number of non-state actors have sought to develop mass casualty bio-weapons. The Japanese apocalyptic cult Aum

Shinriyko worked hard to develop anthrax and botulinum toxin bio-weapons, but fortunately was unsuccessful.[23] Documents and computer hard drives seized during the March 2003 capture of Khalid Shaikh Mohammed, a key operational planner for al-Qaeda, revealed that the organization had recruited a Pakistani microbiologist, acquired materials to manufacture botulinum toxin, and developed a workable plan for *Bacillus anthracis* production.[24] The biological sophistication of al-Qaeda and other non-state terrorist groups is inexorably increasing.[25] During the Soviet period, Russian bio-weapons scientists successfully weaponized smallpox, *Bacillus anthracis*, and other bio-weapons on an industrial scale. Today, many of these scientists are languishing in a crumbling scientific system, are not being paid well, and are recruitment targets for other countries or terrorist networks.

The challenge of preventing and responding to bio-terrorism

The unique characteristics of bio-weapons enhance their appeal to those seeking to damage the US, Europe or other nations. Bio-weapons pose a strategic threat to the transatlantic community for which our vast experience with nuclear safeguards, security and deterrence unfortunately does not prepare us. Preventing and responding to bio-terrorism will require a new approach that advances efforts along three distinct, mutually reinforcing tracks: bio-safety, non-proliferation, and bio-defense.

Bio-safety involves measures to prevent the accidental release or theft of pathogens from laboratories and medical facilities. Non-proliferation involves measures that make it more difficult for nation-states, terrorists or criminals to obtain and use deadly pathogens and toxins by focusing on horizontal proliferation (i.e. efforts by non-state actors to acquire bio-agents) and vertical proliferation (i.e. efforts by states themselves to acquire such agents). Finally, bio-defense involves measures of medical and public health preparedness and emergency response to effectively counter a bio-attack or outbreak should either of these preventative measures fail.

Traditionally, non-proliferation has been an issue for the diplomatic community, while bio-safety and bio-defense have been the preserve of the medical, public health, and bioscience communities. (After September 11 and the subsequent anthrax attacks in the US, bio-safety and bio-defense efforts were redoubled.) In an age of catastrophic terrorism and with the potential power of biological weapons, however, true security will require a broad-based protection-in-depth that advances on all these fronts simultaneously, and engages these disparate communities together.[26]

Issues of bio-safety

To protect the health of laboratory workers and the public, the biomedical community has developed standards and procedures to minimize the risk of accidents. Work involving pathogens themselves or clinical samples from infected patients (e.g. blood, sputum) is guided by these standards, which define proper laboratory procedures, the design of bio-containment laboratories, the keeping of detailed records, and safe protocols for transporting potentially dangerous samples.

Since the anthrax attacks of 2001, policymakers in the US have focused more intently on bio-safety issues. As a result, the requirements to monitor laboratory stocks, physical security, and distribution of pathogens on the "select agent" list of potential bio-weapon pathogens maintained by the US Government have increased significantly.[27] Laboratory accidents do have the potential to trigger outbreaks with international implications, as was seen in late 2003 and early 2004 when three separate outbreaks of SARS were traced to such accidents in Singapore, Taiwan, and China.[28] However, there is also concern that regulations that are too restrictive can hamper research that is critical to finding new treatments and vaccines for these pathogens.[29]

France, Germany, Israel, Great Britain as well as the United States have all passed domestic legislation relating to laboratory security. Additionally, in June 2003 the Council of the European Union (EU) called on EU members to develop best-practice guidelines to promote the enactment of national legislation for controlling dangerous pathogens and toxins.[30] To be effective, however, these disparate national regulations must be comprehensive as well as equivalent, if not necessarily uniform. The alternative is a patchwork of inconsistent regulations, including pockets of weak implementation or enforcement that could result in accidental release of a pathogen or the possible theft of seed stocks by terrorists from poorly protected facilities.[31] Nevertheless, bio-safety regulations have their limitations – laboratories are not the only source of pathogens. Many potential bio-weapons are present in nature (e.g. *Bacillus anthracis*), and new biotechnologies allow pathogens to be created "from scratch," without needing to possess the actual organism, using DNA synthesizing machines and other molecular biology techniques (as has been done, for example, with polio virus[32]). Therefore, these bio-safety precautions must be taken in concert with effective non-proliferation and bio-defense policies.

Issues of non-proliferation

Non-proliferation involves efforts on two fronts: (1) on-the-ground measures to make it difficult for terrorists or criminals to obtain deadly pathogens or toxins from laboratories, which is often termed "horizontal" proliferation; and (2) efforts to prevent states themselves from acquiring or developing bio-weapon capabilities, which is often termed "vertical" proliferation. The latter also involves issues of arms control.

Efforts to block horizontal proliferation have been advanced primarily through better on-the-ground security measures. However, the fact that microbial pathogens exist naturally in the environment and that small samples (even a single organism) can be grown into large quantities means that biological organisms cannot be controlled as effectively, or in the same manner, as fissile materials. Since no technology or procedure can ensure the quantitative accounting of pathogens in a laboratory collection, applying the controls based on nuclear safeguards and auditing of weapon stockpiles to biological laboratories would create a false sense of security while seriously impeding legitimate research. It is therefore essential to develop a new security paradigm tailored to the unique characteristics of microorganisms and the vulnerabilities of the facilities that work with them.[33]

A major problem for non-proliferation efforts is the former Soviet bio-weapons program. The Soviet empire not only left behind 30,000 nuclear warheads and enough highly enriched uranium and plutonium to make 60,000 more, together with 40,000 metric tons of chemical weapons; it also left behind the knowledge to produce and deploy industrial-scale quantities of an array of biological weapons – including the smallpox virus.[34] Russia's dysfunctional economy and eroded security systems have undercut controls on these weapons, material and know-how, and increased the risk that they could flow to terrorist groups or hostile forces. It is a matter of clear self-interest for Europeans and North Americans to make sure that the members of the bioscience research community in the former Soviet Union (some of whom were former bio-weaponeers) can earn a living and participate in the global scientific community, and not be tempted to join those who would use their talents against us.

To this end, the US and its partners have worked with Russia to develop a range of initiatives to deal with this challenge. The leading program is the Cooperative Threat Reduction (CTR) program, also known as the Nunn–Lugar program. The Nuclear Threat Initiative (a non-governmental organization) is also active, and an EU–Russia cooperative program for non-proliferation and disarmament exists as well. Together, these programs offer a variety of targeted efforts to improve the security of pathogenic collections held at former Soviet bio-weapons facilities, ensure safe storage and handling of pathogens at microbiological research centers, promote collaborative research designed to prevent proliferation of bio-weapon-related biotechnology, improve transparency, and enhance force protection capabilities. Details regarding the full dimension of these programs are beyond the scope of this essay, but are readily available.[35]

Efforts to deal with the former Soviet Union's bio-security legacy have been uneven. At the June 2002 G8 Summit, the European Union, Canada, France, Germany, Italy, Japan, Russia, and the United Kingdom pledged to match US funding of non-proliferation programs – $10 billion over ten years. The G8 also announced the creation of a Global Partnership to confront the threat posed by the potential proliferation of nuclear, chemical, and biological weapons and materials emanating from the former Soviet Union. Since 2002, membership in the Partnership has been extended to a number of new donors. The Partnership's scope has also been extended to areas beyond the former Soviet Union. Unfortunately, even though leading European nations have now accepted the need to share the burden, commensurate with Europe's financial capacities, actual pledges made by the other G8 partners remain below their commitments, and few of the funds pledged have been allocated for actual Global Partnership projects. Moreover, these efforts remain heavily focused on nuclear non-proliferation, with some attention to chemical issues. Biological non-proliferation and bio-safety largely remain orphans of this effort. Except for a US commitment of $54 million for improved safety and security of dangerous pathogen collections in Russia, Kazakhstan, Uzbekistan, and Georgia, only France (€5 million) and Sweden ($130,000) have allocated any of their Partnership funds for work in the biological realm. The European Commission, Germany, the UK, Japan, Russia, Finland, the Netherlands, Norway and Switzerland have not allocated any of their Partnership funding to bio-safety or bio-weapons non-proliferation issues.[36] Moreover, efforts in Russia have been hampered by the fact that while cooperation is ongoing in most facilities involved in the former Soviet biological weapons program, four former military facilities continue to refuse to cooperate with the Nunn–Lugar program.[37]

Another attempt to limit the proliferation of dual-use biotechnologies is the Australia Group, an informal consortium comprised of the US, most European nations, the European Commission, Argentina, Australia, New Zealand, Japan, and South Korea, which seeks to harmonize national export controls on dual-use chemical and biological materials and laboratory equipment. The group was established in 1985 following the widespread use of chemical weapons by Iraq during the Iran–Iraq war, but has since turned its attention to biological weapons as well. Significantly, it has also complemented its traditional focus on state-level proliferation with greater emphasis on non-state actors. The Australia Group's effectiveness is limited, however, due to the informal, non-binding nature of the organization's efforts.[38]

These operational efforts to enhance non-proliferation are complicated by the challenges facing biological arms control treaties. The crux of the problem is that it is very difficult to distinguish between offensive and defensive efforts. There are no internationally recognized boundaries between "offensive" and "defensive" biological research and development programs – essentially, all of biomedical research and laboratory equipment is dual-use. The only criterion is intent, which is an exceedingly difficult benchmark. For the past 30 years, the primary arms control focus of the international community has been on vertical proliferation. The centerpiece of such efforts is the 1972 Biological and Toxin Weapons Convention (BWC), signed by 145 nations, which bans the development, production, stockpiling, acquisition, and transfer of biological weapons.[39] As discussed above, the various attributes of bio-weapons, however, make verification exceedingly difficult, and the BWC does not in fact include provisions for verification.

Efforts to craft a monitoring protocol were initiated by BWC members in 1994. These negotiations, which were slow and difficult, were halted in 2001 when the US Government rejected a draft protocol, introduced a series of proposals intended to serve as alternatives to a legally binding, multilateral accord, and called for an end to the negotiations. US officials declared the draft protocol to be a "blind alley," arguing that it was not intrusive enough to detect clandestine biological weapons activities yet was too invasive to safeguard proprietary or classified information held by the pharmaceutical companies or government labs that would be inspected under the proposed protocol.[40]

The US position has unleashed a vigorous debate and contributed to transatlantic dissonance on the issue. Key allies argued that despite the draft protocol's limitations, it was still a useful step forward. The British Government, for example, while also expressing its preference for stronger measures to ensure compliance and transparency, made the point clear:

> ... the Protocol would have delivered significant benefits for transparency, monitoring and deterrence in key dual-use areas capable of misuse ... It would as such help to deter and investigate suspected non-compliance, whether concerning the activity of a particular facility, an alleged use of biological weapons or a suspicious outbreak of disease.[41]

In short, despite a range of initiatives, the overall picture is of an international effort that is suffering from the fact that essentially all of biology is dual-use and, unlike the nuclear arena, cannot be divided into clear offensive and defensive activities. In spite of these challenges, non-proliferation efforts can play a role in increasing global security, but there is a growing gap between the progress that is being made and the scope and urgency of the bio-weapons threat.

Issues of bio-defense

In contrast to issues of bio-safety and non-proliferation, the international challenges of bio-defense – efforts by medical and public health professionals to prepare for and respond to a bio-weapon attack – have received comparatively little attention with respect to transatlantic collaboration. Yet, given the challenges of preventing a bio-attack, bio-defense and crisis response efforts are critically important. While other global security threats (e.g. nuclear, chemical, radiological) have an immediate effect, and response efforts can only "pick up the pieces," the incubation period of most infectious diseases means that many of the people infected in the attack could be saved if an effective public health and medical response were to be mounted. It is even possible that the existence of a robust transatlantic (or international) response capability could serve to deter a bio-terrorist attack.

The ability to mount an effective bio-defense requires that government leaders have adequate situational awareness of the epidemic so that they can lead their publics and make good decisions. The leaders must also have at their disposal a robust medical response capability that will require both trained personnel and effective drugs, vaccines, and other medical counter-measures. These requirements are made even more challenging by the likely need to cooperate across borders to defend multiple national populations.[42]

Attaining situational awareness during an epidemic will be difficult given the pervasive uncertainties of size, scope, and timing that characterize an epidemic, especially one with the reload potential of a deliberate attack by a thinking enemy. In addition, in the transatlantic community, political leaders and even some national security and health officials are unfamiliar with bio-weapons and have limited direct experience with large epidemics of infectious disease – natural or intentional. A robust public health system is critical to attaining situational awareness of an ongoing outbreak, yet for years the nations of the transatlantic community have largely neglected their public health infrastructure. Even with the multibillion dollar investment in US public health since September 2001, significant shortfalls in bio-defense preparedness still remain due to decades-long neglect.[43] This uncertainty and lack of public health capacity will pose considerable challenges when international leaders are pressed to coordinate their actions.

Moreover, a bio-terrorist attack in Europe is likely to generate immediate tension among EU, national, and local authorities, given Europe's multi-jurisdictional setting.[44] Officials are likely to be tentative or uncertain in their initial response, and the lines of jurisdictional "competency" or author-ity are likely to be unclear, to differ, or to conflict. Similar issues are likely to arise between federal and state/provincial authorities within North America. The SARS epidemic in 2002–2003, for example, underscored that the EU is not institutionally prepared to deal with rapidly moving trans-national diseases. While the EU and member states had a system in place to monitor the spread of the SARS virus, they had no system for advising – let alone deciding – on EU-wide measures to contain it.[45] The recent integra-tion into the European Union and NATO of new, largely poorer member nations with uneven bio-terrorism preparedness capabilities could further enhance transatlantic vulnerability to infectious disease unless such integra-tion incorporates more systematic pan-European and transatlantic efforts to enhance infectious disease and bio-terrorism preparedness coordination.[46]

The ability to mount an effective medical response to a bio-attack is severely limited due to the developed world's neglect of infectious disease and public health for several generations. Health care is treated increasingly as a business; disaster and epidemic preparedness has often been neglected as an expensive "luxury." The economics of health care and just-in-time effi-ciencies have eliminated all surge capacity from hospitals in the US, and the situation is very similar in Europe. Hospitals today are simply not prepared for an influx of several dozen, let alone several thousand, ill and potentially contagious patients who will need complex treatment in an intensive care unit setting.[47] During the SARS outbreak in Toronto, only a few hundred cases crippled the health-care system for the entire five-million-plus person metropolitan region, and the city had to send out an urgent call to Canada and the US for volunteer doctors and nurses to shore up the system.[48]

In addition to a lack of medical response capacity, there is a severe lack of the tools required by doctors and nurses to tend to the ill – drugs, vaccines, diagnostic tests, and other countermeasures – and there is almost nothing in the pharmaceutical development pipeline. Claire Fraser, a prominent biologist and President of the Institute for Genomic Research (TIGR) in the US, recently wrote:

> The decisions within the pharmaceutical industry to abandon infectious disease research programs, which reflect today's economic reality, are coming at a time when the specter of antibiotic-resistant organisms is growing ever larger ... Our arsenals against microbial foes are inadequately stocked, and we are vulnerable not only to deliberate attacks but to natural outbreaks of emerging and reemerging diseases.[49]

There are only five major vaccine manufacturers in the world,[50] and a recent study found that of the 506 new drugs currently under development by the 22 largest pharmaceutical and biotech companies, only six were antibiotics.[51] Developing a new drug takes 5–15 years and costs several hundred million dollars (one prominent estimate puts the price tag at over $800 million).[52] The cost of development coupled with small markets in the developed world have driven pharmaceutical companies away from treatments for infectious disease and towards blockbuster drugs against chronic diseases with multi-billion dollar annual sales. The US Government's BioShield, a mechanism enabling the government to purchase $6 billion of bio-defense countermeasures over ten years,[53] is an important first step. However, given the size of the drug industry (a half-trillion dollar global market[54]), even $6 billion will likely not be enough to radically redirect drug developers or fill the antibiotic, antiviral, and vaccine pipelines. In addition, money alone will not solve this problem; a coherent countermeasure strategy in which industry, academia, and government work together as partners will be key.

Challenges to transatlantic bio-defense

The challenges of effective medical and public health preparedness and response at the national level are magnified significantly when considering the international aspects of preventing or responding to a fast-moving epidemic caused by an intentional attack of a contagious pathogen by a thinking enemy. Infectious disease does not recognize national borders. The international response to such a crisis will be influenced in particular by three key issues: transparency of information, movement of people, and sharing of resources. In each area there is serious need for more effective intra-European and transatlantic coordination, as well as coordinated transatlantic pressure to advance broader efforts within international bodies.

Transparency of information

Maintaining continual, open flows of information between public health officials, community physicians, security officials, and political leaders to provide situational awareness during an outbreak response is difficult yet essential. Even in a single metropolitan area, situational awareness and uniform decision-making can be a challenge – as was seen during the 2001 anthrax attacks, when public health agencies from Washington DC, Virginia, and Maryland initially could not agree on recommendations for treatment of anthrax, even though many of the sick and potentially exposed worked in one jurisdiction and lived in another. The Virginia and Maryland authorities followed the federal guidance from the Centers for Disease Control (CDC), while Washington DC officials did not.[55] This problem could be magnified many times when multiple nations are involved, due to considerations of national pride, economics, and security. Yet transparency is critical for the epidemiological investigation required to map and control the outbreak. In addition, knowing what neighboring nations are planning to do, especially how they plan to care for their citizens (e.g. vaccination plans), will also be critical for leaders to maintain public trust and confidence. If neighboring nations or close allies were to take dramatically different actions in repose to an epidemic or bio-attack, in order to maintain public confidence national leaders should be able proactively to explain these differences (and not be forced to react to news reports of actions in other nations).

The 2003 SARS outbreak offers a sobering example of how nations may react to an emergent epidemic within their nation. Although effective communication across national borders is critical to managing an epidemic, Chinese officials did not disclose the growing outbreak to the World Health Organization (WHO) until 10 February 2003, three months after it began on 16 November 2002 in Guangdong province. As the SARS outbreak spread outwards from East Asia to Europe and the Americas, the WHO became more and more concerned about the lack of Chinese cooperation. Ultimately, the WHO broke with normal protocols requiring it to act only in concert with local authorities, and felt compelled to express unilaterally its "strong concern over inadequate reporting" of SARS cases by the Chinese Government.[56] Four days after that WHO announcement – a full five months after the outbreak began – China fully acknowledged the dimensions of the epidemic, announced a "war on SARS," and initiated aggressive action.[57] Unfortunately, the five-month delay contributed to the spread of SARS to dozens of countries, ultimately resulting in over 8,000 infections and approximately 800 deaths. In this case, unilateral action by the WHO may have effectively prompted a nation to act, but only after the epidemic had spread beyond national boundaries.

Subsequent epidemics have shown that other governments have not necessarily learned China's lesson – issues of economics, trade, or national pride can still impact leaders' judgments in this arena. It took weeks for Thailand, the world's fourth largest poultry exporter, to reveal that it had chicken flocks infected with avian flu in early 2004. The Thai Prime Minister was accused of attempting quietly to contain the outbreak so as to not harm the nation's exports.[58] In the end, as happened with SARS, this lack of transparency only worsened the situation.

Currently, nations have limited tools to guarantee that their neighbors are acting transparently. The WHO is severely restricted in its ability to act independently of a national government. Generally, it must be invited into a nation, and must gain permission to investigate affected regions. The SARS outbreak has prompted the WHO's governing body, the World Health Assembly, to increase the authority of the WHO to act more independently to respond to an epidemic – new International Health Regulatons to codify these authorities were approved in May 2005.[59]

Not only is the international community as a whole ill-equipped to deal with information transparency during a bio-attack or other mass epidemic, the nations of the Atlantic Alliance themselves are also poorly prepared to cope with this challenge. There are some rudimentary mechanisms in place. The Euro-Atlantic Disaster Response Coordination Centre (EADRCC) was created in 1998 as the focal point for coordinating disaster relief efforts of the 46 Euro-Atlantic Partnership Council (EAPC) nations, but these efforts are not integrated into broader alliance security considerations, and have been focused primarily on technological accidents or natural disasters (such as floods or fires) rather than terrorist attacks.[60] EU nations also operate a series of disease surveillance networks, each managed by a different member nation, but they are designed to monitor disease during "peacetime." The intense pressures that would arise during the response to a bio-terrorist attack would likely stress these systems far beyond what they were designed for. It is not clear that the EU is institutionally prepared to deal, in Europe, with the pressures of a transnational, rapidly moving disease epidemic caused by a bio-attack, much less to provide assistance to other regions, including the US.[61] Additionally, the pre-existing public heath and infectious disease communications networks that do exist in the EU operate primarily between technical experts in public health or disaster preparedness. There is little direct contact with senior decision-makers or political leaders. After a bio-terrorist attack, however, communications and decision-making would immediately become strategic and should involve senior-level political leaders in affected nations.

The likely unevenness of European and transatlantic response was highlighted in September 2003 by Exercise Global Mercury, an international "table-top" simulation conducted under the auspices of the G7's Global

Health Security Action Group to test communications between national health agencies in the event of a smallpox outbreak. EU member states focused on implementation of their national plans, the international aspects of national measures were seldom discussed, and no EU-wide strategy emerged to combat the outbreak. The exercise also highlighted the lack of international considerations in most national smallpox plans, and the difficulties involved in international exchange of information during such an emergency.[62]

Movement of people

Movement of infected people following an attack with a contagious disease could amplify the attack's initial effect, and would complicate the ability to attain situational awareness of the outbreak. As noted above, one of the earliest SARS patients flew from Singapore to New York to Frankfurt before his symptoms became apparent.[63] Unfortunately, there is no good understanding of how restriction of movement across international borders could help (or hurt) the response to an international bio-terror attack, and no preexisting standards or procedures between nations for restricting movement of people or trade in such contingencies. Many overlapping treaties, such as WTO, NAFTA or bilateral arrangements, obscure the legal framework for action. The Schengen agreement, which provides for free movement of people among 15 European countries, is not clear whether its emergency clause permitting temporary closure of borders could be triggered by a public health crisis. There is even less clarity within Europe, across the Atlantic, and internationally on procedures to restart international trave and trade once borders have been closed or movement of people restricted.

Sharing of resources

Another great challenge for international bio-terrorism response is the issue of sharing limited medical resources between nations during a crisis. Therapeutic drugs and vaccines will become severely limited during the response to a bio-terrorist attack, and there are restricted pre-existing mechanisms to share these vital resources between nations. Even doctors and nurses can become limiting in a crisis, as was seen during the Toronto SARS outbreak in 2003, when Toronto was forced to put out a call to US physicians and nurses to travel to Canada and care for SARS patients.[64] Stocks of smallpox vaccine are national secrets in many countries, and so complete statistics are difficult to obtain. However, it appears that national efforts to stockpile vaccine are very uneven. Information compiled by the European Commission in 2003 showed that national stockpiles of smallpox vaccine ranged from having one dose per citizen to having enough for one dose per 30 citizens.[65] It is likely that only a handful of nations in the world (US, UK, France,

Germany, and perhaps a few others) have enough smallpox vaccine for their entire population. Many would be dependent on assistance from other countries – but which countries should receive such resources, and based on what criteria (e.g. close allies, a first-come-first-served basis, or every government that shows a need and asks for it)? It would be very difficult for any national leader to send precious vaccine to other nations when his or her own citizens were at risk. Discussions regarding developing a common European stockpile and having a sharing scheme of antibiotics and vaccines failed to lead to substantive action. Most member states, in fact, did not wish to continue these sensitive discussions, as any reform would require significant financial resources for what is still regarded as a low-probability problem.[66] The WHO does maintain a small stockpile of smallpox vaccine left over from the eradication campaign that could be used to combat a smallpox outbreak, and it is working to develop a "virtual" stockpile of vaccine from national stockpiles.[67] Plans for distributing this critical resource in the wake of a smallpox attack, however, are still being developed.

Moving forward

Bio-terrorism poses a daunting series of interrelated security challenges for the transatlantic community. As Europe and North America work to lead an international effort to thwart this threat, primary consideration should be given to the following two factors.

First, there is a window of opportunity, but it is closing. Despite the vast potential for bio-weapons proliferation, thus far the spread of such weapons among states and non-state actors appears to have been limited. The power of biotechnology to do good or ill is increasing at an accelerating rate, and as a result we are on the cusp of exponential change, both in the power of bio-weapons as well as their accessibility to state and non-state actors alike. Effective action now could mitigate the negative impact of this technological trend.

Second, something can be done after an attack to minimize, or potentially eliminate, death and suffering. Drugs, vaccines and other medical countermeasures can save lives if there is a robust medical response capacity. The transatlantic community contains the highest concentration of biomedical talent in the world, as well as the bulk of the global pharmaceutical industry. Concerted efforts to build on this capacity and integrate it with robust governmental decision-making systems will save lives.

With these factors in mind, it is incumbent upon the US and Europe to build on their respective efforts to thwart bio-terrorism by working more effectively across the Atlantic. Efforts to bolster trans-European or transatlantic bio-terrorism preparedness will remain limited until medical, public health, and local civil emergency authorities are more effectively woven into the European integration process and transatlantic civil/homeland defense. High-level political awareness is critical, and commensurate political commitment and monetary resources are required. As former US Senator Sam Nunn has stated:

> We have to realize that we have reached a new realm in the dialectic of new weapons and new defenses. In the evolution of warfare, arrows were countered by shields, swords with armor, guns with tanks, and now biological weapons must be countered with medicines, vaccines and surveillance systems.

The US and Europe should advance a broad-based effort at protection in depth that includes mutually reinforcing initiatives in the areas of biosafety, non-proliferation, and bio-defense.

New steps in bio-safety and non-proliferation

As discussed above, the almost universal "dual use" nature of biological sciences and the prevalence of many dangerous pathogens in nature limit the ability of bio-safety and non-proliferation efforts to prevent a biological attack. Nevertheless, such efforts have an important role to play as the transatlantic community seeks to build a layered defense against this strategic threat, and as cooperative international efforts to develop uniform standards and procedures are underway.

Bio-safety and non-proliferation could both be served by a more integrated global bioscience research community that develops shared standards and norms of behavior. The dual-use nature of bioscience and the inability to draw clear lines around "dangerous" science has led some to suggest that the scientific community should use a self-governance system to manage the gray area of dual-use science, and minimize accidental development of powerful bio-weapons.[68] However, others feel that a more formal regime is necessary – and possible.[69] A recent National Academies of Science report recommended the more flexible self-governance model, and proposed that, in the US, a panel of scientists should evaluate potentially dangerous lines of experimentation and determine if the potential benefits outweigh the costs.[70] The US Government quickly accepted many of the report's recommendations, and established the National Science Advisory Board for Biosecurity (NSABB).[71] The NSABB is still in its planning stages, so it is unclear how the board will carry out its mission, and how effective it will be. Pre-existing efforts that sought to engage scientists in the former Soviet Union (as the Nunn–Lugar CTR programs do) could be expanded and linked with these new calls for the biomedical research community in the US and Europe to consider the dual-use implications of its research. This could create a more unified scientific community, including researchers in the Americas, Europe, the former Soviet Union, and Asia, that is actively working to prevent proliferation of biological weapons.

The Organization for Economic Cooperation and Development (OECD), a group of 31 advanced industrial countries headquartered in Paris, is working to establish a global network of Biological Resource Centers (BRCs) that would act as a virtual lending library of microbial cultures based on harmonized, accredited standards and regulations for bio-safety. These arrangements will be based on voluntary agreement, but those countries failing to meet the standards will be excluded.[72] Efforts by the WHO and professional societies to improve and harmonize national standards in the wake of the recent laboratory accidents with SARS virus should be encouraged.[73]

Other international organizations have also entered the non-proliferation arena. The OSCE has proposed licensing standards and enforcement procedures related to dangerous pathogens and dual-use biotechnology equipment. The World Customs Organization has begun informal information-sharing with Interpol and the World Health Organization to combat the smuggling of biological, chemical, and radioactive materials. The International Maritime Organization plans to negotiate agreements to halt the shipping of biological agents for hostile purposes, and to criminalize the use of biological weapons on maritime vessels.[74] Additionally, as Jonathan Winer discusses in Chapter 6, the G7 responded to the danger of terrorist financing during the 1990s by launching a Financial Action Task Force to set global standards in this area. The FATF provides an interesting model of a networked response to a networked threat, and may offer some lessons learned for networked cooperation in other areas, including bio-weapon non-proliferation efforts involving non-state actors

Standard-setting can also help to invigorate efforts to counter vertical proliferation (i.e. state-sponsored programs). Many diplomatic initiatives have faltered due to failure to articulate an international standard that governments would be expected to meet. Absent identification of and agreement on such standards, governments have little to compel them to take action. Many governments will enact measures that fall short of worthwhile standards either unintentionally, because they cannot decipher the existing regulatory concepts, or intentionally, because they seek to perpetuate illicit activities. The let-each-government-do-as-it-pleases approach will further foster an uneven patchwork of domestic laws and practices that might have little near-term value and could prove difficult to harmonize in the future. Extending international standards and making them decipherable for translation in to national legislation will raise the bar.[75]

Making progress on transatlantic bio-defense

As discussed above, an effective bio-defense must provide situational awareness to decision-makers, and a robust medical response capacity. Although many of the medical and public health preparedness components of an effective bio-defense are nationally focused, infectious disease epidemics do not recognize national boundaries. International bio-defense cooperation – beginning with the nations of the Atlantic Alliance – will be critical to the success of any individual national effort. Key will be closer intra-European cooperation, together with new forms of cooperation between the US and the EU, and between NATO and its partners as well.

A potentially significant EU initiative is the creation of the European Center for Disease Prevention and Control (ECDC) in Sweden, to be operational in 2005. Its mission encompasses elements of bio-safety, non-proliferation, and bio-defense. The ECDC will operate as a network rather than a centralized agency, maintaining only a small office in Sweden. It will run no independent labs, nor will it consolidate any member state disease-control agencies. It will work as a coordinating entity in charge of pooling European resources and reinforcing those existing public health organizations across the European Union that are in charge of controlling communicable diseases.[76] Among other responsibilities, it will provide scientific advice to the EU Commission and national authorities, facilitate epidemiological surveillance and laboratory networking, operate the EU's early warning and response system (EWRS), and support the development of EU-level preparedness planning for health crises "such as an influenza pandemic or a bio-terrorist attack."[77] Although the ECDC has been envisioned as pursuing the same goals as the US Centers for Disease Control and Prevention based in Atlanta, Georgia, and is likely to become a focal point for transatlantic communication on disease surveillance and bio-defense issues, the ECDC will have very different operational capabilities and administrative structures.[78] Most importantly, the prerogative of deciding on a specific course of action in a crisis will still be in the hands of the member states. Nevertheless, the ECDC could serve as an important European partner for the US CDC and other nations if the ECDC is involved a coherent EU-wide decision-making process.

A second, related effort is the Global Health Security Action Group established by the health ministers of the G7 plus Mexico on 7 November 2001 in Ottawa. The group has worked on improving international communications and assistance capabilities in a health crisis, improving non-proliferation protocols for the transfer of pathogens from one laboratory to another, and promoting best practice in such areas as vaccine production and isolation techniques. The Global Health Security Action Group might consider extending its current work, which has been limited primarily to assessing communications in a crisis, to standard setting and medical resource-sharing. It could even engage G7 Interior and Foreign Ministers (in the US case, the Secretaries of Homeland Security and State) to consider the difficult issue of movement of people.

As NATO transforms itself for the twenty-first century, the Alliance's civil defense capabilities should be revamped and given much higher profile with respect to bio-terrorism preparedness and response. The Partnership for Peace and the Euro-Atlantic Partnership Council have undertaken several initiatives in the biological protection field. Potentially, the Euro-Atlantic Disaster Response Coordination Center (EADRCC) could be used as a focal point for an operative effort.

The EU has been working to improve its preparedness. The anthrax attacks in the US, together with uncovered plots to unleash toxins and pathogens in Europe, have combined with the March 11 Madrid attacks to prompt EU member states and the European Commission to take several interrelated initiatives to enhance bio-preparedness and response capacity. For example, they have created a bio-terrorism task force,[79] have reinforced mechanisms to share information (e.g. early warning, alert, notification), established detection and classification methods, launched a mechanism for acquiring information on the capacities of laboratory facilities in the member states (as no single state has the laboratory capabilities and resources needed), and assessed the availability of serums and vaccines in the member states.[80] Such efforts are slow, however, and do not match the urgency of the challenge. Moreover, while the EU slowly enhances its operational and technical preparedness, top-level decision-makers and national leaders in Europe have only begun to consider how they might act if they were thrust unexpectedly into an acute crisis-management mode in response to a sudden outbreak of a contagious disease within Europe or in the transatlantic community – something which, unfortunately, could happen today.

Bio-defense is dependent on having drugs, vaccines, and other medical countermeasures available for use by medical and public health officials during a crisis, and, as has been discussed above, there is a critical lack of such medicines today. The transatlantic community possesses the bulk of the world's academic and industrial biomedical research community. Integrating these scientists and drug development experts into a coherent, targeted transatlantic effort to develop new bio-defense and infectious disease countermeasures would be a powerful tool to lower the threat of bio-terrorist attack. Such an effort should have a long-term goal of accelerating the drug development process overall and developing new countermeasures that can contribute to the elimination of the lethal effects of epidemics caused by bio-weapons.[81] The bioscience community is inherently international. A recent study has found that cross-border collaborations in the biosciences are growing, and are important to the development of new medicines. The authors of the study also recommended that national bio-defense efforts should encourage such international collaboration, not discourage it for fear of aiding proliferation.[82] The US Congress has tasked the National Institutes of Health (NIH) with the development of new bio-defense countermeasures, and has provided the agency with approximately $3.3 billion for intra- and extramural bio-defense research funding since 2001, with another $1.7 billion expected in 2005.[83] Unfortunately, this scale of investment in bio-defense research has not been mirrored in Europe.

Accomplishing the goal of taking infectious diseases and bio-terror agents "off the table" will require enormous creativity, organization, and investment. Leaders on both sides of the Atlantic should strive to link US Government research efforts in infectious disease and bio-defense with Europe's, perhaps through the EU's "framework program" of scientific funding. Such a linkage, combined with a robust strategy that adequately engages and directs academic, industrial, and government researchers, could result in the development of the medicines needed not only to reduce the threat of bio-terrorism in the transatlantic community, but perhaps also to eliminate the scourge of infectious disease worldwide.

Conclusion

It is perhaps impossible to protect fully against any biological attack. The goal must be to enhance the resilience of European and North American societies to large-scale biological attacks so that it is not worth mounting them. There is an opportunity for transatlantic leadership on this issue, but time is not on our side. It is urgent that Europeans and Americans address the threat now.

Issues of public health must become mainstream issues of diplomacy and national security. This means offering opportunities in government for experts in these matters – the interface between governments and biomed-ical experts in academia and industry must become tighter. We will not succeed without a critical mass in governments of those who understand the science and can understand the threat. Europe and America have phenome-nal capability in bioscience, medicine, and public health. Whether it can be mobilized and directed quickly enough to prevent or minimize the effects of a big bio-terrorist attack is an open question. Can we switch the advantage to the defense? Absolutely. But it is a matter of will and imagination.

Notes

1 See G. Koblentz, "Pathogens as weapons: the international security implications of biological warfare," *International Security*, 28(3), Winter 2003/2004. For tech-nical background on biological weapons, see Office of Technology Assessment (OTA), *Proliferation of Weapons of Mass Destruction: Assessing the Risks*, Washing-ton, DC: US Government Printing Office, 1993, pp. 71–117.
2 Office of Technology Assessment, op. cit., pp. 53–54.
3 B. Broad, "A nation challenged: the spores; terror anthrax resembles type made by US," *New York Times*, 3 December 2001.
4 T. V. Inglesby, T. O'Toole, D. A. Henderson *et al.*, "Anthrax as a biological weapon, 2002," *Journal of the American Medical Association*, 287, 2236–2252.
5 This is unlike plutonium and highly-enriched uranium, the essential ingredi-ents for nuclear weapons, which are synthetic materials that do not exist in nature and are difficult and costly to produce.
6 Koblentz, op. cit. This is in contrast to about a hundred restricted nuclear sites around the world containing weapons-grade fissile materials.
7 J. Miller, "Next to Old Rec Hall, a 'germ–making plant'," *New York Times*, 4 September 2001.
8 This stands in stark contrast to the elaborate efforts in place to track and control the materials needed to build nuclear weapons. For further details see Koblentz, op. cit., and J. B. Tucker, *Biosecurity: Limiting Terrorist Access to Deadly Pathogens*, Washington, DC: US Institute of Peace, November 2003.

9 D. A. Edwards and C. Dunbar, "Bioengineering of therapeutic aerosols," *Annual Review of Biomedical Engineering*, 4, 2002, 93–107.

10 D. B. Levin and G. V. De Amorim, "Potential for aerosol dissemination of biological weapons: lessons from biological control of insects," *Biosecurity and Bioterrorism*, 1(1), 2003, 37–42.

11 Tucker, op. cit.; K. Alibek and S. Handelman, *Biohazard*, New York: Random House, 1999.

12 Tucker, op. cit.; Koblentz, op. cit.

13 See G. Kwik J. Fitzgerald, T. V. Inglesby, and T. O'Toole. "Biosecurity: responsible stewardship of bioscience in an age of catastrophic terrorism," *Biosecurity and Bioterrorism*, 1(1), 2003, 27–35.

14 J. B. Petro, T. R. Plasse and J. A. McNulty, *Biosecurity and Bioterrorism*, Vol. 1(1), 161–168.

15 R. Danzig, *Catastrophic Bioterrorism – What Is To Be Done?* Washington, DC: Center for Technology and National Security Policy, National Defense University, August 2003.

16 A January 2003 workshop hosted by the CIA and the National Research Council brought together bio-scientists and members of the intelligence community to discuss the signatures (or "observables") that would indicate the presence of an offensive bio-weapons program using sophisticated biotechnologies. The bio-scientists indicated in the strongest terms that there would be no such signatures – biotechnologies are all dual-use. An official summary of this meeting is available online at www.fas.org/irp/cia/product/bw1103.pdf (accessed 22 September 2004).

17 Tucker, op. cit.

18 R. Danzig, op. cit.

19 R. Murch, *Biosecurity and Bioterrorism*, 1, 2003 117–122. B. Budowle, S. E. Schutzer, A. Einseln *et al.*, "Building microbial forensics as a response to bioterrorism," *Science*, 26 September 2003, 1852–1853.

20 WHO update 95-SARS: Chronology of a Serial Killer, available online at: www.who.int/csr/don/2003_07_04/en/ (accessed 20 September 2004).

21 To begin to address this gap, a table-top exercise called *Atlantic Storm* was convened 14 January 2005 by the Center for Biosecurity of UPMC, the Center for Transatlantic Relations of Johns Hopkins University, and the Transatlantic Biosecurity Network. *Atlantic Storm* simulated a summit of transatlantic leaders forced to respond to bioterrorist attacks on multiple nations. The exercise focused on the high-level strategic, political, and security challenges that heads of government will be confronted with as they respond to the unique security threat of bio-terrorism. Further information on the exercise is available online at http://www.upmc-biosecurity.org./ and http://www.transatlantic.sais-jhu.edu See also J. Miller, "Exercise finds US unable to handle germ war threat," *New York Times*, 26 April 1998, p. A1; T. V. Inglesby, R. Grossman and T. O'Toole, "A plague on your city: observations from TOPOFF," *Clinical Infectious Diseases*, 32(3) 2001, 436–445; and T. O'Toole, M. Mair, and T. V. Inglesby, "Shining light on dark winter: lessons Learned," *Clinical Infectious Diseases*, 34(7), 2002, 972–983.

22 According to the US Government, roughly a dozen countries, including Iran and North Korea, are thought to have offensive bio-warfare efforts underway. US Department of State, International Information Programs, "Statement of Under Secretary of State for Arms Control and International Security John Bolton to the Fifth Review Conference of the Biological Weapons Convention," Geneva, Switzerland, 19 November 2001, available online at: www.state.gov/t/us/rm/janjuly/6231.htm.

23 D. E. Kaplan, "Aum Shinriyko," in J. Tucker (ed.), *Toxic Terror*, Cambridge: MIT Press, 2000.

24 Cited in Tucker, *Biosecurity*, op. cit; B. Gellman, "Al Qaeda near biological, chemical arms production," *Washington Post*, 23 March 2003, p. A1. Case studies of terrorist groups interested in biological weapons can be found in J. B. Tucker (ed.), *Toxic Terror*, op. cit., and W. S. Carus, *Bioterrorism and Biocrimes: The Illicit Use of Biological Agents in the 20th Century*, Washington, DC: National Defense University, April 2001.

25 J. B. Petro and D. Relman, "Understanding threats to scientific openness," *Science*, 12 December 2003, 1898.

26 For additional perspectives, see M. L. Ostfield, "Bioterrorism as a foreign policy issue," *SAIS Review*, 24(1) 2004, 131–146.

27 Available online at www.cdc.gov/od/sap/ (accessed 21 September 2004); D. Malakoff, "Congress adopts tough rules for labs," *Science*, 31 May 2002, 1585–1587.

28 D. Normile and G. Vogel, "Early indications point to lab infection in new SARS case," *Science*, 19 September 2003, 1642–1643; D. Normile "Second lab accident fuels fears about SARS," *Science*, 2 January 2004, 26; D. Normile, "Mounting lab accidents raise SARS fears," *Science*, 30 April 2004, 659–660.

29 *Biotechnology Research in an Age of Terrorism*, Committee on Research Standards and Practices to Prevent the Destructive Application of Biotechnology, National Research Council, 2004; D. Malakoff and M. Enserink, "Biodefense: researchers await government response to self-regulation plea," *Science*, 17 October 2003, 368–369.

30 *House of Cards: The Pivotal Importance of a Technically Sound BWC Monitoring Protocol*, Washington, DC: Stimson Center, 2001.

31 Tucker, *Biosecurity*, op. cit.

32 J. Cello, A. V. Paul and E. Wimmer, "Chemical synthesis of poliovirus cDNA: generation of infectious virus in the absence of natural template," *Science*, 9 August 2002, 1016–1018.

33 J. D. Steinbruner and E. D. Harris, "Controlling dangerous pathogens," *Issues in Science & Technology*, 19(3) 2003; 47–54; G. Kwik, J. Fitzgerald, T. Inglesby, and T. O'Toole, "Biosecurity: responsible stewardship of bioscience in an age of catastrophic terrorism," *Biosecurity and Bioterrorism*, 1(1), 2003, 27–35; *Biotechnology Research in an Age of Terrorism*, op cit.

34 K. Alibek and S. Handelman, *Biohazard*, New York: Random House, 1999.

35 Joint US–Russian research is being conducted at 49 former biological weapons production facilities, and security improvements are underway at four biological weapons sites. See the statement by Senator Richard Lugar at the National Press Club, 11 August 2004, available online at: www.lugar.senate.gov/nunnlugar. html. The suggestion has also been made to expand European involvement in these programs, perhaps by expanding the scope of the EU's Joint Action plan toward Russia as the basis of an EU equivalent to CTR and a mechanism for coordinating bilateral arrangements between EU states and third countries. See D. Feakes, "The emerging European disarmament and non-proliferation agenda on chemical and biological weapons," *Disarmament Diplomacy*, 65, 2002.

36 For a detailed official outline of funding commitments and projects by country, see G8 Consolidated Report of Global Partnership Projects, available online at: www.g8usa.gov/pdfs/GPConsolidatedReportofGPProjectsJune2004.pdf. A related initiative is the Proliferation Security Initiative (PSI), a multilateral effort established in 2003 to interdict weapons and materials of mass destruction. More than 60 nations, including Russia, have associated themselves with this effort, but it too focuses primarily on nuclear issues. See the EU country

report in Volume 3, *International Responses*, of R. Einhorn and M. Flournoy, *Protecting Against the Spread of Nuclear, Biological and Chemical Weapons*, Washington, DC: Center for Strategic and International Studies, 2003.

37 For an independent assessment of the Global Partnership's progress, see the CSIS monitoring effort, available online at: www.sgpproject.org/GP%20Scorecard.pdf.

38 Available online, at www.australiagroup.net/ (accessed 14 September 2004); Koblentz, op. cit.; Tucker, *Biosecurity*, op. cit.

39 Available online at: www.opbw.org/ (accessed 20 September 2004); www.state.gov/t/ac/trt/4718.htm (accessed 20 September 2004).

40 "The draft protocol that was under negotiation for the past seven years is dead in our view. Dead, and it is not going to be resurrected. It has proven to be a blind alley." US Department of State, International Information Programs, "Bolton briefing on the biological weapons pact," transcript of press conference, 20 November 2001, available online at: www.usinfo.state.gov/topical/pol/terror/01112003.htm. See also Ambassador Donald Mahley, "Statement by the United States to the Ad Hoc Group of Biological Weapons Convention States Parties," Geneva, Switzerland, 25 July 2001, available online at: www.state.gov/t/ac/rls/rm/2001/5497.htm For a review of US participation in the negotiations over a verification protocol to the BWC, see M. Leitenberg, *Biological Weapons and "Bioterrorism" in the First Years of the 21st Century*, Center for International and Security Studies, School of Public Affairs, University of Maryland. Paper prepared for conference on "The Possible Use of Biological Weapons by Terrorist Groups: Scientific, Legal and International Implications," ICGEB, Landau Network, Ministry of Foreign Affairs, Rome, April 16, 2002, paper updated to 15 May 2002.

41 See *Strengthening the Biological and Toxin Weapons Convention: Countering the Threat from Biological Weapons*, UK Foreign and Commonwealth Office.

42 Koblentz, op. cit.; Tucker, *Biosecurity*, op. cit.

43 *Ready or Not? Protecting a Public's Health in an Age of Bioterrorism*, Washington, DC: Trust for America's Health, December 2003.

44 B. Sundelius and J. Grönvall, "Strategic dilemmas of biosecurity in the European Union," *Biosecurity and Bioterrorism*, 2, (1), 2004, 17–23.

45 EU Health and Consumer Protection Commissioner David Byrne noted that SARS was a "wake-up call" for Europe to get better prepared and to substantially enforce cooperation at an EU level.

46 R. J. Coker, R. A. Atun, and M. McKee, *The Lancet*, 363, 2004, 1389–1392.

47 The mean occupancy rate of US intensive care units (where many of the seriously ill victims of a bio-attack will need to be treated) in the largest US hospitals has been estimated to be 93 per cent. J. S. Groeger, K. K. Guntupalli, M. Strasberg *et al.*, *Critical Care Medicine*, 21, 1993, 279–291.

48 L. K. Altmann, "The doctor's world; behind the mask, the fear of SARS," *New York Times*, 24 June 2003.

49 C. M. Fraser, "An uncertain call to arms," *Science*, 16 April 2004, 359.

50 They are Merck and Co., Aventis Pasteur, GlaxoSmithKlein, Wyeth, and Chiron.

51 B. Spellberg, J. H. Powers, E. P. Brass *et al.*, *Clinical Infectious Diseases*, 38, 2004, 1279–1286.

52 J. A. DiMasi, R. W. Hansen, and H. G. Grabowski, *Journal of Health Economics*, 22, 2003, 151–185.

53 US Public Law 108–276.

54 IMS *World Review*, 2004.

55 E. Gursky, T. V. Inglesby and T. O'Toole, *Biosecurity and Bioterrorism*, 1, 2003, 97–110.

56 "Learning for SARS," Washington, DC: Institute of Medicine, 2004.
57 "Learning for SARS," Washington, DC: Institute of Medicine, 2004.
58 A. Sipress, "Thailand admits mistakes in handling of bird flu outbreak," *Washington Post*, 28 January 2004.
59 C. H. Conde, "WHO seeks to change rules on contagious diseases," *International Herald Tribune*, 28 April 2004.
60 There have been some limited efforts to shift the EADRCC from its focus on natural disasters to premeditated attacks. The field exercise "Dacia 2003" in October 2003, proposed by Romania, focused on consequence management following a terrorist attack using a Radiological Dispersion Device ("dirty bomb"). Unfortunately, this remains a rather isolated example. For more information see "Dacia 2003", available online at: www.nato.int/eadrcc/2003/dacia/index.htm.
61 Sundelius and Grönvall, op. cit
62 S. Vedantam, "WHO assails wealthy nations on bioterror," *Washington Post*, 5 November 2003. For the full report, see *Global Mercury Report*, available online at: www.doh.gov.uk/cmo/exerciseglobalmercury/globalmercuryreport.PDF.
63 Available online, at www.who.int/csr/don/2003_07_04/en/ (accessed 20 September 2004).
64 L. K Altmann, "Behind the mask, the fear of SARS," *The New York Times*, 24 June 2003.
65 See Sundelius and Grönvall, op. cit.; Tucker, op. cit; Tegnell, op. cit.; Leitenberg, op. cit.
66 Ibid.
67 The WHO currently has several hundred thousand doses of vaccine, but studies have shown that those doses likely could be diluted 1 : 5 without losing efficacy. Available online, at www.who.int/csr/disease/smallpox/preparedness/en/ (accessed 20 September 2004).
68 G. Kwik *et al*, op. cit.
69 J. D. Steinbruner and E. D. Harris, op. cit.
70 *Biotechnology Research in an Age of Terrorism*, op cit. D. Malakoff and M. Enserink, op cit.
71 Available online, at www.biosecurityboard.gov/index.htm (accessed 20 September 2004).
72 See the OECD report, *Biological Resource Centers: Underpinning the Future of Life Sciences and Biotechnology*. Online, available at: www.oecd.org/dataoecd/26/19/31685725.pdf.
73 Available online at: www.who.int/csr/labepidemiology/projects/biosafetymain/en/ (accessed 14 September 2004); D. Normile, "SARS experts want labs to improve safety practices," *Science*, 3 October 2003, 31.
74 For a review of various agreements, see Tucker, *Biosecurity*, op. cit., and Koblentz, op. cit.
75 Tucker, *Biosecurity*, op. cit.
76 The agency will likely start in 2005 with a core staff of as few as 40 people and then grow to a full force of 100 people by 2007. See N. Stafford, "European CDC closer to reality," *The Scientist* website, available online at: www.biomedcentral.com/news/20031204/04/; A. Tegnell, P. Bossi, A. Baka, F. Van Loock, J. Hendriks, S. Wallyn, and G. Gouvras, "The European Commission's Task Force on Bioterrorism," *Emerging Infectious Diseases*, October 2003. Online, available at: www.cdc.gov/ncidod/EID/vol9no10/03–0368.htm. See also "European Centre for Disease Prevention and Control (ECDC)," European Union website, available online at: europa.eu.int/comm/health/ph_overview/strategy/ecdc/ecdc_en.htm.

77 "European Centre for Disease Prevention and Control (ECDC)," European Union website, available online at: europa.eu.int/comm/health/ph_overview/ strategy/ecdc/ecdc_en.htm.
78 Stafford, op. cit.; Tegnell, op. cit.; "European Centre for Disease Prevention and Control Proposed," European Public Health Alliance website, available online at: www.epha.org/a/585.
79 A. Tegnell, P. Bossi, A. Baka *et al.*, *Emerging Infectious Diseases*, 9, 2003, 1330–1332.
80 Available online, at http://europa.eu.int/comm/health/ph_threats/Bioterror-isme/bioterrorisme_en.htm (accessed 20 September 2004). "European Centre for Disease Prevention and Control Proposed," European Public Health Alliance website. Online, available at: www.epha.org/a/585.
81 B. T. Smith, T. V. Inglesby, and T. O' Toole, *Biosecurity and Bioterrorism*, 1, 2003, 193–202.
82 K. Hoyt and S. Brooks, "A double-edged sword: globalization and biosecurity," *International Security*, 28(3), 2003–2004, 123–148.
83 A. Schuler, "Billions for biodefense: federal agency biodefense funding, FY2001–FY2005," *Biosecurity and Bioterrorism*, 2(2), 2004, 86–96, available online at: www.niaid.nih.gov/biodefense/ (accessed 21 September 2004).

3 Preventing nuclear terrorism by means of supply-side security

Morten Bremer Maerli[1]

Just prior to Christmas Eve 2003, scores of casually dressed government nuclear scientists with sophisticated radiation detection equipment hidden in briefcases and golf bags began scouring five major US cities for radiological, or "dirty," bombs.[2] The teams crisscrossed the cities, taking measurements 24 hours a day. Suddenly, after a week of probing, the searchers received their first and only radiation detection at a downtown storage in Las Vegas. The finding sent a jolt of tension through the nation's security apparatus. Even the White House was notified. The FBI agents were on to something big, protecting the homeland against international terrorism. But the "dirty bomb" soon turned out to be a therapeutic radium source, inadvertently stored by a homeless man.

What does this flustered exercise tell us? Certainly not only that Christmas was ruined for many hardworking agents. The most important lesson is that detection of a dirty bomb or a nuclear explosive in a busy urban environment is challenging. Once an assembled nuclear explosive or fissile material reaches its country of destination, it may be too late for interception.

This chapter assesses the evolving threat of nuclear terrorism and appropriate measures to meet this peril. It starts by clarifying the many facets and (misrepresented) forms of nuclear terrorism. A subsequent risk assessment deals with different aspects of the threat, but with a special focus on the possible technical capability of nuclear terrorists. The chapter shows that rather than heightened vigilance and high-tech forensics in possible target areas, the focus needs to be on nuclear terrorism prevention by means of supply-side security at potential sources of illicit fissile material. If non-state actors have access to sufficient quantities of highly enriched uranium (HEU) or plutonium, the production of crude nuclear explosives is likely to be within their reach. The inevitable conclusion must be that "homeland security" starts abroad.

The single most formidable obstacle to would-be nuclear terrorists is access to fissile material. The risk of nuclear terrorism can hence best be reduced through adequate control, protection, and elimination of excessive stocks of weapon-usable fissile material. The gap, however, between the nuclear terrorist threat and the international response is widening.[3] The chapter therefore presents some specific policy recommendations for how to reduce the risk through proper nuclear material management. It concludes with a discussion on why and how European and American actors must work together: Nuclear terrorism represents a global threat that calls for multilateral solutions. The most suitable means to be applied is a combination of formalized arms control and *ad hoc* nuclear security initiatives. The backbone of this joint effort could be strong transatlantic cooperative threat reduction, building upon decades of mutual security assistance and well-established political and organizational connections.

What is "nuclear terrorism"?[4]

The possible modalities of terrorist attacks related to nuclear and radiological substances may be divided into four categories:[5]

1   Nuclear weapons
2   Nuclear materials
3   Nuclear facilities
4   Radiation sources/radiological dispersal devices.

The scenarios with potentially the gravest consequences are (1) where a complete nuclear weapon is seized by rogue elements – a preferred scenario for Hollywood thrillers – or (2) where nuclear materials get stolen for the subsequent fashioning of a nuclear explosive device. A nuclear detonation will result in huge physical *and* psychological damages. Even a crudely assembled nuclear explosive (like at Hiroshima) can produce devastating effects due to the heat, pressure, and radiation generated.[6] Generally, it is assumed that nuclear weapons are subject to stringent standards of physical security and control, and stealing an intact nuclear explosive may be harder than anticipated.[7] Delivery and use represent further challenges for potential perpetrators, and Scenario (1) is hence not part of the following assessment.

Scenario (3) involves the deliberate attacking of nuclear power plants, other nuclear facilities or nuclear spent fuel transports, to cause radioactive releases and societal disturbances. The major threat associated with nuclear facilities involves the theft or diversion of nuclear material from the facility, a hostile takeover, or a physical attack or act of sabotage. If such an attack were to cause either a meltdown of the reactor core or a dispersal of the spent fuel waste on the site, the power plant would be a source of radiological contamination, and resulting fires could intensify the dispersion of radioactive material.

In Scenario (4), terrorists may combine highly radioactive nuclear material with conventional explosives to create radiological dispersal devices – so called "dirty bombs." Radiological dispersion devices could expose people to radiation as, for instance, radioactive laboratory waste or spent nuclear fuel would be wrapped around a conventional explosive and detonated, spreading poison and contamination. Alternatively, radioactive materials may be dispersed to the environment after the (mechanical) crushing or cracking of transportation casks for high-level radioactive materials. Pulverized radioactive substances in particular may be distributed fairly easily, once the source shielding and containment are disabled. However, while the radiation *could* kill during such scenarios, the primary impact on health and life would be through long-term effects (like cancer development).[8]

The associated psychological impact of any acts of radiological terrorism or attacks on nuclear facilities could be strong, and possibly magnified through media coverage. The prospect of panic and mass evacuation of urban centers should not be excluded. However, in the absence of any nuclear chain reaction and hence release of vast amounts of energy, "nuclear terrorism" may not be the appropriate term for such forms of terror. Nor would any commercial nuclear power plants ever become a "nuclear bomb." Hence, neither Scenario (3) nor Scenario (4) is given further consideration here.

Throughout this analysis, nuclear terrorism is therefore strictly understood as being a scenario involving non-state actors with improvised nuclear explosive devices, or ambitions in this direction.

The threat of nuclear terrorism

No terrorist group has been known publicly to have ever developed or deployed a nuclear device. Scholars argue about the severity of the threat. According to some, the possibility that terrorists could acquire a nuclear weapon and explode it in a US city is real, and the lack of TV screens flickering gruesome pictures around the world in the wake of nuclear terrorist activities is merely due to a "lack of means, rather than a lack of motivations."[9] Such views appear predicated upon the belief that the gruesome scenes from lower Manhattan on 11 September 2001 are only the prelude of far worse tragedies to come.

The spectacular attacks of September 11 were all performed with conventional terrorist means. However, the magnitude, crudeness, and efficacy with which these actions were carried out could point in the direction of future large-scale terrorist use of weapons of mass effect (WME).[10] More people died in one day on September 11 than in 35 years of sub-state terrorism in Western Europe.[11] On 11 March 2004, Europe received its dreadful taste of large-scale terrorist violence when the multiple assaults in Madrid killed nearly 200 people.

According to other scholars, however, nuclear terrorism is "an overrated nightmare,"[12] and while chemical, biological, or radiological terrorism is likely to occur, nuclear terrorism is unlikely to do so, as it is too difficult.[13] Others dismiss the risk of large-scale nuclear terrorist violence in their country on the grounds of internal factors such as geography, politics, and security policy.[14] Even vagabond fissile material is said to only "slightly increase the likelihood of nuclear terrorism."[15]

Indeed, conventional means are likely to remain the weaponry of choice for most terrorists.[16] Such means could still more than effectively serve their goals. There are practical, strategic, and perhaps even moral constraints against the use of nuclear explosives. Unconventional means and methods of violence with new technical requirements and unknown outcomes – and thus an increased risk of failure – could be less appealing to non-state actors. Unsuccessful actions may waste resources, kill members of the terrorist groups, increase the risk of revelation and retaliation, embarrass the terrorist organization, and reduce support amongst followers – all putting the very existence of the group, and its cause, at stake.

The use of weapons of mass effect could, moreover, stigmatize the group – labeling members forever as uncompromising terrorists – and render any political aspirations hard to accomplish. The constraints against WME-use are particularly severe for terrorists who are concerned with their constituents (like social revolutionary and national separatist terrorists).[17] Therefore, there has always been a huge gap between the potential of a weapon and the ability and/or the will to employ it by terrorists.[18] Yet this is not the time for complacency.

A change of motivations and tactics

While the majority of terrorist groups will stick to traditional terrorist means and known tactics, *some* groups may be ready to step up to a new level of violence. After September 11, the notion that "terrorists want a lot of people watching and listening, not a lot of people dead"[19] is questionable. A mix of interrelated developments transpire.[20]

First, terrorists' motivations are changing. A new breed of terrorists appears more inclined than terrorists of the past to commit acts of extreme violence. These new terrorists may range from *ad hoc* groups motivated by religious conviction or revenge, to violent right-wing extremists and apocalyptical cults. Second, chemical, biological, and nuclear weapons could be especially valuable to terrorists without traditional political goals, but who instead seek divine retribution, to display prowess, or simply to kill large numbers of people.

Third, terrorists will generally choose their technology to exploit the vulnerabilities of a particular society. Modern societies are particularly susceptible to weapons that are capable of killing many people at one time. Moreover, as governments implement sophisticated security measures against terrorist attacks, terrorists may find more powerful weapons appealing, as a way to overcome such countermeasures. Fourth, with the break-up of the Soviet Union and corrupt nuclear scientists in states on the fringes of international law,[21] black markets may now offer unprecedented access to weapons components and know-how. Fifth, additional terrorist attacks may be spurred by copycat efforts of new groups seeking both inspiration and ideas from previous large-scale terrorist violence.

A high-profile terrorist group with nuclear intentions is al-Qaeda, the organization of Osama bin Laden. According to R. James Woolsey, former Director of the Central Intelligence Agency, bin Laden has been trying to obtain enriched uranium for seven or eight years.[22] The trail for the bombings of the US embassies in Nairobi, Kenya, and Dar es Salaam, Tanzania, in August 1998, shed new light on bin Laden's and al-Qaeda's nuclear weapon intentions.[23]

The biological and chemical programs of the Japanese Aum Shinrikyo cult that culminated in the Tokyo metro attack have been highly publicized. Less well known is the nuclear weapon program of the group. Natural uranium was acquired from the sect's properties in Australia, and markets were explored to purchase nuclear technology via front trading companies.[24] Apparently, this fissile material production path, normally chosen by states with vast resources and well-developed nuclear infrastructure, turned out to be less than fruitful for Aum Shinrikyo. Why this arduous (state) approach was chosen remains unclear.[25]

Even if the risk of nuclear terrorism may still be low, the possible level of physical destruction, fatality, and injury is so great in and of itself that the potential for terrorist acquisition and use of nuclear devices warrants serious consideration – and optimum countermeasures.

Nuclear terrorism risk assessments

Terrorism countermeasures have traditionally included political governance, socio-economic measures, communications and educational efforts, military interventions, judicial and legal measures, and law-enforcement and intelligence activity.[26] In the US, measures against terrorism have been put together under the rubric of "homeland security," whose strategic objectives (in order of priority) are to prevent terrorist attacks within the United States, to reduce US vulnerability to terrorism, and to minimize the damage and recover from attacks that do occur.[27] These measures are all likely to play a role, small or large, in fighting future acts of terrorism. Their use, efficiency, and costs will differ significantly, however. The respective countermeasures must be scrutinized and prioritized accordingly.

Here, a simple terrorism risk assessment model, considering the different elements of the nuclear terrorism threat, could prove useful. At the outset, it should be acknowledged that terrorist abilities rest on a combination of intentions and capabilities. The greatest danger of large-scale killing occurs when the group or individual is not only motivated, but also has technical capabilities, easily exploitable opportunities, and a minimum of restraints.[28] Hence, highly motivated groups possessing the proper means to perform nuclear terrorism represent the highest risk. Equivalently, low motivation and low capability represents a low nuclear terrorist probability, and hence a low risk. In the complete absence of either motivation or means, the probability of nuclear terrorism becomes zero.

Similar considerations could be made for societies' vulnerabilities to terrorism. "Vulnerability" may be regarded as the (societal) ability to withstand injury, or its ability to recover from damage. Operationally, vulnerability could be defined as "a function of the reciprocal multiplicative relationship between risk and preparedness."[29] Society is most vulnerable when risk is high and preparedness is low; by the same token, it is least vulnerable when risk is low and preparedness high. An absence of targets, or a high level of resistance, could reduce the risk of nuclear terrorism.

Hence, as reflected in the US homeland security strategy, terrorism threats, and thus proper countermeasures, have to be continuously monitored against terrorists' motivations and means, and against the resistance of the society and possible targets (see Figure 3.1).[30]

These dimensions of terrorist risk and their implications for proper responses to the threat of nuclear terrorism will be discussed in the following section.

Nuclear terrorist motivations

Terrorists are conscious actors who develop calculated strategies to achieve their objectives.[31] They should not be viewed as irrational madmen, thirsting for enemy blood. Terrorists make their own rational choices between different options and tactics, based on the limitations and possibilities of the respective situations. Hence, contemporary terrorism prevention may involve an element of persuasion and an opportunity to change terrorist motivations.

By making acts of terrorism more costly (both politically and managerially) and by making non-violent (democratic) means more rewarding, a shift in the motivations and acts of non-state actors may occur, especially among

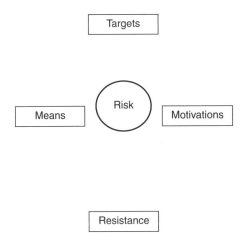

Figure 3.1 Dimensions of terrorism risks.

those with political and negotiable goals. Coercion may play a role, as the prospects of massive retaliation and possible annihilation of the group might also influence terrorists' priorities. However, modern terrorism is not easily deterred.[32] It could even be stimulated by absolute military superiority and actions.[33] Military force may backfire. Using peaceful and non-military means towards less ferocious intentions, on the other hand, is likely to be a long-term effort, with uncertain outcomes.

To base nuclear terrorism countermeasures primarily on changing motivations could therefore be a challenging – and daring – endeavor.

Nuclear terrorism targets

The number of targets for a nuclear terrorist detonation is close to infinite. Depending on the aims of the terrorists (e.g. intimidation, large-scale killing, destruction, economic damage, or blackmail), any densely populated area would do. The immensely destructive power of nuclear explosives makes attempts to harden potential targets superfluous. While some military installations are constructed to withstand nuclear attacks, a similar level of protection for the majority of civilian buildings is not an option. In short, attempting to reduce nuclear terrorist susceptibility by protecting all potential targets is neither practicable nor sensible.

Nuclear terrorism resistance

A second approach to reducing vulnerability to acts of terrorism is to increase societal resistance by enhancing surveillance and intelligence, or by improving emergency preparedness and response capabilities.

From a medical point of view, however, interventions in the aftermath of a nuclear terrorist attack may provide very limited remedies. The effect of even a sturdy third layer of nuclear terrorism preparedness is likely to be correspondingly low. Where chemical and biological agents at least offer *some* opportunities for protection and medical response, there is very little protection against the pressure, heat, and radiation from a nuclear detonation.[34] Structural chaos and breakdown in logistics and capacities will further limit the effects of any post-event response. The possibilities for meaningful mitigation are very minor.

The vulnerability to terrorism may also be reduced through heightened vigilance and high-tech forensics to detect evolving plots. This, however, is not enough to deter all would-be nuclear perpetrators.[35] The probability of successful border detection may depend on the terrorists' own skills, and their level and sophistication of (technical) control. In the wake of rumors about al-Qaeda's alleged progress toward obtaining a nuclear or radiological weapon in Afghanistan, hundreds of new and sophisticated radiation detection sensors were deployed to US borders, overseas facilities, and points around Washington DC The ability of the sensors to detect nuclear material, however, may be limited. In reality – as seen in the search described in the introduction to this chapter – efforts to detect and interdict nuclear smugglers are unlikely to reduce the likelihood of successful transfers to anywhere close to zero.[36]

Besides, while pursuing terrorism resistance through public surveillance and intelligence, tighter societal control may result and fundamental civil liberties might be at risk. US citizens can now be locked up for merely asserting that they are part of a terrorist plot.[37] The term "enemy combatants" has been introduced into the civilian sphere to detain perceived suspects without charges, keep them in secret, and hold them incommunicado, denying them counsel. In the aftermath of a nuclear terrorist attack, basic human rights may be further compromised to manage the chaos and to track down the perpetrators. Intelligence and sting operations carry with them other inherent limitations and uncertainties.[38]

Hence, *national* approaches to nuclear terrorism security could be dubious endeavors. Once the fissile material has entered the country of destination, law-enforcement officers may not only be fighting in vain against a relatively undetectable enemy; they may also be fighting against the clock. The closer nuclear terrorists are to succeeding, the more arbitrary and uncertain the countermeasures put in place seem to become. Not only will the number of locations, means of transportation, and persons to control increase dramatically: finding the infamous needle in the haystack, in this case unirradiated fissile material, may also be extremely hard – the radiation signatures are weak, the quantities needed for a workable nuclear device are limited, and the number of possible targets and locations for assembling are many.

For assembled nuclear explosives, radiation signatures from the fissile material are likely to be better masked due to the metal casing of the explosive device, making radiological detection even harder.[39] As a test, a 6.8 kg cylinder of depleted uranium metal was smuggled into the United States on two occasions without being detected.[40] Admittedly depleted uranium has a lower specific activity than highly enriched uranium (HEU),[41] but weapons-grade uranium may also very well have passed through US Customs unnoticed, despite recent security upgrades at the borders and elsewhere. To terrorists, the limited radiation emanating from the fresh fissile material could render shielding and advanced laboratory facilities superfluous during its handling.

A final key factor that should affect decisions about nuclear terrorism resistance is that the nature of the terrorist threat and the targets, weapons, and means of delivery will change over time, often in response to successful countermeasures. Terrorists will adapt to the defenses in place, and seek the weakest spots known.[42] Boosting societal resistance against nuclear terrorism is hard.

Nuclear terrorism means

This leaves us, in effect, with the option of denying terrorists the means to carry out their acts of violence; other approaches to terrorism risk reduction may simply not provide the required levels of protection. Neither is this task straightforward. Nuclear explosive technology is no longer a secret shared by a few. Designing and fabricating a nuclear gun-type explosive is not likely to be an overwhelming task for a non-state actor.[43]

Uranium and plutonium, however, are the essential ingredients of any nuclear explosive. Hence, denying terrorists these materials offers a unique opportunity for nuclear terrorism prevention.[44] A survey of likely steps leading to an act of nuclear terrorism shows that cutting off the supply of these means will effectively reduce the probability of nuclear terrorism to zero.[45] As such, it represents *the* nuclear terrorism chokepoint; this is the step in the pathway to nuclear terrorist capabilities that can most directly and reliably be stopped.

Technical aspects of the threat of nuclear terrorism are explored further in the following section.

Assessing the means of nuclear terrorism

Establishing nuclear explosive capabilities demands a series of technical steps that would be challenging for both states and non-state actors. However, technical considerations show that the production of crude nuclear explosive devices is within reach of non-state actors. The first-generation nuclear weapons were produced 60 years ago. At that time, such weapons represented high-tech, cutting-edge technology. Today they are not only old, but also primitive. General designs of crude nuclear explosives, capable of producing yields in the kilotonne range, are out in the public domain.

Like any other actors with nuclear ambitions, terrorists need to go through a series of steps to establish functioning nuclear explosive capabilities. Each step is demanding. Any nuclear aspirant must:[46]

1   Develop a design for its nuclear device or obtain such a design from a nuclear weapon state
2   Produce the fissile material for the core of the device or obtain it from an external source and then shape the fissile material into appropriate nuclear parts
3   Fabricate, or obtain from outside, the non-nuclear parts of the device, including the high-explosive elements and triggering components that will detonate the nuclear core
4   Verify the reliability of these various elements individually and as a system
5   Assemble all of these elements into a deliverable nuclear armament, a process commonly referred to as "weaponization."

Consequently, and despite the revelations of an illicit nuclear technology network with Pakistani roots, building a well-functioning nuclear device may represent significant challenges for terrorists, as well as for states with well-funded and sophisticated programs.[47] Such endeavors would have to include skills, specialized brain-power (e.g. metallurgical experts and specialists in explosives and electronics), money, facilities, equipment, and of course fissile material. Aspiring nuclear bombers would, moreover, have to study how to optimize the design. Although the basic scientific and technical principles of making nuclear weapons are relatively well-known, details and "tricks" can be very hard to duplicate in practice.[48]

However for past state nuclear programs, most of the resources have been used in the production of fissile material.[49] Moreover, the technical difficulties are very strongly dependent on the complexity of the device non-state actors choose to develop.[50] As the complexity of the nuclear design decreases, so do the technical challenges associated with the design of auxiliary components. As a result, a modest program aiming simply at producing a limited number of crude nuclear explosives may circumvent the need for extensive know-how. Requirements in terms of yield, safety, delivery, and performance of a terrorist nuclear explosive are, moreover, likely to be much lower than for traditional state (military) nuclear weapons.[51]

The different standards of nuclear explosives

Two basic designs of crude nuclear explosives are likely to be adequate for most purposes of a terrorist group intent on nuclear terrorism. Both designs were used in the first generation of nuclear weapons produced, and could almost certainly be fielded without a nuclear testing program.[52] The late Luis W. Alvarez, a Nobel Laureate in Physics and a prominent nuclear weapon scientist in the Manhattan Project, emphasized the simplicity of constructing a nuclear explosive with highly enriched uranium (HEU):[53]

> With modern weapons-grade uranium, the background neutron rate is so low that terrorists, if they have such materials, would have a good chance of setting of a high-yield explosion simply by dropping one half of the material onto the other half. Most people seem unaware that if separated HEU is at hand it's a trivial job to set off a nuclear explosion . . . even a high-school kid could make a bomb in short order.

The Alvarez statement may also very well describe the fundamental differences between a nuclear weapon wielded by a terrorist and one possessed by a state. While potential nuclear terrorists would probably go for an undefined "high-yield explosion," military nuclear weapons must meet an array of requirements before fielded. The highly differing requirements for performance and delivery can make weapons designed to meet the "terrorist nuclear weapon standards" less technically challenging than those for nuclear weapons states.

First, as shown in Figure 3.2, a state will be at least as concerned with the nuclear device *not* going off during storage and transportation as it will with optimizing the yield and detonation of the weapon. The "one-point safety" requirements of the US to prevent accidental detonations of nuclear weapons are one example. This set of strict requirements is designed to ensure that a nuclear explosion will not result if any point on the conventional explosive that surrounds the fissile material is accidentally detonated. While safety is a must for states, such concerns may be given less consideration by terrorists, especially by groups with a strong affection for martyrdom.

Second, reliability concerns may be equally low amongst terrorists. While an ignition failure or a fizzle yield might be unfortunate from the viewpoint of terrorists, it could potentially have a profound impact on the security of a state in, for example, a nuclear offensive mode. Credible deterrence, moreover, rests upon a nuclear arsenal that is known to function as intended. States, in other words, do not compromise with the reliability of their nuclear weapons. For terrorists, however, even a nuclear "fizzle" may suffice. Any explosion in the lower kiloton range represents an unprecedented terrorist yield (and failed plutonium weapons may also serve as radiological dispersion devices). States, on the other hand, want fairly accurate and known yields, to predict damage and the number of weapons needed.

Third, weapons for military use are normally required in fairly large numbers, and they must be delivered by conventional military means (missiles, mortars etc.). The most important constraining factors for state nuclear

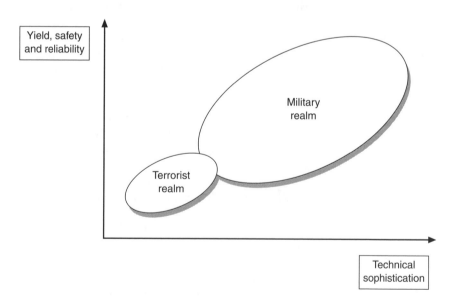

Figure 3.2 Terrorist and state military nuclear explosives compared.

weapons are often the weight capacity of the delivery vehicle and the space available to carry the weapon (i.e. the diameter and length of a nosecone, or the length and width of a bomb bay). Developing reliable delivery systems and slender nuclear explosives is technically challenging and expensive. Crude terrorist nuclear devices, however, will easily fit into a van or even an automobile for subsequent detonation, possibly in densely populated areas. Other non-military means of delivery might involve trucks, hot-air balloons, ships, or simply a complete assembling of the nuclear device inside a garage or an out-of-the-way residence.[54]

Relevant bomb making information

A US veteran weapon designer has noted that "the scientific knowledge and computational expertise required for nuclear weapon design is now widely dispersed."[55] Six decades after Hiroshima and Nagasaki, this should hardly come as a surprise. Knowledge of nuclear weapon design is so prevalent that trying to maintain a shroud of secrecy around it no longer offers adequate protection.[56] The rapid spread of technological knowledge may advance terrorists' weaponization attempts. Indeed, in a 1960s experiment conducted by the US Government, three newly graduated students were asked to develop a nuclear weapon design using only publicly available information. The students performed their task successfully. In the years since, much more information has entered the public domain, probably making similar efforts today even simpler.

Relevant information on the production of nuclear weapons can be found in the technical literature. *The Los Alamos Primer: The First Lectures on How to Build an Atomic Bomb* was declassified and published in 1992.[57] The book originated as a series of five lectures, given to the physicists of the Manhattan Project at its commencement, outlining the theoretical foundations of bomb-making. Also within the information mass on the Internet, potential nuclear weapon producers can find useful sites. While these are not likely to be "step-by-step" descriptions for nuclear weapon acquisition, aspects of the openly available information are likely to assist and even guide potential bomb-makers in the process.

Access to fissile material

The vast production of fissile materials during the Cold War has today left the world with a staggering legacy of three million kilograms of weapons-usable material. Two-thirds of this material is produced for military purposes,[58] and more than half of the quantity is in excess of national security needs.[59] Nuclear weapon states are exempted from safeguards. Miniscule amounts of fissile material – slightly above 2 percent of all highly enriched uranium – are subjected to international control by the International Atomic Energy Agency (IAEA).

The huge quantities of fissile materials and reports of lax security and accountancy of nuclear materials raise concerns about the possibility of a successful diversion of significant quantities of weapons-usable materials, particularly in the former Soviet Union. In January 2001, a bipartisan panel mandated by the US Secretary of Energy assessed the security of Russia's nuclear materials. The conclusions of the panel were not encouraging:

> The most urgent unmet national security threat to the United States today is the danger that weapons of mass destruction or weapons usable material in Russia could be stolen and sold to terrorists or hostile nation states and used against American troops abroad or citizens at home.[60]

In February 2002, representatives of the US intelligence community confirmed to Congress that "weapons-grade and weapons-usable nuclear materials have been stolen from some Russian institutes."[61] Law enforcement representatives assessed that undetected smuggling had occurred, although they were unable to define the extent or magnitude of such thefts. Specialists from Russian law enforcement bodies have identified poor physical protection as the primary causes of nuclear thefts, along with the acute shortage of funds allocated for nuclear material protection, control, and accounting (MPC&A).[62] The ratio of prevented to successful thefts remains uncertain due to insufficient accounting of nuclear material at some facilities, and the failure to carry out an overall national fissile material inventory exercise.

According to the US Department of Energy, 603 tonnes of highly enriched uranium and plutonium – enough to produce almost 40,000 nuclear bombs – are at risk of nuclear material theft in Russia.[63] This material can be used directly in a nuclear weapon without further enrichment or reprocessing. The material is considered to be highly attractive and liable to theft because it is not very radioactive and is therefore relatively safe to handle, and it can easily be carried by one or two people in portable containers or as components from dismantled weapons. Security upgrades now protect roughly 50 percent of Russia's fissile material outside nuclear weapons. Only 26 percent of the protected material is protected by the necessary comprehensive security systems.[64] One estimate indicates that if current rates are not accelerated, Russia's nuclear material will not be completely secure until 2029.[65]

According to the IAEA's Illicit Trafficking Database,[66] about 600 illicit trafficking incidents have taken place since 1 January 1993.[67] Of these, about 400 incidents have been confirmed by states. A little less than half of the confirmed cases (175) have involved nuclear material, including 18 cases with highly enriched uranium or plutonium. In none of the incidents was the quantity of seized nuclear material enough to produce a workable nuclear explosive, and no endpoint, or buyers, have been identified. Yet one successful transfer of high-quality nuclear material could be one too many; the thefts present a disturbing picture.

A closer look reveals that the fraction of HEU and plutonium taken today represents a similar proportion of cases to that in the early 1990s, indicating a persistent market, or at least a remaining interest in fissile materials. Second, successful transfers will never be registered, and the dark figures behind the smuggling remain unknown. An optimistic detection rate of 10 percent indicates, for instance, nearly 200 smuggling events involving plutonium or highly enriched uranium. Third, some of the material seized traveled across wide distances and through several border crossings. Germany was particularly exposed during the mid-1990s, possibly as a result of a hyped nuclear market where sellers and middlemen anticipated finding buyers for their dangerous goods in Central Europe. However, even today, Swedish authorities admit that their national capabilities to detect illicit nuclear material are inadequate.[68] Finally, the seized quantities may be test samples for larger amounts of material that is readily available for sale.

Implications for nuclear terrorism prevention

Strategies must be devised to reduce the risk of nuclear terrorism. First and foremost, international cooperation to improve the security of nuclear material in Russia must be enhanced. At many Russian nuclear installations, the standards of physical protection and nuclear material accountancy fall below those in the West. Ongoing international activities and opportunities to increase nuclear security are presented in the following sections.

International efforts: ongoing activities

In the post-Cold War environment, some states are providing practical security assistance to other states in order to reduce common threats. Since the early 1990s, a range of new nuclear security initiatives has been initiated.

Bilateral programs, mostly US–Russian, have ranged from those aimed at securing or destroying weapons and weapons-usable materials in the former Soviet Union, combating trafficking in illicit nuclear materials, and engaging out-of-work weapons scientists, to those focused on physically downsizing Russia's nuclear weapons complex. The Cooperative Threat Reduction (CTR) Program is designed to help the countries of the former Soviet Union destroy and protect nuclear, chemical, and biological material and weapons, and associated infrastructure. The program emanates from the Soviet Nuclear Threat Reduction Act of 1991, championed through Congress by Senators Nunn and Lugar.[69] Today, the CTR constitutes the backbone of US non-proliferation assistance programs. American efforts to "globalize" and extend Cooperative Threat Reduction activities to states outside the former Soviet Union have been initiated.[70]

The European Union, for its part, runs the TACIS program, which assists states of the former Soviet Union in various fields, largely to improve nuclear safety. On 17 December 1999 the EU Council adopted a Joint Action for Non-proliferation and Disarmament in the Russian Federation, using the Cooperative Threat Reduction Program of the United States as a model. However, its funding is still modest, and the nuclear security initiatives of the Union remain fragmented and meek. This may soon change. The EU Strategy against Proliferation of Weapons of Mass Destruction,[71] adopted in December 2003, specifically mentions the reinforcement of EU cooperative threat reduction programs with other countries by increasing funding beyond 2006. The strategy, moreover, calls for enhancing the security of sensitive materials, and for supporting multilateral organizations in charge of verification activities.

The terrorist attacks of 11 September 2001 also spurred a wave of multilateral security initiatives. In March 2002, the IAEA Board of Governors endorsed an action plan designed to upgrade worldwide protection against acts of terrorism involving nuclear and other radioactive material. In approving the plan, the Board recognized that the first line of defense against nuclear terrorism is the strong physical protection of nuclear facilities and material.[72]

The plan covers eight areas: physical protection of nuclear material and nuclear facilities; detection of malicious activities (such as illicit trafficking) involving nuclear and other radioactive material; strengthening of state systems for nuclear material accountancy and control; security of radioactive sources; the assessment of safety- and security-related vulnerabilities at nuclear facilities; response to malicious acts or threats thereof; the adherence to international agreements and guidelines; and enhancement of program coordination and information management for matters relating to nuclear security.

In June 2002, the G8 countries launched the Global Partnership against the Spread of Weapons and Materials of Mass Destruction. Under this initiative, G8 countries will support specific cooperation projects, initially in Russia, to address issues of non-proliferation, disarmament, counter-terrorism, and nuclear safety. Among the priority concerns are the destruction of chemical weapons, the dismantlement of decommissioned nuclear submarines, the disposition of fissile material, and the employment of former weapons scientists. The G8 countries committed themselves to raising up to $20 billion to support such projects over the next ten years. Some non-G8 countries, among them Norway, joined the partnership later.[73] Related efforts include the Proliferation Security Initiative, and the Global Threat Reduction Initiative.[74]

In parallel, the UN Security Council adopted Resolution 1540.[75] The Resolution strengthens the international non-proliferation regime by calling upon all states "to promote the universal adoption and full implementation, and, where necessary, strengthening of multilateral treaties to which they are parties, whose aim is to prevent the proliferation of nuclear, biological or chemical weapons." The Resolution specifically demands that states

"Develop and maintain appropriate effective measures to account for and secure nuclear, chemical, or biological weapons and materials", "Develop and maintain appropriate effective physical protection measures", and "Develop and maintain appropriate effective border controls and law enforcement efforts" to prevent illicit trafficking in these materials. The Resolution also mandates states to adhere to the Convention for Physical Protection of Nuclear Material.

Some of the requirements relate to physical security; others come into play in international export controls and the prevention of proliferation of enrichment and reprocessing technologies. In sum, UNSC Resolution 1540 provides an unprecedented opportunity to pursue the mutually reinforcing goals of disarmament and non-proliferation within the most inclusive and legitimate multilateral body in the world, the UN Security Council, filling a gap that has emerged in existing arms control and non-proliferation agreements.[76]

International opportunities: recommendations for supply side nuclear security

Cutting off the supply of fissile material could be the most vigorous nuclear terrorism countermeasure. The more material produced and the more material that remains without proper accountability and protection, the higher the risk of nuclear terrorism. To reduce the risk of nuclear terrorism risk reduction, the following steps could be considered:

- *Accelerate, unblock, and upgrade fissile material security programs.* A decade after the instigation of international security upgrades, most sensitive fissile material in Russia has not been dealt with. While unprecedented work has been carried out, much remains to be done to accelerate, unblock, and upgrade existing fissile material security programs to reduce the nuclear threat legacy of the Cold War.
- *Expand funding for fissile material security.* Physical protection and control of fissile material is the primary line of defense and best deterrent to non-state actors with nuclear ambitions. As nuclear physical security activities are accelerated and expanded, the burden should be shared by more than one donor (i.e. the US). The G8 Global Partnership offers an appropriate avenue for concerted, coordinated, and collective security upgrades. UNSC Resolution 1540 may provide the formal framework needed.
- *Improve nuclear transparency and accountability.* Nuclear programs and stockpiles remain shrouded in secrecy. This is hardly the best way to ensure responsible nuclear husbandry and international recognition of the security challenges associated with the excessive stocks of fissile material. Nuclear weapons-state declarations and data exchanges on national nuclear material stockpiles should be stimulated, as should non-intrusive verification of sensitive fissile material (see below).

- *Establish nuclear stockpile inventories.* Proper accountability is crucial to nuclear security. Current uncertainties in fissile material holdings can only exacerbate the nuclear terrorist threat. An overall Russian stockpile inventory exercise should be launched, sponsored if necessary by international donors.

- *Accelerate down-blending of Russian highly enriched uranium.* The US and Russia are working cooperatively to eliminate Russian HEU through down-blending to low enriched uranium (LEU) and subsequent use in nuclear power plants. Eventually, 500 tonnes of fissile material will be rendered unusable for nuclear explosives. The efforts, however, should be accelerated and expanded to include additional stocks of Russian HEU that are vulnerable to theft.

- *Improve and implement non-intrusive verification of stockpiles.* Proper accounting of existing stocks of fissile material is a perquisite for control and possible stockpile reduction. To meet international and domestic nonproliferation and disarmament demands, technical communities are now examining a variety of non-intrusive verification measurements on nuclear items with sensitive or classified properties. Important progress has been made on joint plutonium verification. Efforts should be initiated to expand non-intrusive verification on stocks of fissile material declared as excess by the nuclear-weapon states.

- *Assess ongoing nuclear security programs and approaches.* More than a decade of cooperation in international nuclear security offers a cornucopia of experiences. These should be assessed and best practices identified. Particularly successful programmes, like the joint naval security upgrades,[77] could provide important inputs for fruitful working approaches and strategies in other ongoing and future cooperative nuclear security programs.

- *Establish and implement mandatory standards of physical protection of fissile material and nuclear installations.* While safeguards aim at deterring state nuclear proliferation, physical protection is the primary barrier against potential nuclear terrorists. Yet despite recent updating, the international standards for physical protection are non-mandatory and probably too weak to meet contemporary nuclear terrorist threats.

- *Expand physical protection information-sharing and international peer reviews.* Domestic standards and practices for physical protection differ widely. While sensitive information is protected, physical security experiences and best practices should be shared in international fora, to raise the general level and norms of nuclear security.[78]

- *Expedite international efforts to put material declared excess to national needs under international (IAEA) control.* Both the US and Russia participate in the Trilateral Initiative, which arranges for stocks of fissile material in excess of national needs to be put under international control. As yet, however, no weapons-usable material has been submitted under the initiative, even though earlier technical and political challenges have been solved and the IAEA, US and Russia have signed a working agreement.

- *Make all nuclear arms reductions truly irreversible.* The principle of irreversibility, i.e. that material and weapons taken out from the arsenals of nuclear-weapon states should be irrevocably rendered unusable for the purposes of nuclear explosives, is essential for reducing the threat of nuclear terrorism. If destruction of the fissile material is not an option, deals should be struck for international control and/or irrevocable disposal of fissile material.[79]

- *Commence negotiations on a fissile material cut-off treaty.* Ending the production of weapons-usable material would create an upper boundary to the number of nuclear explosives possibly produced by states or terrorists. A verifiable fissile material cut-off treaty (FMCT) is a prerequisite for genuine stockpile reductions and hence a reduced threat of nuclear terrorism. For the FMCT, effective verification is technically feasible. The obstacles are political in nature.

- *Reinvest in the nuclear non-proliferation regime.* The Nuclear Non-proliferation Treaty (NPT) is an international regime put in place not only to reduce the military and political role of nuclear weapons; through its disarmament and non-proliferation provisions it also offers, *inter alia*, a specified scheme for the handling, control, and elimination of fissile material, along the steps outlined above. Its role is weakening, however, not least because leading states are turning away from their own nuclear disarmament and non-proliferation commitments.

Each of the suggested measures alone may not prevent future acts of nuclear terrorism. However, they are likely to be mutually self-reinforcing and eventually sufficient to establish the norms and standards needed to avoid further proliferation of fissile material, by states and to non-state actors, and thus to prevent nuclear terrorism.

Transatlantic nuclear terrorism prevention

The challenges posed by nuclear terrorism are substantial, and require both immediate and sustained efforts by national governments and international organizations.[80] Europe and America should work jointly to meet evolving nuclear threats, through a combination of *ad hoc* international nuclear security cooperation and formalized nuclear non-proliferation activities. A shift in prioritization and initiatives is, however, required on both sides of the Atlantic.

What Europeans should do to further transatlantic efforts to prevent nuclear terrorism

With US assistance over the past decade, Russia has made unprecedented progress in securing dangerous weapons and material. However, while much more needs to be done, the Cooperative Threat Reduction (CTR) Program remains a highly politicized issue in Washington. While some activities receive small financial increases, others remain static, and still others are targeted for spending cuts. This stems, in part, from the embarrassingly low participation and support of other donor states, in particular European ones.

European CTR funding is still modest, and the programs still lack the comprehensiveness, coordination, and political visibility needed to become a genuine vehicle for improved nuclear security in Russia. The new EU Strategy may change the picture, as well as prioritization. So far, emphasis has been on cooperative nuclear safety. Europe should hence seize the opportunity to help build viable nuclear security initiatives, for instance under the auspices of the G8 Global Partnership. Indeed, as Europeans face new terrorist tolls, genuine efforts to diminish the nuclear terrorist threats should be in their interests. A surge in illicit trafficking incidents in nuclear materials in the 1990s, and Europe's proximity to and close ties with Russia, could moreover facilitate funding of future nuclear security measures.

In response to the terrorist attacks in Madrid, European Union ministers have appointed an EU Counterterrorism Coordinator. The Coordinator works under the EU's Foreign Policy and Security Chief Javier Solana, and is answerable to the Council of Ministers (i.e. to the EU's national governments, not to the European Commission).[81] For now, the EU has rejected the idea of establishing a "European CIA." A competent and focused intelligence community, however, is essential for any successful interception of terrorism plots in the making. While Europe has long traditions of intelligence sharing and cooperation (e.g. through Europol), improved cross-border – including transatlantic – collaboration could be vital, both for improved threat assessments and for information sharing. Most important, however, is Europe's ability to safeguard and promote its preferences for the strengthening of international order through effective multilateralism and global adherence to relevant treaties.[82]

What Americans should do to further transatlantic efforts to prevent nuclear terrorism

Evidence of state-to-state nuclear proliferation and the possible prospect of state-to-non-state nuclear support have been in the forefront of US security debates and policy priorities. In the beginning of 2004, for instance, President George W. Bush called for strengthening parts of the international regime to stem further nuclear proliferation.[83] Important efforts like the Proliferation Security Initiative have also been launched. Many of these proposals are positive, not least as they recognize the importance of international cooperation and multinational mechanisms to stem nuclear proliferation.

However, the Bush Administration sees traditional arms control as "largely the agenda of the past."[84] Strong unilateral currents may hence run the risk of undermining the international nuclear non-proliferation regime.[85] The implications for the threat of nuclear terrorism could be harsh: without the international non-proliferation regime, terrorists are likely to find it easier to gain access to nuclear explosives.[86] In tandem, the US nuclear posture fails to address the risk of nuclear terrorism in an adequate manner, by ignoring the need for adequate measures to safeguard and, as needed, dispose of the hundreds of tons of excess nuclear weapon material.[87] In sum, the US national strategy on nuclear issues has seemed destined to reduce international cooperation in enforcing non-proliferation commitments, rather than enhance it.[88]

According to the US National Security Strategy, issued in September 2002, the United States must "deter and defend against the threat before it is unleashed."[89] US military and civilian agencies must therefore "possess the full range of operational capabilities to counter the threat and use of WMD by states and terrorists."[90] Building upon the December 2001 Nuclear Posture Review,[91] some of the weapon capabilities advocated therein are nuclear.[92] By expanding the nuclear target list, the new posture explicitly increases the nuclear threat to possible US adversaries.[93] In short, rather than reflecting an updated strategy for minimizing the demand for nuclear explosives and material, the current US nuclear posture adds an unknown amount to inducements for nuclear proliferation.[94]

Moreover, very limited consideration is given to following up on the practical steps on nuclear disarmament and non-proliferation from the 2000 Review Conference of the Nuclear Non-proliferation Treaty (NPT). The viability of the NPT may rest upon the successful implementation of these steps. Now, however, the US is in direct or indirect violation of a majority of the 13 practical steps for nuclear disarmament and non-proliferation agreed by consensus by all treaty members. At the 2005 Review Conference, no reference was made to the steps by the US delegation.

This can only further marginalize an already heavily strained regime. Rather than fulfilling its own commitments under the NPT, the US focus has shifted from eliminating nuclear explosives and material, to eliminating certain regimes that may have them, today or in the future. In this selective and coercive counter-proliferation strategy some nuclear weapons are tolerated, even encouraged, and others are not. Universal norms and treaties then become a hindrance to US freedom of action, instead of serving as strategic levers in the battle against non-proliferation.[95]

Blunt US disregard of such a central multilateral non-proliferation mechanism as the NPT is not only a huge paradox in an era when possible nuclear proliferation and terrorism is at the top of the international security agenda. It is also a dangerous approach likely to increase the role of nuclear weapons and the availability of fissile materials – and thus the risk of nuclear terrorism. Rather than emphasizing domestic (i.e. "homeland") security solutions to the threat of nuclear terrorism, the US needs again to look abroad and to redirect political prestige, interest, leadership, and funds to sustained international cooperation in nuclear security upgrades at facilities at risk. A genuine political reinvestment in an ailing nuclear non-proliferation regime is, moreover, vital, as nuclear counterterrorism and nuclear non-proliferation are inescapably linked.

Conclusion

In the global fight against nuclear terrorism, the US and the EU need to work together to identify the real threats and to establish joint approaches and platforms to stem nuclear proliferation. A global terrorist threat calls for international solutions. The two continents share common goals of non-proliferation, nuclear stability, and, of course, the prevention of terrorism. Efficient transatlantic nuclear terrorism prevention requires political leadership, as well as awareness of and a focus on optimum countermeasures.

Nuclear terrorism risk reduction starts abroad. Countermeasures should emphasize denying terrorists the means to carry out their acts of violence, i.e. highly enriched uranium and plutonium – the essential components of any nuclear explosive. Technical barriers to the construction of crude nuclear explosives should not be regarded as sufficient to avoid nuclear terrorist havoc. Terrorists will have far less stringent requirements regarding their nuclear explosives in terms of reliability, safety, security, and delivery, than do states. Detection of a nuclear terrorist plot in the making is challenging. In a "War on Nuclear Terrorism," there is hence the need to shift the focus from possible state or non-state *demands* for nuclear explosives to the protection and control of vulnerable *supplies* of excessive stocks of fissile material.[96]

For *ad hoc* nuclear security and nuclear non-proliferation initiatives, common cooperative principles have, for instance, been spelled out by the G8 in conjunction with their Global Partnership. More important, however, is a mutual recognition of the role and importance of institutionalized, multilateral arms control as an essential means towards nuclear security. It is crucial to avoid a further marginalization of the Nuclear Non-Proliferation Treaty. For US policymakers in particular, it has become fashionable to dismiss arms control and non-proliferation as ineffective. Such attitudes can only exacerbate the threat of nuclear terrorism.

Notes

1 Christian-Marius Stryken at the Norwegian Institute of International Affairs (NUPI) and Anja Dalgaard-Nielsen at the Danish Institute for International Studies (DIIS) provided valuable comments during the preparation of this chapter. Great appreciation is due also to authors of the other chapters in this book, for useful inputs at a joint workshop in February 2004. Any errors or inaccuracies are, of course, my own responsibility.

2 J. Mintz and S. Schmidt, "'Dirty bomb' was major New Year's worry. Scores of nuclear scientists scoured five US cities", *Washington Post*, 7 January 2004, available online at: www.msnbc.msn.com/Default.aspx?ID=3896656&p1=0.

3 On this gap see, for example, the range of opening statements for the IAEA Symposium on International Safeguards: Verification and Nuclear Material Security Vienna, Austria, October 29–November 1, 2001, with a special session on "Combating nuclear terrorism," available online at: www.iaea.org/worldatom/Press/Focus/Nuclear_Terrorism/.

4 This section builds in part on a text by the author for the NATO PROJECT SST.CLG.978964, "Terrorist attacks on nuclear power plants and nuclear material transports."

5 For a brief description of the different forms of nuclear and radiological terrorism, see, for example, W. Potter and L. Spector, "The real sum of all fears," *Los Angeles Times*, 11 June 2002.

6 An explosion of even low yield could kill hundreds of thousands of people. A relatively small bomb, say 15 kilotons, detonated in a city center could immediately kill upwards of 100,000 inhabitants, followed by a comparable number of deaths in the lingering aftermath. Massive quantities of fissile material exist around the world. Sophisticated terrorists could fairly readily design and fabricate a workable atomic bomb once they had managed to acquire the precious deadly ingredients. From B. Blair, "What if terrorists go nuclear?" Center for Defense Information, 21 October 2001, available online at: www.cdi.org/terrorism/nuclear.cfm. For more on the issue of terrorists and crude nuclear weapons, see, for example, M. B. Maerli, "Relearning the ABCs: terrorists and 'weapons of mass destruction'," *The Nonproliferation Review*, Summer 2000.

7 Center for International Security and Cooperation, "Nuclear explosion fact sheet. Nuclear terrorism: risks and realities", CISAC, Stanford University 2003, available online at: www.ldml.stanford.edu/cisac/pdf/Nuc_explosion.pdf.

8 A radiological device detonated by terrorists would require the evacuation and decontamination of the immediate area, disrupting the (local) economy and societal life. Given the relative simplicity of constructing a dirty bomb and the vast availability of radioactive materials, scenarios involving radioactive substances have been assumed to be more probable than other acts of nuclear terrorism. Around the world there is a large number of unwanted radioactive sources, many of them abandoned, others under no regulatory control. Only a fraction of the sources, however, represents real security threats. See C. D. Ferguson, T. Kazi, and J. Perera, *Commercial Radioactive Sources: Surveying the Security Risks*, Occasional Paper, Center for Nonproliferation Studies, Monterey, CA, no. 11, January 2003, available online at: www.cns.miis.edu/pubs/opapers/op11/index.htm.

9 Opening sentence in M. Bunn, J. P. Holdren, and A. Wier, *Securing Nuclear Weapons and Materials: Seven Steps for Immediate Action*, Report of the Project Managing the Atom, Belfer Center for Science and International Affairs, John F. Kennedy School of Government, Harvard University, 2002, available online at: www.ksgnotes1.harvard.edu/BCSIA/MTA.nsf/www/N-Terror.

10 Traditionally, biological, chemical, and nuclear weapons are collectively grouped in the "Weapons of Mass Destruction" (WMD) category. However, the destructive powers of the weapons differ significantly and the term "Weapons of Mass Effect" (WME) may be more appropriate. Moreover, such a term may also better cover the likely psychological consequences of their uses. See M. B. Maerli, "The real weapon of mass destruction: nuclear, biological and chemical warfare in the era of terrorism and 'rogue' states," Atlanterhavskomiteen, Security Policy Library, no. 1, January 2003, available onlne at: www.atlanterhavskomiteen.no /publikasjoner/sp/2003/1.htm.

11 P. Wilkinson, "Overview of the Terrorist Threat to International Security," *Terrorism and Disarmament*, DDA Occasional Papers, No. 5, October 2001.

12 K. H. Kamp, "An overrated nightmare," *The Bulletin of the Atomic Scientists*, 52(4), 1996, 30–34.

13 G. Cameron, "Nuclear terrorism reconsidered," *Current History*, April, 2000, 154–157.

14 B. Anet, *Nuclear Terrorism: How Serious a Threat to Switzerland?* Fact Sheet, Spiez Laboratory, Defense Procurement Agency, available online at: www.vbs.admin.ch/acls/e/current/fact_sheet/nuklearterrorismus/pronto/.

15 K. H. Kamp, "Nuclear terrorism is not the core problem," *Survival*, 40(4), 1998–99, 171–175.

16 D. C. Rapoport, "Then and now: what have we learned?" *Terrorism and Political Violence*, 13(3), 1999, xv.

17 J. M. Post, "Differentiating the Threat of Radiological/Nuclear Terrorism: Motivations and Constraints." Paper presented at the International Atomic Energy Agency (IAEA) Symposium on International Safeguards: Verification and Nuclear Material Security Vienna, Austria, 29 October–1 November 2001.

18 Rapoport, "Terrorism and weapons of the Apocalypse," *National Security Studies Quarterly* V(3), 1999, 49–67.

19 A phrase coined by Brian Michael Jenkins – see, for example, his chapter "International terrorism: a new mode of conflict" in D. Carlton and C. Schaerf (eds), *International Terrorism and World Security*, London: Croom Helm, 1975, p. 15.

20 J. Stern, *The Ultimate Terrorist*, Cambridge: Harvard University Press, 1999.

21 Early in 2004, Pakistan's top nuclear scientist, Abdul Qadeer Khan, confessed to having leaked nuclear secrets to other states.

22 E. Lane and K. Royce, "Bin Laden tried to obtain enriched uranium," *Newsday*, 19 September 2001.

23 For an informative overview of these efforts and summary of testimonies from the trial, see K. McCloud and M. Osborne, "WMD Terrorism and Usama Bin Laden," Center for Nonproliferation Studies, CNS Reports, 2001, available online at: www.cns.miis.edu/pubs/reports/binladen.htm.

24 M. B. Maerli, "Relearning the ABCs: terrorists and 'weapons of mass destruction'," *Nonproliferation Review*, 7(2), 2000, 108–119.

25 The cult's opportunistic path, described in G. Cameron, "Multi-track microproliferation: lessons from Aum Shinrikyo & Al Qaeda," *Studies in Conflict and Terrorism*, 22, 1999, 277–309, may offer some explanations.

26 To identify and classify preventive and counter-terrorist measures, the Terrorism Prevention Branch of the United Nations Office on Drugs and Crime has developed a set of eight categories from a "Toolbox of Measures to Prevent and Suppress Terrorism." A detailed summary description of these may be found in A. Schmid, "Statement at the Inter-Agency Co-ordination Committee Meeting on the Illicit Cross-Border Movement of Nuclear and Other Radioactive Material," International Atomic Energy Agency, Vienna, 26–27 May 2003.

27 United States Office of Homeland Security, *National Strategy for Homeland Security*, Washington DC, July 2002, available online at: www.whitehouse.gov/homeland/book/nat_strat_hls.pdf.

28 J. V. Parachini, "Putting WMD terrorism into perspective," *Washington Quarterly*, 26(4), 2003, 37–50.

29 A. Hedge, "Major hazards and behaviour", in W. T. Singleton and J. Hovden (eds.), *Risk and Decisions*, Chichester: Wiley, 1987, pp. 148–149.

30 The risk assessment model is taken from the presentation by Dr John-Erik Stig Hansen at the Conference "Homeland Security. Bridging the Transatlantic Gap", sponsored by The Danish Institute of International Studies, the Johns Hopkins SAIS Center for Transatlantic Relations, and the Norwegian Institute of International Affairs in Copenhagen, 19–21 September 2003.

31 T. Bjørgo (ed.), "Root causes of terrorism," *Proceedings from an International Expert Meeting,* Norwegian Institute of International Affairs, Oslo, 9–11 June 2003.

32 A. H. Cordesman, *Defending America: Asymmetric and Terrorist Attacks with Radiological and Nuclear Weapons,* Washington DC: Center for Strategic and International Studies, 23 September 2001, available online at: www.csis.org/burke/hd/reports/NucTerr010923.pdf.

33 B. Urquhart, "World order and Mr Bush", *The New York Review of Books,* 9 October 2003.

34 M. B. Maerli, "The real weapon of mass destruction: nuclear, biological and chemical warfare in the Era of Terrorism and 'Rogue' States," Atlanterhavskomiteen, *Security Policy Library,* no. 1, January 2003, available online at: www.atlanterhavskomiteen.no/publikasjoner/sp/2003/1.htm (accessed 30 October 2003).

35 G. Vogel, "Crime and (puny) punishment," *Science,* 298, 2002, 952.

36 G. T. Allison, O. R. Coté Jr, R. A. Falkenrath, and S. E. Miller, *Avoiding Nuclear Anarchy. Containing the Threat of Loose Russian Nuclear Weapons and Fissile Material,* CSIA Studies in International Security No. 12, Cambridge: MIT Press, 1995.

37 The case of Jose Padilla is indicative. Padilla is a US citizen who was taken into custody in Chicago in May 2002, after returning from Pakistan. He is suspected of being part of a "dirty bomb" plot by al-Qaeda, but as of early 2004 the US Government had not pressed any charges against him. The US Government insists that military-style rules like the enemy combatant doctrine now apply to US citizens, even on US soil, because al-Qaeda has "made the battlefield the United States." *The New York Times,* "The 'Enemy Combatant'", editorial, 20 November 2003. A principal decision on the issue by the US Supreme Court is expected in mid-2004.

38 In the words of Sir Stephen Lander, past director of MI5, the British Secret Service, "intelligence is about secret information others want to keep secret. 100 per cent success is never achieved." Quoted by R. Hutchinson, in *Weapons of Mass Destruction. The No-Nonsense Guide to Nuclear, Biological and Chemical Weapons Today,* London: The Orion Publishing Group Ltd, 2003, p. 196.

39 A. H. Cordesman, op cit.

40 Natural Resources Defense Council, *The ABC News Nuclear Smuggling Experiment: The Sequel. The Continuing Saga of NRDC's Uranium Slug and the Potential Consequences,* Fact Sheet, revised 11 September 2003, available online at: www.nrdc.org/nuclear/furanium.asp.

41 The specific activity (the radioactivity per unit mass) of the uranium isotopes in depleted uranium is about 15 million becquerel per kg (15×10^6 Bq/kg). This is approximately 40 percent lower than that of naturally occurring uranium (25×10^6 Bq/kg) and about 150 times less than that of enriched uranium (approximately 2.3×10^9 Bq/kg).

42 Committee on Science and Technology for Countering Terrorism, *Making the Nation Safer. The Role of Science and Technology in Countering Terrorism,* National Research Council, Washington DC: National Academies Press, 2002.

43 A. Narath, "The Technical Opportunities for a Sub-national Group to Acquire Nuclear Weapons", Paper Presented at the XIV International Amaldi Conference on Problems of Global Security, Certosa Di Pontignano, Siena, Italy, 27–29 April 2002.

44 M. B. Maerli, *Crude Nukes on the Loose? Preventing Nuclear Terrorism by Means of Optimum Nuclear Husbandry, Transparency, and Non-Intrusive Fissile Material Verification,* Phd dissertation, Faculty of Mathematics and Natural Sciences, University of Oslo, Norway, March 2004.

45 M. Bunn, A. Wier, and J. P. Holdren, *Controlling Nuclear Warheads and Materials: A Report Card and Action Plan*, Washington, DC: Nuclear Threat Initiative and the Project on Managing the Atom, Harvard University, March 2003, available online at: www.bcsia.ksg.harvard.edu/publication.cfm?program=STPP& ctype=book&item_id=262.

46 Carnegie Analysis, "Going nuclear: what it takes to build a bomb," 6 November 2001. The analysis is based on R. W. Jones, M. G. McDonough, T. Dalton, and G. Koblentz, *Tracking Nuclear Proliferation: A Guide in Maps and Charts*, Washington, DC: Carnegie Endowment for International Peace, 1998.

47 A. H. Cordesman, op cit.

48 D. Albright, "Secrets that matter," *Bulletin of the Atomic Scientists*, 56(6), 2000, pp. 57–62.

49 D. MacKenzie and G. Sinardi, "Tacit knowledge, weapons design and the uninvention of nuclear weapons," *American Journal of Sociology*, 101(1), 1995, 44–99.

50 A. Narath, "The Technical Opportunities for a Sub-national Group to Acquire Nuclear Weapons", Paper Presented at the XIV International Amaldi Conference on Problems of Global Security, Certosa Di Pontignano, Siena, Italy, 27–29 April 2002.

51 M. B. Maerli, A. Schaper, and F. Barnaby, "The characteristics of nuclear terrorist weapons," *American Behavioural Scientist,* 46(6), 2003, 731–732.

52 P. D. Zimmerman, "Technical barriers to nuclear proliferation," in Z. S. Davis and B. Frankel (eds), *The Proliferation Puzzle: Why Nuclear Weapons Spread (And What Results),* London: Frank Cass, 1993, pp. 345–356.

53 L. W. Alvarez, *The Adventures of a Physicist*, New York: Basic Books Inc., 1987.

54 J. Boutwell, F. Calogero, and J. Harris, "Nuclear terrorism: the danger of highly enriched uranium (HEU)," *Pugwash Issue Brief*, 2(1), 2002, available online at: www.pugwash.org/publication/pb/sept2002.pdf.

55 Quoted by M. Hoenig, "Terrorists going nuclear," in Y. Alexander and M. Hoenig (eds), *Super Terrorism. Biological, Chemical, and Nuclear*, Ardsley: Transnational Publishers, Inc., 2001, p. 32.

56 J. M. Deutch, "The nuclear threat," in Y. Alexander and M. Hoenig, ibid.

57 R. Serber, *The Los Alamos Primer: The First Lectures on How to Build an Atomic Bomb*, Berkeley: University of California Press, 1992.

58 D. Albright and K. O'Neill (eds), *The Challenges of Fissile Material Control*, Washington DC: Institute for Science and International Security, 1999.

59 D. Albright, F. Berkhout, and W. Walker, *Plutonium and Highly Enriched Uranium 1996. World Inventories, Capabilities and Policies,* SIPRI, Stockholm: Oxford University Press, 1997.

60 See *A Report Card on the Department of Energy's Nonproliferation Programs with Russia,* Secretary of Energy Advisory Board, 10 January 2001, available online at: www.hr.doe.gov/seab.

61 National Intelligence Council, *Annual Report to Congress on the Safety and Security of Russian Nuclear Facilities and Military Forces, February 2002,* quoted in T. Z. Collina and J. B. Wolfsthal, "Nuclear terrorism and warhead control in russia," *Arms Control Today*, April 2002, available online at: www.armscontrol.org/ act/2002_04/colwolfapril02.asp.

62 V. A. Orlov, "Exports control and nuclear smuggling in Russia," in G. K. Bertsch and W. C. Potter (eds), *Dangerous Weapons, Desperate States*, New York: Routledge, 1999.

63 United States General Accounting Office, *Security of Russia's Nuclear Material Improving; Further Enhancements Needed*, GAO–01–312, February, 2001.

64 K. Luongo and W. Hoehn, "An ounce of prevention," *Bulletin of the Atomic*

Scientists, 61(2), 2005. Online, available at: www.thebulletin.org/article.php? art_ofn=ma05luongo.

65 Senator Richard Lugar at the Nuclear Threat Initiative Conference: "Reducing the Threats from Weapons of Mass Destruction and Building a Global Coalition Against Catastrophic Terrorism," Moscow, Monday 27 May 2002.

66 The database is part of an information exchange program among IAEA member states, with some 80 states participating. The member states report and confirm incidents of illicit trafficking on their territories, and provide background information to the cases. Additional information from open sources is included when appropriate. Available online at www.iaea.org/NewsCenter/News/2004/ iaea_database.html

67 G. Anzelon, "Improving the Knowledge Base on Nuclear Terrorism Threats," paper presented at the IAEA Symposium on International Safeguards: Verification and Nuclear Material Security Vienna, Austria, 29 October–1 November 2001.

68 G. Arbman, A. Axelsson, R. Bergman, L. Melin, A. Ringbom, L. Oliver, L. Widlund, L. Wigg, and G. Ågren, *Primitiva Kärnladdningar – ett realistisk hot?* (Crude Explosive Devices – A Real Threat?, in Swedish), FOI-R-0735-SE, Totalförsvarets forskningsinstitut, December 2002.

69 For more on the CTR program, see www.dtra.mil/ctr/ctr_index.html or www.defenselink.mil/pubs/ctr/.

70 S. Squassoni, *Globalizing Cooperative Threat Reduction: A Survey of Options,* Congressional Research Service, 15 April 2004, available online at: www.fpc.state. gov/documents/organization/32006.pdf.

71 For more on the Strategy, see www.ue.eu.int/uedocs/cmsUpload/st15708. en03.pdf.

72 International Atomic Energy Agency, "IAEA Board of Governors approves IAEA Action Plan to combat nuclear terrorism", Press Release 2002/24, 19 March 2002, available online at: www.f40.iaea.org/worldatom/Press/P_release/ 2002/prn0204.shtml.

73 For more on this, consult "Strengthening the Global Partnership", available online at: www.sgpproject.org.

74 The Global Threat Reduction Initiative (GTRI) enhances national programmes to identify, secure, remove, and/or facilitate the disposition of vulnerable nuclear and other radiological materials and equipment around the world – as quickly and expeditiously as possible – that pose a threat to the international community. A related effort is the US Megaports initiative, aimed at detecting, deterring, and interdicting illicit trafficking in nuclear and other radioactive materials.

75 UN Security Council Resolution 1540, adopted by consensus on 28 April 2004. For the resolution text, see www.state.gov/t/np/rls/other831990.htm.

76 A. Millar and M. B. Maerli, *Nuclear Non-Proliferation and UNSC Resolution 1540*, Policy Briefs on the Implementation of the Treaty on the Non-Proliferation of Nuclear Weapons, the Norwegian Institute of International Affairs (NUPI), April 2005, available online at: www.nupi.no/IPS/filestore/PolicyBriefsApril 2005.pdf.

77 For more on these endeavors, see M. B. Maerli, "US–Russian Naval Security Upgrades. Lessons learned and the way ahead," *Naval War College Review*, 56(4), 2003, 19–38.

78 For instance, the IAEA initiative to organize country-wise physical protection peer reviews (International Physical Protection Advisory Service, IPPAS) should be expanded.

79 The latest strategic nuclear arms reduction treaty, the Strategic Offensive

Reductions Treaty (SORT), does not include provisions for destruction of nuclear warheads or fissile material. As such, it offers very little toward reducing the nuclear terrorist threat. SORT has no milestones or intermediate goals, no provisions for destroying fissile material or delivery systems, and verification has no role in assuring compliance. Apart from the obligation not to have more than 2,200 strategic nuclear warheads by 31 December 2012, it is actually hard to see how SORT can be violated.

80 W. C. Potter, "Non-State Actors and Nuclear Weapons," Paper Prepared for the Monterey Nonproliferation Strategy Group, Monterey, California, 15–17 November 2003.

81 A. Roxburgh, "Q&A: EU 'terror tsar'," BBC, 26 March 2004, available online at: www.news.bbc.co.uk/1/hi/world/europe/3550543.stm.

82 On these preferences, see J. Solana, "A Secure Europe In A Better World," Statement for the Common Foreign And Security Policy European Council, Thessaloniki, 20 June 2003, available online at: www.ue.eu.int/pressdata/EN/reports/76255.pdf.

83 In his speech at the US National Defense University, Bush proposed steps for augmenting the existing treaty-based regime in some areas where it faces systemic shortcomings, most notably on export controls. Secondly, he declared that efforts should be pursued for strengthening the regime where it faces problems that can be addressed by internal reforms. In addition to urging other states to expand their internal control of nuclear proliferation activities, Bush specifically proposed broadening the scope of the Proliferation Security Initiative; expanding the Nunn–Lugar Cooperative Threat Reduction Program; curtailing the sale of enrichment and reprocessing equipment; refusing to sell equipment for civilian nuclear programmes to countries that fail to observe the IAEA's Additional Protocol on safeguards; establishing a new special committee under the IAEA Board of Governors for safeguards and verification; and finally, denying positions on the IAEA Board of Governors to states that are under investigation for illicit nuclear activities (Spring 2004, 3).

84 L. Brooks, "New Security Challenges for a New Century," Remarks given at the Conference on International Security Challenges and Strategies in the New Era, Sandia National Laboratories, Albuquerque, NM, 23 April 2003, available online at: www.nnsa.doe.gov/na-20/docs/intersecurstrat.pdf.

85 S. Lodgaard, "Good news for non-proliferation? The changing relationship between Russia, NATO and the NPT", *Disarmament Diplomacy*, 69, 2003, available online at: www.acronym.org.uk/dd8dd69/69op02.htm; J. du Preez, "The impact of the Nuclear Posture Review on the international nuclear nonproliferation regime", *Nonproliferation Review*, 9(3), 2002, 67–81; J. Cirincione, "How will the Iraq war change global nonproliferation strategies?" *Arms Control Today*, 33(3), 2003, available online at: www.armscontrol.org/act/2003_04/cirincione_apr03.asp; G. Perkovich,, "Bush' nuclear revolution", *Issue Brief*, Carnegie Endowment for International Peace, 6(4), 14 March 2003.

86 J. Holum, "Assessing the new US–Russian pact," *Arms Control Today*, 32(5), 2002, available online at: www.armscontrol.org/act/2002_06/holumjune02.asp.

87 M. May, "An Alternative Nuclear Posture," Background Paper for the Pugwash Workshop on Tactical Nuclear Weapons, Sigtuna, Sweden, 24–25 May 2002, available online at: www.stanford.edu/~mmay/Nuclear_Posture.html.

88 G. Perkovich, op cit. President Bush' 2005 budget request includes a cut in the Nunn–Lugar Program and the Administration has not acted quickly in the past to remove bureaucratic barriers to this critical program. S. A. Baynard, "How to thwart a nuclear black market", *Newsday*, 10 March 2004, available online at: www.newsday.com/news/opinion/ny-vpbay103701753mar10,0,6014295.story.

89 United States of America, *National Security Strategy of the United States of America*, September 2002, available online at: www.whitehouse.gov/nsc/nss.pdf.

90 United States of America/the White House, *United States National Strategy to Combat Weapons of Mass Destruction*, December 2002, available online at: www.whitehouse.gov/news/releases/2002/12/WMDStrategy.pdf.

91 The Nuclear Posture Review is classified. Excerpts made available reveal the establishing of a New Triad composed of offensive strike systems (both nuclear and non-nuclear), defenses (both active and passive), and a revitalized defense infrastructure (including a strengthening of US nuclear testing capabilities) that will provide new capabilities in a timely fashion to meet emerging threats. From GlobalSecurity.org, 2001.

92 M. Butcher, *What Wrongs Our Arms May Do. The Role of Nuclear Weapons in Counterproliferation*, Report issued by the Physicians for Social Responsibility, Washington, DC, August 2003, available online at: www.psr.org/documents/psr_doc_0/program_4/PSRwhatwrong03.pd. In May 2003, the US Senate lifted the ban on "mini-nuke" research and development. The time required to resume nuclear testing has been shortened to 18 months or less. On the possible US development of new nuclear weapons, see C. D. Ferguson and P. D. Zimmerman, "New nuclear weapons?" *Research Story of the Week*, Center for Nonproliferation Studies, 29 May 2003, available online at: www.cns.miis.edu/pubs/week/030528.htm.

93 M. May, op cit. The Pentagon has apparently produced contingency plans for pre-emptive use of nuclear weapons against several new states. F. Barnaby, *How to Build a Nuclear Bomb and Other Weapons of Mass Destruction*, London: Granta Books, 2003.

94 J. du Preez, op cit.

95 J. Cirincione, op cit.

96 There is, as a vivid example, a need to compare the $1 billion spent over more than a decade for the Nunn–Lugar Cooperative Threat Reduction Program with the $87 billion for less than a year in Iraq. R. Garwin in A. Hendels, "Scientist Claims Arms Reduction Is Best Defense," *The Stanford Daily*, 10 March 2004.

4 Critical infrastructure protection and cyber-terrorism
Mass destruction or mass annoyance?

James A. Lewis

With the end of the Cold War, national security analysts began to reassess the source and nature of threats that nations would face in the future. In the United States, a series of influential commissions issued reports whose common conclusion was that the US faced new kinds of opponents who would use unconventional, asymmetric modes of attack against the US homeland.[1]

The emphasis on asymmetric threats and unconventional attacks in these reports reflects, in part, the understanding that no nation will be able to challenge NATO member states in a conventional military confrontation. Vulnerable civilian targets and unconventional weapons will be more attractive to new kinds of opponents. Weapons of mass destruction form the principal threat, especially given the potential for their delivery by "unconventional" means (such as commercial vehicles or cargo containers rather than missiles), but some of the reports also identified "catastrophic" cyberattack as a new area of risk. Information systems and the communications infrastructure – a new, dynamic, and poorly understood element of the economy – were seen as a special area of vulnerability.

Policies for homeland security in the US and Europe must address a variety of threats, real and imagined. This creates a dilemma for constructing policy for any single nation, much less cooperation among nations. Many threat analyses are based on chains of assumption rather than evidence, and stem from what analysts believe *could* happen rather than what is *likely* to happen. The root of the dilemma lies in the need to balance the risks and potential damage of an attack against the probability that such an attack could be successfully carried out. There are bureaucratic and political incentives to discount probability in arguing for attention and for funds, but a serious policy process will attempt to rank threat not only by the maximum consequences but also by a reasonable assessment of whether attackers will choose to use a weapon, how likely the weapon is to work, and what the damage will be if an attack using this weapon succeeds.

This chapter undertakes that assessment for cyber-terror. It reviews US and European efforts in cyber-security, examines the likelihood of catastrophic attack, and reviews the motives of terrorists and the vulnerabilities of different infrastructures. Finally, based on an assessment that the cyber risk has been overstated, it suggests possible areas for transatlantic cooperation.

In the late 1990s, several Defense Department exercises, along with a number of computer security incidents, seemed to point to significant danger from cyber-attack. The exercises involved teams of skilled computer specialists who were given *carte blanche* in hypothetical scenarios to penetrate computer networks and create havoc. The ease with which their attacks did this (in theory) created a sense of urgency that reinforced the conclusion that the US faced a serious new risk.[2] The growing awareness of network vulnerabilities led US officials to become concerned that foreign nations or other potential opponents could launch attacks against Defense Department computer networks, against which the US was woefully unprepared.

Analyses of asymmetric, unconventional attack assumed that potential military competitors would be attracted to the use of cyber-weapons, as would "rogue states" and "non-state actors" antithetical to the West or its interests. Cyber-weapons were thought to be particularly attractive for asymmetric attacks because they can be difficult to trace and because the cost of launching an attack can be relatively low.

These concerns over the risk of catastrophic cyber-attack and electronic Pearl Harbors shaped much of the initial thinking on homeland security before the attacks of 11 September 2001. In response, the US created a new bureaucratic structure for cyber-security and began a process to develop a national strategy for securing cyber-space. The 1998 Presidential Decision Directive 63 (PDD-63) directed agencies to take necessary steps to ensure the continuity and viability of critical infrastructures, and ordered development of a national strategy for critical infrastructure that highlighted cyber vulnerability. Since the attacks of September 11, these efforts have been merged and subsumed – some might say submerged – into the larger work of the Department of Homeland Security. That Department (supported by recent work in the Intelligence Community) has decided that the risks of physical attacks against infrastructure far outweigh the risk of cyber-attack, and DHS has de-emphasized the cyber threat, prompting a debate in the US over whether more attention needs to be paid to the vulnerability of critical infrastructures to cyber-attack.[3]

In Europe, work to improve Internet security began as an element of a larger effort to build a European information society. Internet security issues were seen primarily through a business and commercial lens (rather than the defense and counterterror focus used in the US). Internet security was left primarily to private sector efforts, reinforced by EU-funded research programs among European institutions. The goals of these private sector efforts have been to build an information society and to meet European regulations on privacy and Internet content. Since September 11, internal security concerns, rather than economics, have become increasingly significant in discussions among and within European governments. The terrorist bombings in

Madrid in March 2004 strengthened these concerns, but, as in the US, counter-terrorism and physical security overshadow cyber-security.

There has been extensive consultation between the US and Europe on cyber-security, including cooperation between Computer Emergency Response Teams (CERTs), industry groups, and government agencies. Law enforcement and commercial channels for cooperation have been particularly important. European efforts at cyber-security tend to be advanced as part of the European Commission's larger strategy for building an information economy or, in some instances, as part of internal security activities of national authorities responsible either for e-government efforts or for internal security (where the Commission has had little or no authority).[4] Network security to enable the information society has been more important for Europe than critical infrastructure protection. In Europe as in the US there has been a relative lack of progress in determining how best to tie cyber security to the larger problems of critical infrastructure protection and homeland security

The notion that nations are vulnerable to cyber-attack rests on a central set of assumptions: critical infrastructures are dependent on computer networks, and if these computer networks are vulnerable, the infrastructures that use these networks are equally vulnerable. Attacks that disable these computer networks will cause terror or deal crippling blows to industrial nations. All of these assumptions are flawed. While computer networks are vulnerable to attack, critical infrastructures are not equally vulnerable. Infrastructures and nations are not dependent on computer networks that can be disabled by cyber-strikes. Catastrophic cyber attack is not realistic now or for the foreseeable future.

These erroneous assumptions should be placed in the context of a larger debate over whether the US and other nations have overestimated the probability of certain kinds of attack and the risks they face. Discussions of homeland security often include a range of improbable attack scenarios against which we are urged to defend. The counterargument to the low probability of a particular attack or weapon is that some forms of attack are so horrific and so potentially damaging that we should prepare for them even though there is only a small chance of their being carried out successfully. The outcome of this debate has real implications for resource allocation, and for intrusive and constraining new regulations. The general conclusion is that it is better to err on the side of security, but in the case of cyber-security, a focused and minimalist approach may be sufficient.

To assess this conclusion for cyber-security, we need to consider three elements. The first is the ability of cyber-attack to create terror or to damage economic or military performance. The second is the motives and rationales for various kinds of opponents to use cyber-weapons, and the third is the vulnerability of critical infrastructure to cyber-attack.

The ability of cyber-attack to create terror or damage economic or military performance

The theory of cyber-attack is that it will come with little or no warning and have catastrophic consequences. This is not new. Fear of surprise and a crippling blow has marked strategic thinking since the 1940s, in response to the twin shocks of devastating attacks on US military forces throughout the Pacific and the collapse of defenses in Western European nations. Elements common to these shocks included rapid and unexpected erosion of the defenders' position, the use of new technologies against which defenders were relatively unprepared, and exploitation of unexpected vulnerabilities by attackers which contributed to the scale and pace of defeat. NATO and the US spent considerable effort to avoid a repetition of *blitzkrieg* or Pearl Harbor, and it is not surprising that this has carried over into the new post-Cold War security analysis.

The theory of cyber-attack has also been shaped by the concepts of strategic warfare, which emphasize the need to attack and destroy an opponent's industry and civil infrastructure. These concepts emerged from the trenches of the World War I, when it became apparent that seeking victory over a modern industrial nation by defeating its military forces could only result in a grinding war of attrition. European strategists like Douhet and Trenchard argued that aerial bombing attacks against critical infrastructure well behind the front lines would disrupt and cripple an enemy's capacity to wage war and provide a shortcut to victory.

Their theories were put to the test in the 1940s. Massive aerial bombing raids were conducted for years against infrastructure and industry. However, surveys of the results of attacks, contrary to expectation, found that industrial societies are far more resilient than is commonly assumed. The US found similar results from aerial bombardment during the Vietnam War. Counterintuitively, the political effect of aerial attack on civilian infrastructure and populations was often to harden and increase popular support for continued resistance. Cyber-attacks, which create virtual rather than physical damage, would be even less likely to achieve catastrophic or decisive results.

One survey concluded that "whatever the target system, no indispensable industry was permanently put out of commission by a single attack. Persistent re-attack was necessary." This is important, for in a cyber-attack, once a hacker has gained access and the damage is done, the target usually responds quickly to close off the vulnerability that allowed that attack and to bring systems back on line. Terrorists would need to attack multiple targets simultaneously for long periods of time to have any effect, and it is likely that they would be unable to sustain such attacks in the face of a defender's response. For hackers, terrorist groups or nation states, multiple sustained attacks on critical infrastructure is not a feasible scenario. This is particularly the case for nation states, where the risk of discovery of what would be seen as an act of war outweighs any advantage gained from cyber-attacks on infrastructure.

In the larger context of economic activity, power outages, air traffic disruptions, and other cyber-terror scenarios occur routinely and do not damage national security or create terror. On a national or regional level, where dozens or even hundreds of different systems provide critical infrastructure services, failure can be a routine occurrence at the system or regional level, with service denied to customers for long periods of time. If the goal is to prevent cyber-attacks from costing a single day of electric power or water service, we have set an unnecessarily high standard. If a cyber-attack does not cause damage that rises above the threshold of routine disruption, it will not achieve the political or military effect its perpetrators would desire. From a strategic perspective, attacks that do not degrade national capabilities are not significant.

Many cyber-attack scenarios also assume an unlikely degree of passivity among defenders. In most cases of system failure, efforts to respond, repair, and restore begin almost at once. Absent the shock and horror of conventional attacks, the effect of a cyber-event could be very short-lived as government officials and private companies scramble to restore service. The same surveys of the effect of bombing attacks on civilian targets and critical infrastructure also found that "The speed and ingenuity with which they [the target] rebuilt and maintained essential war industries in operation clearly surpassed Allied expectations."[5] The experience of the twentieth century and the first few years of this century show that people are extraordinarily resilient and inventive in response to attacks, and in their capability to restore services and production. Cyber-weapons, which do not compare to WMD or conventional explosives in their destructive capability, therefore pose a very limited threat.

In recognition that cyber-attacks themselves might pass unnoticed, there has been speculation that a cyber-attack could have useful "multiplier effects" if undertaken simultaneously with a physical attack. This sort of simultaneous combination of physical and cyber-attacks may be attractive to terrorists. For example, a cyber-attack that disrupted a local 911 system shortly before an explosion could compound damage and shock. This sort of coordination would reinforce and multiply the effect of a physical attack. However, there are again untested assumptions in this scenario. The most important of these is that a defender would not compensate by using other means of communications. There is considerable redundancy in communications (voice radio, fixed telecommunications, mobile telephones, broadcast services are more important for public information, and less vulnerable to hacking, and emergency responder communications do not rely on computer networks).

In short, the utility of cyber-weapons and the vulnerability of industrial societies to attack have been overstated. While there are real risks in cyberspace, these are business risks that accrue more to individual firms rather than to nations.

Motives and rationales for opponents to use cyber-weapons

Among the potential opponents faced in homeland security, non-state actors pose the greatest threat. In their current form, entities like al-Qaeda are made up of clusters of smaller, like-minded groups (flat structures, no hierarchy, many leaders). Very often, the attackers are integrated into civil society. Their operations often fall outside the legal structure created for conflict between states. They have the ability to exploit commercial networks and technologies to achieve a global presence. They are less likely to respond (at least in the near term) to deterrence. These factors make them more elusive and more dangerous, but also reduce the likelihood that they will use cyber-weapons.

This is because they are motivated by a virulent anti-Western or anti-modern ideology, and their immediate goals are violence and destruction. Terrorists seek to inflict psychological and physical damage on their targets in order to make a political statement and achieve a political effect. If terrorism is an act of violence to achieve a political end, will terrorists use a weapon whose effects may not be noticed or are at best gradual and cumulative? A captured al-Qaeda training manual, *Military Studies in the Jihad against the Tyrants*, notes that explosives are the preferred weapons of terrorist because "explosives strike the enemy with sheer terror and fright." Explosions are dramatic, create fear, and do lasting damage. They meet certain psychological needs of those who are attracted to terrorism. Cyber-attacks would not have the dramatic and political effect that terrorists seek. A cyber-attack, which might not even be noticed by its victims, or which might be attributed to routine delays or outages, will not be the preferred weapon of terrorists.

Despite a decade of major terrorist activity, there have been no reports of cyber-attacks. Since 2001, the United States, the United Kingdom, Germany, Spain, and other nations have discovered active terrorist cells operating within their borders. These cells were planning attacks against civilian and military targets in the US. Most of these plans intended to use conventional explosives and gunfire, but terrorists reportedly also considered bio-toxins, and chemical or radiological weapons. None of these cells, however, are reported to have planned attacks using cyber-weapons. The only reference to the use of cyber-weapons came in 2002, when a fundamentalist cleric who resides in London and who has been a spokesperson for al-Qaeda threatened attacks against US economic infrastructure using all sorts of technologies, including the Internet, but to date, these attacks have not been launched.[6]

This absence of cyber-attack is indicative, and must be an element in the calculation of larger risks to homeland security. There have been many hundreds of terrorist attacks.[7] These attacks conformed to the predictions that new opponents would exploit vulnerabilities, use commercial technologies, and aim at creating shock and horror. Where the attacks differed from the predictions of earlier analyses was that they avoided the use of exotic technologies and weapons. Moreover, in the last decade more than 200,000 computer security incidents have been reported in the US.[8] None of these computer security incidents has damaged infrastructure, created panic or terror, or affected US military capabilities. A quantitative assessment of risk would assign a low probability to cyber-attack.

It can be argued, of course, that previous experience is not an adequate guide to future risk. Homeland security strategists, in ordering their priorities, can judge the utility of experience by taking note of three computer attacks against infrastructure that can be confirmed:[9]

1   A teenage boy hacked into a telephone computer switch in 1998 and disabled it for six hours, preventing the air traffic control tower at a regional airport in Massachusetts from using its main radio transmitter or from remotely activating runway lights. The air traffic tower had a back-up radio system, and there was no disruption to air traffic.[10]

2   In 2000, an ex-employee of the company that installed a sewage management system for the Maroochy Shire Council in Australia was able to hack into the sewage treatment plant's computer network and use his insider knowledge to pump sewage into a stream. He succeeded after numerous break-in attempts, all of which went unnoticed by Council authorities. Australia's environmental protection agency reported that "the creek water turned black and the stench was unbearable for residents." Despite the stench, terror did not ensue and there were no injuries or permanent damage.[11]

3   The Slammer worm reportedly damaged financial and government services, including 911 emergency response systems. These reports were overstated. Some credit card company and bank networks were affected for a few hours; others were not, and continued their weekend operations unabated. Slammer did not damage 911 systems. Slammer slowed the computers that dispatchers use to log 911 calls. Dispatchers in the affected Washington State jurisdictions have a back-up system (pen-and-paper logs) in the event of power failures or other problems. They used this when Slammer affected their computers. Response times by the 911 system and emergency services were not affected.[12]

These are serious offenses, but they are not terrorism. Neither attack produced fatalities, injury or permanent damage. They had none of the political or psychological effects desired by terrorists. Terrorism requires overt, public acts of violence that create widespread shock and horror. These incidents (along with any of the thousands of other computer security incidents) did not have this effect, and cannot be regarded as terrorist acts or threats to national security.

It is worth considering the calculus that a terrorist group may go through when it plans an operation. Their calculus is different from ours, but not necessarily less rational. They consider risk, commitment of resources, and opportunity cost in undertaking an operation. Terrorist groups weigh these factors against the likelihood of an operation achieving their aims. Operations with a high profile and a high probability of success will be preferred. Measuring this probability involves a number of factors, including an estimate of the psychological reaction to the attack, the difficulty of mounting the operation, and the reliability of the weapon to be used. Attackers will choose to avoid unfamiliar or unreliable weapons, given the cost (in resources and time) of mounting an operation that results in little or no damage. From this perspective, terrorists are likely to prefer proven weapons such as conventional explosives or proven tactics like hijacking.

Terrorist groups – al-Qaeda, Hamas, and others – do make significant use of the Internet, but as a tool for intra-group communications, intelligence collection, fund-raising, and propaganda. Their members have acquired the skills needed for these functions. Terrorists, who in the past often resorted to bank robbery to fund their operations, may also be taking advantage of the Internet to steal credit card numbers or valuable financial data.[13] Some experts go so far as to say that terrorists may avoid cyber-weapons because of the potential risk it could pose to their own operations and communications.[14]

It is possible that a potential opponent could have hacked into systems and planted "time bombs" or other disruptive programs that could be set into operation in the event of a crisis. This sort of approach is likely to be more attractive to a nation state for *in-extremis* situations than to a non-state actor like al-Qaeda. In the event of a conflict with the United States, a country may feel it has nothing to lose from triggering a cyber-attack, and that even a temporary disruption may be worth the cost. This is likely an overestimation by potential opponents – cyber-attacks would not reduce US military effectiveness – but it may be the only scenario where cyber-attack might be attractive.

The vulnerability of critical infrastructure to cyber-attack

Scenarios where computer attacks disable electrical grids, water systems, emergency response networks, air traffic control or major industries remain surprisingly common in public discussions of homeland security. One problem with these scenarios is that they remain entirely hypothetical. Previous sections discuss why there has been no use of cyber-weapons despite numerous terrorist attacks. This section asks what the results would be even if a cyber-weapon were used. Many of the existing analyses that predict "electronic Pearl Harbors" assume that there is a close connection between the physical and the cyber. In most instances, however, this connection seldom exists.

- Public water systems are often cited as a likely target for cyber-attack.[15] However, the use of diverse network technologies and systems architectures complicates the terrorists' task. The American Waterworks Association's assessment of the terrorist threat to water supplies placed "physical destruction of the system's components to disrupt the supply of water" as the most likely source of infrastructure attack.[16]

- Electrical utilities are a frequent target for hackers, but these attacks have not disrupted service.[17] Blackouts do not create terror. The State of California de-regulated its electrical power market, leading to months of blackouts and brownouts and a clear economic cost, but this was neither crippling nor terrifying. The failure of the Northeast electrical grid in August 2003 was embarrassing, but also did not create panic or damage national security. The Information Assurance Task Force of the President's National Security Telecommunications Advisory Committee concluded that "Physical destruction is still the greatest threat facing the electric power infrastructure. Compared to this, electronic intrusion represents an emerging, but still relatively minor, threat."[18]

- Cyber-attacks against air traffic systems to disrupt flights and endanger passengers and crews are a frequently cited threat.[19] However, computer networks do not operate aircraft, so hackers cannot take over a plane. Air traffic control does not depend on computer networks to manage air traffic. The high level of human involvement in flight operations and air traffic control makes cyber-attacks improbable.

- Although the Internet was designed to be robust and survivable during nuclear war, its current configuration is likely to have points of failure that could be exploited to create system-wide disruption. Even if could be disrupted for considerable periods, this would be unlikely to result in terror or long-term economic damage. Not all of the thousands of networks that comprise the Internet would be equally affected. Individuals would turn to alternate means of communications. Most industrial countries now have access to three or four different modes of communications, such as wireless and satellite links, providing redundancy and making communications more robust than a decade ago. Individual companies, however, may need to examine their operations and develop plans for continuity of operations in the event of disruption.

- The emergency response system is also a favorite target for theorists of cyber-terrorism. In the US this is the 911 telephone system, to respond to requests for police, fire and ambulance services. One US cyber-attack exercise ("Eligible Receiver" in 1997) developed a scenario where attackers sent a flood of email messages instructing people to call 911 for important information, in order to overload the system, and it is possible that in conjunction with a bombing or other physical attack this could act as a temporary "force multiplier" for terrorists.

- Manufacturing and economic activity are increasingly dependent on computer networks, and cyber-crime and industrial espionage are new dangers for economic activity. However, the evidence suggests that at a macro level, manufacturing is not vulnerable to cyber-attack.[20] Some companies would experience increased losses; others would not. Some major manufacturers now report that as a result of defensive measures they have taken, viruses are now only "nuisances."[21]

• Information operations and information superiority are critical for military operations, but no nation has military forces that are dependent on vulnerable computer networks. A RAND study conducted for the US Air Force on military operations and information vulnerabilities noted "while most of the current topical interests has focused on the newer, trendier threats to information systems, particularly computer hacking and associated disruption and manipulation . . . our analysis showed that some of the 'old-fashioned' threats pose a greater danger . . ."[22]

Three factors greatly reduce risk from cyber-attack. First, while computer networks are vulnerable, critical infrastructures that use these computers are not equally vulnerable. Gaining access to an infrastructure's computer network does not translate into control of the infrastructure or an ability to damage it. The infrastructures usually identified as cyber targets still require a physical presence and human intervention for most vital control mechanisms. Second, and more importantly, nations are robust and resilient in responding to attacks. A cyber-attack unaccompanied by physical damage or casualties would generate a quick response to repair and restore. Third, the increasing interdependence and interconnectivity of national economies provides a degree of redundancy and an ability to accommodate disruption and failures. All of these factors make it difficult for remote computer attacks to disrupt critical functions. If there were cyber-attacks, the effect on national security would be very limited.[23]

The risk lies in the potential for change. Risks could increase over time as the Internet is incorporated into a wider range of routine operations and activities. The most likely source for vulnerabilities in the future will lie in the upgrading or modernization of IT and control systems. Critical infrastructure systems that are currently secure because they rely on proprietary networks or manual controls will be less secure if they move to using public networks and remote, IP-based controls. This will occur on a company-by-company or even facility-by-facility basis within selected infrastructures. The most important function in relation to cyber-security and critical infrastructure protection is to monitor change to determine when vulnerabilities will appear.

The greatest risk at this time from cyber-attack lies in the potential to manipulate stored data or gain access to valuable information – e.g. espionage, theft of intellectual property or financial data, or vandalism. This poses a greater risk than infrastructure attacks. Intelligence collection techniques for the Internet differ significantly from earlier technical collection techniques. The global Internet significantly lowers the "cost-of-entry" for collectors and analysts, who can now be located around the globe and who can rely on inexpensive, commercially available equipment. Terrorist groups appear to use the Internet to collect information on potential targets.[24] This is very different from cyber-attack, in that in the event of a successful penetration of a computer network, a terrorist group will want to be as unobtrusive as possible.

This is not a static security situation. The vulnerability of critical infrastructure to cyber-attack may change as societies move to a time[25] when more daily activities have become automated and rely on remote computer networks, and as industrial and infrastructure applications move from dedicated, proprietary networks to greater use of the Internet and Internet protocols for their operations. These changes will increase vulnerabilities if countries do not make efforts to improve network security and make sure that critical infrastructures use hardened, redundant systems. One key issue for homeland security, including transatlantic cooperation in homeland security, is to monitor the potential for new vulnerabilities as the use of computer networks grows, and to develop strategies to avoid them.

Reassessing homeland security priorities

This picture of the cyber-threat calls for a reassessment of homeland security priorities. Planning and cooperation for cyber-security should be subsumed and integrated into a larger critical infrastructure effort. A useful first step is to identify what is actually critical. Current lists of critical infrastructures are too imprecise, and the result has been a dilution of efforts to build security. Identifying which infrastructures are actually critical, in the sense that a disruption of their operations would cause immediate problems for the economy, public safety or defense, is essential for constructing an effective defense.

The concept of criticality involves temporal and geographic elements. If there will be immediate problems for public safety or national defense when a system goes off-line, it is critical. Problems that emerge days, weeks or months after an attack allow for the marshaling of resources to respond, and are not critical. Also, national infrastructures are composed of many local pieces, not all of which are equally critical or equally vulnerable. Specific parts of the larger infrastructure, or "nodes," provide critical support, not entire networks or industries. For cyber-attack, the implication is that we are facing a smaller and more manageable problem. Not all industries, infrastructures or networks must be hardened or held to higher security standards. For cyber-security, the primary concern for agencies responsible for homeland security is to determine if any critical infrastructure vulnerabilities have been created by computer networks. These vulnerabilities have been asserted many times, but it is troubling that even after several years of work we cannot now say where or what they are with the precision required for effective defense.

Transatlantic cooperation

Transatlantic cooperation fits in this kind of reassessment. To cooperate, homeland security agencies on both sides of the Atlantic will need to identify transatlantic (e.g. shared) infrastructures and determine if there are vulnerabilities. Any assessment will likely find only a limited subset of transatlantic infrastructures – there is no transatlantic power grid, for example – that will probably involve only finance, communications, and transportation (cargo and air traffic). Intra-European cooperation on securing infrastructure should be a higher priority than transatlantic homeland security (as there is a much greater degree of interconnectedness), but agencies on both side of the Atlantic would benefit from working together to develop and share information on and solutions for vulnerabilities.

Structuring this cooperation poses a challenge. Solutions for transatlantic homeland security will depend less on traditional military alliances and more upon new forms of cooperation among intelligence and law enforcement agencies and, potentially, agencies charged with the new mission of homeland defense. In line with the suggestion that cyber-security works best as part of a larger strategy for critical infrastructure protection, planning for cyber defense may best be accomplished by inclusion in a larger structure for cooperation in homeland defense, and for sharing information and intelligence.

The emergence of a single European entity complicates efforts to build a cooperative arrangement. Before Maastricht, economics and trade were the purview of the European Commission, and security and defense functions were the prerogative of the member states. The still-evolving division of responsibility for security functions between the Commission and the member states means that, for a interim period of unknown duration, the US may need to pursue multiple and overlapping initiative with both member states and Brussels.

Disparities in national approaches to security between the US and Europe, and among European nations, also complicate building a cooperative approach.[26] It is still easier for the US to cooperate bilaterally with member states in intelligence, which forms a central part of any homeland security or critical infrastructure partnership. Cyber-security and critical infrastructure protection touch upon all three pillars of European cooperation (single market, common foreign and security policy, Justice and Home Affairs), but of these and in contrast to the US, it is security policy that has been given the least weight. European institutions for security and intelligence remain immature, and even the member states at times seem reluctant to devolve too much authority in these issues to Brussels. The current (albeit evolving) constraints on the EU's role in security and law enforcement will limit its ability to be a partner across the range of homeland security activities.

In the past, transatlantic defense cooperation would have been a matter for NATO, but the EU is building itself a role in defense. The European Commission's broad regulatory authority over key infrastructures makes Brussels a logical place to develop critical infrastructure protection. The effort to create a common and coordinated European approach to law enforcement and counter-terrorism (which has advanced following the March 11 attacks in Madrid) will also give it useful authorities and provide a new basis for cooperation with the US Finally, as European energy, transport, telecommunications, and financial networks continue to interconnect, the Commission offers the best venue to build a common homeland defense, among EU members, with the United States and, potentially, with NATO.

This means that some key questions for a transatlantic approach to homeland security will depend on resolution of political issues involved in European integration: the assignment of responsibilities for security and intelligence between member states and Brussels, and the relations of the European entity with the US and with NATO. To move ahead, it may be necessary to find new ways to combine or coordinate transatlantic efforts in law enforcement and intelligence (which operate at the member state level) with efforts at economic infrastructure protection (which operate to a greater degree at the Community level).

Recent European developments that will shape future cooperation include the creation of ENISA (the European Network and Information Security Agency) and the adoption of the Framework Decision on Attacks against Information Systems. The European Union authorized the creation of ENISA in February 2003. The new agency issued its first work program in early 2005, and it hopes to be fully functional in 2006. In its first work program, ENISA writes that until its creation in 2003, "Europe had no systematic cross-border co-operation on networking and information security as there was no mechanism which could ensure an effective response to transnational and global security threats." ENISA hopes to provide this mechanism. It is not a regulatory agency, and its authorities are carefully proscribed so as to not pre-empt national authorities or other EC regulatory or standards bodies, but one ENISA goal is to help the European Commission, member states, and the business community meet "the requirements of network and information security, including present and future Community legislation."[27]

Located in Greece, ENISA's mission is to "contribute to the development of a culture of network and information security for the benefit of the citizens, consumers, enterprises and public sector organisations of the European Union, consequently contributing to the smooth functioning of the internal market." ENISA provides "a centre of expertise" that collects information, promotes cooperation and raises awareness.[28] ENISA plays an advisory role and, given the current limitations on its functions, cannot be the primary partner in a transatlantic homeland cyber-security effort.

This additional legislation includes the Framework Decision on Attacks Against Information Systems.[29] The Framework Decision, which was adopted after six years of discussion by the European Commission's Council on Justice and Home Affairs (JHA) at the end of February 2005, is an element of the larger EU law enforcement and security strategy, and its counter-terror efforts. It complements other EU initiatives on data protection and information security. It requires member states to establish in their national laws criminal offenses for illegal access to an information system or illegal interference with an information system. It also requires member states to join the existing G8 network of operational points of contact on high tech crime.[30]

By harmonizing EU member state practices for cyber-attacks, the framework will make transatlantic cooperation easier, but neither the framework nor ENISA clearly place the EC as the preferred partner for cooperation. For the moment, the best approach to transatlantic cooperation may still require the US to work simultaneously with the Commission, with individual member states, and through other multilateral vehicles such as NATO.

ENISA and the Framework also do not fully resolve the differences in US and European approaches to cyber-security. Europe and the US face the same problem from different directions. This problem is to integrate cyber-defense into a comprehensive strategy for critical infrastructure protection. To achieve this larger strategic vision, Europe will need to assign greater weight to security, rather than economic issues, and the US will need to reassess improbable scenarios of cyber catastrophe and, perhaps, move closer to the European emphasis on regulatory agencies and law enforcement. For both sides of the Atlantic, putting cyber-defense into a larger strategic context requires first mapping any interrelationship between computer networks and critical infrastructure vulnerabilities, determining where additional measures for homeland security are needed (including some subset of cooperative transatlantic measures), and then taking action to ensure that these measures are put in place.

Conclusion

From a transatlantic perspective, it is impossible to separate-cyber security and critical infrastructure protection from the larger questions of political and security cooperation. A fully effective transatlantic approach to critical infrastructure protection and "cyber terrorism" will require better understanding of how intelligence, security, and law enforcement cooperation will work in the context of European integration. It will also require a precise assessment of which threats require a transnational defense, and which threats are most important.

This review suggests that computer network vulnerabilities pose an increasingly serious economic problem, but that the threat to security is overstated. Modern industrial societies are more robust than they appear. Critical infrastructures, especially in large market economies, are distributed, diverse, redundant, and self-repairing. In all cases, cyber-attacks are less effective and less disruptive than physical attacks. Computer network vulnerability and critical infrastructure vulnerability are not equal, and conventional forms of attack, more in line with terrorist objectives and capabilities, pose a greater risk. As an intelligence and law enforcement problem cyber-security is increasingly important, but cyber-attack is a secondary concern for homeland security.

At first glance, these conclusions seem counterintuitive. We all realize that information is transforming our societies and becoming central to their activities. However, we also live in a harsh time, and an assessment that looks at cyber-attack not from the perspective of peacetime but from the perspective of disruption and damage found in war suggests that cyber-attack is neither a tool for victory nor a fatal vulnerability that could lead to catastrophe or defeat. Faced with resource constraints and many immediate tasks, homeland security agencies need to consider this in their planning. While they must ensure careful efforts to determine where critical infrastructures are vulnerable and where computer networks should be hardened, cyber-attack or cyber-terror should not be a primary concern.

Notes

1 These reports include: Joint Security Commission, *Redefining Security: A Report to the Secretary of Defense and the Director of Central Intelligence*, February 1994; Defense Science Board, *Report of the Defense Science Board Task Force on Information Warfare – Defense (IW-D)*, November 1996, *Countering the Changing Threat of International Terrorism: Report of the National Commission on Terrorism Pursuant to Public Law 277, 105th Congress, Transforming Defense: National Security in the 21st Century: Report of the National Defense Panel*, December 1997; The President's Commission on Critical Infrastructure Protection, *Critical Foundations: Protecting America's Critical Infrastructure*, October, 1997.

2 The *Los Angeles Times*, in reviewing some of these exercises, concluded in 1999 "the evidence suggests a certain amount of hype and hysteria have overshadowed the reality of cyberspace." The magazine *Federal Computer Week* reported on 27 September 1999 that media coverage of one exercise, Moonlight Maze, is "a combination of outright fabrications, distortions and incorrect quotations . . . military secrets were not compromised."

3 Ted Bridis, Associated Press, "DHS Cybersecurity Chief Abruptly Resigns, Cites Frustrations," 1 October 2004, available online at: www.siliconvalley. com/mld/siliconvalley/news/editorial/9811404.htm; D. Verton, "DHS cyber division taking shape, despite concerns about waning influence," *Computer World*, October 2003, available online at: www.computerworld.com/security topics/security/story/0,10801,85589,00.html. M. Savage, "House Approves New Cybersecurity Post," *SC Magazine*, April 2005, available online at: www.scmagazine.com/news/index.cfm?fuseaction=newsDetails&newsUID=cc52 e9a3–b663–4319–98a5–78ff929a2b67&newsType=News.

4 "Communication of 28 May 2002 from the Commission to the Council, the European Parliament, the Economic and Social Committee and the Committee of the Regions – The eEurope 2005 action plan: an information society for everyone."

5 Interviews with senior executives from Verizon and Con Edison, the telephone and electric companies at the World Trade Center (and telephone service

provider at the Pentagon) found that both companies' work forces immediately and spontaneously regrouped to begin repair operations within hours of the attack, and worked around the clock to restore service. Surveys by the United States of the effect of aerial bombardments in Europe and Vietnam found that industrial societies are impressively resilient and capable of overcoming damage. See, for example, US Strategic Bombing Survey, *Summary Report (European War)*, 1945, available online at: www.anesi.com/ussbs02.htm.

6 Experts: Don't Miss Cyber attack Warning. Available online at: www.computerworld.com/securitytopics/security/story/0,10801,76000,00.html.

7 Department of the, Patterns, Global Terrorism, available online at: www.state.gov/s/ct/rls/pgtrpt/2000/; www.usinfo.state.gov/topical/pol/terror/01103131.htm; www.library.nps.navy.mil/home/tgp/chrono2001.htm; www.state.gov/s/ct/rls/pgtrpt/2000/2452.htm.

8 RT/CC statistics, 1998–2005, available online at: www.cert.org/stats/cert_stats.html#incidents.

9 Richard M. Smith, personal communication with the author.

10 US Department of Justice, "Juvenile computer hacker cuts off FAA tower at regional airport – first federal charges brought against a juvenile for computer crime," 18 March 1998, available online at: www.usdoj.gov/criminal/cybercrime/juvenilepld.htm.

11 L. Tagg, "Aussie hacker jailed for sewage attacks," 1 November 2001; available online at www//cooltech.iafrica.com/technews/837110.htm.

12 R. M. Wells, "Dispatchers go low-tech as bug bites computers," *Seattle Times*, 27 January 2003, available online at: www.archives.seattletimes.nwsource.com/cgi-bin/texis.cgi/web/vortex/display?slug=webworm27m&date=20030127.

13 There have as yet been no reported incidents of terrorist-linked financial hacking.

14 Vincent Cannistraro, a former CIA counter terrorism chief, quoted in *Computer World* in November 2002, available online at: www.computerworld.com/securitytopics/security/story/0,10801,76000,00.html.

15 B. Gellman, "Cyber attacks by al Qaeda feared: Experts: terrorists at threshold of using Web as deadly tool," *The Washington Post*, 27 June 2002.

16 G. DeNileon, "The who, what why and how of counter-terrorism issues," *American Water Works Association Journal*, 93(5), 2001, 78–85; available online at www.awwa.org/Communications/journal/Archives/J501es3.htm; see also S. Berinato, "Debunking the threat to water utilities," *CIO Magazine*, 15 March 2002, available online at: www.cio.com/archive/031502/truth_sidebar2.html.

17 Riptech Internet Security Threat Report, July 2002, available online at: www.securitystats.com/reports/Riptech-Internet_Security_Threat_Report_vII.20020708.pdf.

18 Information Assurance Task Force of the National Security Telecommunications Advisory Committee, available online at: www.aci.net/kalliste/electric.htm.

19 P. Larissa, "When Cyber Hacktivism Meets Cyberterrorism," SANS Institute, 19 February 2001, "Examples of cyber terrorist actions can include hacking into an air traffic control system that results in planes colliding..."

20 K. Bradsher, "With Its E-Mail Infected, Ford Scrambled and Caught Up," *The New York Times*, 8 May 2000.

21 Riptech Internet Security Threat Report, July 2002, op cit.

22 G. C. Buchan, "Implications of information vulnerabilities for military operations," in Z. M. Khalilzad and J. P. White (eds), *The Changing Role of Information in Warfare*, Santa Monica, CA: Rand, 1999; see also E. Lichtbau, the *Los Angeles Times*, April 24, 2002, which reported that the Chinese Army "does not have the capability to carry out its intended goal of disrupting Taiwanese military

and civilian infrastructures or US military logistics using computer virus attacks" and is limited to the "temporary disruption of sectors that use the Internet." Available online at: www.landfield.com/isn/mail-archive/2002/Apr/0138.html, and http://www.internetnews.com/dev-news/article.php/10_1023131.

23 While the vulnerability of critical infrastructure and countries to cyber-attack is low, the vulnerability of individual companies may be high if they experience the loss of intellectual property, financial data or reputation as a result of cyber-attack. This does not, however, translate into damage to national security.

24 This should not be construed as an argument for censorship or the removal of information from websites. The economic and political benefits of openness and making information available to the public outweigh, in almost all cases, the potential costs of espionage.

25 See Computer Science and Telecommunications Board, National Research Council, *Embedded, Everywhere: A Research Agenda for Networked Systems of Embedded Computers*, Washington, DC: National Academy Press, 2001

26 J. L. Clarke, "Securing the European homeland," *Journal of Homeland Security*, September 2003. Online, available at: www.homelandsecurity.org/journal/articles/clarke.html

27 ENISA, *Work Programme 2005: Information Sharing is Protecting*, February 2005, pp. 3–5, available online at: www.enisa.eu.int/doc/pdf/management_board/decisions/work_programme_2005.pdf.

28 European Network and Information Security Agency. Available online at: www.enisa.eu.int/about/activities/index_en.htm.

29 The final text can be found online at www.register.consilium.eu.int/pdf/en/04/st15/st15010.en04.pdf.

30 European Commission, Brussels, 19 March 2002, "Council Framework Decision on attacks against information systems". Available online at: www.europa.eu.int/eur-lex/en/com/pdf/2002/com2002_0173en01.pdf.

5 Border and transportation security in the transatlantic relationship

Rey Koslowski[1]

Recent terrorist attacks on the US and Europe linked to al-Qaeda have either targeted transportation systems (Spanish trains and French oil tankers) or weaponized forms of transportation, whether truck bombs at US embassies in Kenya and Tanzania, the boat bomb used against the *USS Cole*, or commercial airliners smashing into the World Trade Center and the Pentagon. These attacks have starkly revealed security vulnerabilities of global transportation systems and national border controls. At least two of the September 11 hijackers used altered passports, one of the hijackers entered with a student visa but never showed up for class, three stayed in the US after their visas had expired, and several purchased fraudulent documents on the black market that primarily services illegal migrants. The Madrid train bombings on 11 March 2004 not only demonstrated the vulnerabilities of European rail transportation systems; they also highlighted weaknesses in European border security. An al-Qaeda-affiliated group linked to the Madrid bombing, Ansar al-Islam, had a human smuggling and document fraud operation to fund terrorist actions and smuggle its own members into countries such as Spain and Iraq.

Given that some of the al-Qaeda members who planned and executed the September 11 plot lived in Europe and were recruited there, it is clear that European immigration and border control policies are crucial to US homeland security. Border control officials working on both sides of the Atlantic realize that transnational threats posed by terrorist networks require stepped-up international cooperation. While the split between the US and individual EU member states, such as France and Germany, over the Iraq war led some commentators to declare US–European relations as being in crisis, these EU member states were busily signing shipping-container security agreements and exchanging information with US border control authorities. Indeed, there has been significant transatlantic cooperation on border and transportation security, and there is potential for much more. Does it make sense to speak of "transatlantic homeland security?" With respect to border control and transportation, it certainly does.

This chapter examines the US and EU responses to the attacks of September 11 and March 11 in the area of transportation and border security, the reverberations of US homeland security policy initiatives in Europe, and the progress in transatlantic cooperation with respect to trade and travel between the US and Europe. The chapter specifically addresses the security of containerized shipping and passenger air travel, and the future of visa-free travel between the US and EU member states. It concludes by considering the impact of transatlantic cooperation in border and transportation security, as well as possible steps toward further cooperation.

Border security in the US and EU

In response to the attacks of 11 September 2001, the United States initiated a reorganization of government largely aimed at improving border and transportation security. European Union member states tightened border controls and accelerated integration in Justice and Home Affairs, but did not engage in similar wholesale reorganization. Jonathan Stevenson[2] has argued that EU member states were less inclined to take dramatic steps in response to the September 11 attacks because Europeans perceive the threat of terrorism differently than Americans do, largely due to the type of terrorism Europeans have lived with for the past three decades. Attacks by groups like the Provisional Irish Republican Army and Basque separatists have largely been limited in scope, with the intention of keeping open the possibility of negotiations to meet political objectives. In contrast, al-Qaeda's objective has been to inflict mass casualties against US military and civilian targets in order to cripple the US Government and the US economy, and, if possible, to use weapons of mass destruction in these attacks. Moreover, European foot-dragging could be explained by the belief that the US, not Europe, was al-Qaeda's primary target. The March 11 Madrid bombing disabused policymakers of that belief and prompted the European Council to establish the position of an EU counter-terrorism coordinator and take even more measures to strengthen border security. Indeed, evaluation of the nature of the terrorist threat and the sense of urgency in combating it may be increasing among European policymakers and publics at the same time that perception of a terrorist threat is fading across the Atlantic as the years tick by without another attack on the US homeland. With respect to border and transportation security, differing levels and kinds of action have not simply been a function of differing threat perceptions, but also of differing institutional arrangements, policy approaches, social norms, and political constraints.

In the wake of the September 11 attacks, the Bush Administration quickly established the Office of Homeland Security within the White House, under the leadership of Tom Ridge, to coordinate the anti-terrorism and border control efforts of key agencies spread across several cabinet-level departments of the federal government. At the time, the Bush administration opted against a complete reorganization of government along the lines envisioned in the Hart–Rudman Commission[3] report – a merger of the

Coast Guard, US Customs Service, and the US Border Patrol (a part of the Immigration and Naturalization Service (INS) into the Federal Emergency Management Agency to form a new Department of National Homeland Security. Congressional Democrats and Republicans proposed such a merger, but the Bush Administration appeared to limit its action to reforming the INS by separating its enforcement functions from service functions.[4] Homeland Security Director Tom Ridge then supported a plan to combine the law enforcement arm of the INS with the Customs Service in late April 2002. Unbeknownst to the top managers in the INS and Customs Service, who were preparing plans for the INS reorganization at the time, a small group within the White House was working on a government reorganization that went beyond what the Hart–Rudman Commission recommended.

The new Department of Homeland Security (DHS) merged 22 previously separate agencies into the new department's four "directorates" and three "elements" on 1 March 2003. The Border and Transportation Security (BTS) Directorate provides executive direction, oversight, coordination, and policy guidance to US Customs and Border Protection (CBP), US Immigration and Customs Enforcement (ICE), the Transportation and Security Administration (TSA), and the Federal Law Enforcement Training Center (FLETC). The BTS Directorate also oversees the United States Visitor and Immigrant Status Indicator Technology (US-VISIT) program, which is the entry–exit tracking system that collects digital photograph and fingerprint scan biometrics from those individuals traveling on a non-immigrant visa to the United States, and which runs watch list checks on the data collected. When the "legacy" INS was divided up, the US Border Patrol and immigration inspectors went to US Customs and Border Protection, immigration investigators and detention services went to Immigration and Customs Enforcement (ICE), and the remainder formed the US Citizenship and Immigration Services (USCIS), one of the three "elements" (along with the Coast Guard and Secret Service) whose directors all report to the Deputy Secretary of Homeland Security.[5]

Prodded by Congressional critics who questioned the efficacy of a new department without a clear mission, the Bush Administration in July 2002 issued a "National Strategy for Homeland Security" that states:

> A single entity in the Department of Homeland Security will manage who and what enters our homeland in order to prevent the entry of terrorists and the instruments of terror while facilitating the legal flow of people, goods, and services on which our economy depends. The Department and its partners will conduct border security functions abroad to the extent allowed by technology and international agreements."[6]

In a dramatic illustration of the administration's agenda to use new technologies to support risk management-based border controls that were being "pushed out" beyond US territorial boundaries, Richard Falkenrath, Deputy

Assistant to the President and Deputy Homeland Security Advisor, drew an analogy likening the revolution in military affairs of the 1990s to the "revolution in border security" that is now taking place.[7]

There is no exact EU or EU member state counterpart to the US Department of Homeland Security. The new Department of Homeland Security is actually much closer in organization to European interior ministries, which implement most border control functions, than the previous dispersal of border control functions across the US Federal Government. Collectively, the border control divisions of EU member state interior ministries, however, are much larger than their US equivalent, the Bureau of Customs and Border Protection (CBP).[8]

The European approach to border control has also differed significantly from that of the US in that EU member states strictly enforce migration laws within their countries, while there is very little internal enforcement in the US. Legal immigrants as well as European citizens routinely register with the local police when they move to a new address, and carry identity documents that the police may ask to see at any time. Most EU member states require and enforce work permits, and employers are tightly controlled. Migrants who cross the border into the United States illegally are rarely stopped from living and working in the US (there are now approximately ten million), making it much more difficult to find and apprehend an illegal migrant in the US. US immigration control has been tightly focused on the border itself, whereas border control in the EU is layered, extending back from the border and throughout society and the economy.

While national identity cards (IDs) have long been a part of the social fabric of Continental Europe, the US and the UK have a long tradition of resisting national IDs, and this resistance continues in the US. The Bush administration rejected proposals for a national ID card shortly after the September 11 attacks, and if such a proposal were to be put forward, vote counters indicate that it would not receive a majority vote in Congress. In the years since the attacks, there have been no initiatives by the US Government to introduce a national ID or to require biometrics (beyond digitized photographs) from US citizens for identification and travel documents. In contrast, most continental Europeans carry national ID cards, and countries such as Portugal incorporated fingerprint biometrics into their IDs before 11 September 2001. Other EU member states have not incorporated fingerprint biometrics due to social norms against fingerprinting those who have not committed crimes, as well as historical legacies of World War II, which have influenced the debate in Germany. In response to the September 11 attacks, however, Germany's SPD/Alliance90/Green coalition Government proposed strong anti-terrorism legislation. The SPD-led Interior Ministry originally demanded inclusion of fingerprint data in identification documents and passports, while the Greens proposed using hand and facial geometric data. A compromise emerged which left open the type of biometric data used while lifting the ban on fingerprints in the passport law. The September 11 attacks also prompted UK Home Secretary David Blunkett to break with British tradition and propose a national ID card that would include personal data, a digital photo, and a biometric (such as a fingerprint). The draft bill and pilot scheme were introduced in April 2004 to a mixed response.

Moreover, border control policies of EU member states are being integrated into EU institutional structures, and the implementation of border controls by member state interior ministries is increasingly coordinated at a European level. The establishment of a single European market in 1986 increased pressure to eliminate internal borders so that trucks and tourists would not be held up by passport inspections. Since lifting internal borders required the erection of a common external border, a subset of EU member states signed the 1990 Schengen Convention that eliminated border checks among its members at the same time that it called for a common visa policy, harmonization of polices to deter illegal migration, and an automated Schengen Information System (SIS) to coordinate actions regarding individuals who have been denied entry. Title VI of the 1992 Maastricht Treaty formalized long-standing cooperation among the member states regarding border controls, migration and asylum in the "third pillar" devoted to cooperation in Justice and Home Affairs (JHA). The 1997 Amsterdam Treaty incorporated the Schengen Convention into the EU treaties, and set out a plan to integrate policies on visas, asylum, immigration, and external border controls.

In the immediate aftermath of the attacks on the World Trade Center and the Pentagon, the extra-ordinary European Council of 21 September asked member states to strengthen controls at external borders, and also surveillance measures.[9] Shortly thereafter, the Justice and Home Affairs Council began discussions regarding forming a common border police force, which would involve the development of a harmonized curriculum for training border control officials and of a European Border Guard School. Although proposals for a common border guard were blocked at the 2001 December Laeken European Summit, bilateral joint border patrols continued, as did bilateral arrangements for cooperation to deploy assistance to address sudden influxes of illegal migration into fellow member states. Additionally, a new European Agency for the Management of Operational Co-Operation at the External Borders of the European Union agency will coordinate the implementation of common policies by member state border police, although it lacks policymaking or implementing powers of its own.[10]

Like the US, the EU has focused on using information technology to strengthen border controls. The Schengen Information System (SIS) is designed to enforce the common external border and build confidence in this common border so as to enable member states to remove all internal border controls. Integration into the system is necessary for the Schengen Convention to become effective for any signatory. The SIS contains data on illegal migrants, lost and false travel documents, and wanted or missing persons, and approximately ten million people were listed in the SIS, as of June 2002.[11] The SIS can electronically transmit text and figures, but not photos and fingerprints.[12] Since the SIS is only capable of working with no more than 18 member states and cannot handle the increased data processing demands of EU enlargement, the European Commission proposed the Schengen Information System II (SIS II). Scheduled to become operational in 2007, the SIS II will not only increase data capacity, but also be able to store digital images and biometric data and answer police requests within five seconds[13] With rising concerns about illegal migration into Europe and the possibility of terrorists being smuggled into the EU or entering by visa fraud, the European Commission proposed a common online database that would complement secure identity documents,[14] and the Spanish Presidency put forward a proposal to the Council for creating a "Visa Information System".[15] Subsequently, Germany and the Benelux countries proposed a uniform format visa incorporating anti-counterfeit features and biometric data such as fingerprints or iris scans stored on a microchip embedded in the document, and the European Commission proposed the incorporation of biometrics into visas and resident permits for third country nationals.[16] In February 2004, the European Commission put forward a legislative proposal to create a visa information system with the Commission developing a central database system to which member states would link their own national systems. The European Parliament initially balked at the plan, but eventually gave an opinion permitting the legislation to go forward to the Council.[17]

In September 2001, the border control authorities of the EU and its member states collectively had more staff and resources than did the US, and many EU member states had much more proactive polices in certain areas – such as internal enforcement, national identification systems, and airline passenger screening. As indicated above, the staffing gap still persists even after the establishment of the Department of Homeland Security. While European capabilities may be greater than those of the US, they are still primarily organized on a national basis, reflecting the legacy of controlling borders between EU member states – border controls that have largely been lifted with the implementation of the Schengen Convention. Should further bilateral and European-wide agreements be reached, tens of thousands of current EU member state border guards (e.g. a large portion of the German *Bundesgrenzschutz*) may be redeployed to the EU's common external borders to the east as internal border controls with the EU's new member states are lifted in the coming years.

Container security

Delivery of a weapon of mass destruction (WMD) by shipping container is one of the greatest threats posed by transnational terrorism, both to the country on the receiving end of the shipment and to the global transportation system upon which international trade and the global economy depend. Shipping containers carry approximately 90 percent of the world's international trade by value. The volume of trade moving through the United States' 102 seaports has nearly doubled since 1995. Each year, more than 16 million containers arrive in the United States by ship, truck, and rail. Before September 11 about 2 percent of the containers that entered the United States annually were physically opened and inspected,[18] but since September 11 that percentage has increased "significantly."[19] Due to the physical constraints of ports, it is impossible to increase inspections beyond a single digit percentage without bringing international trade to a halt. For example, if more than 8 percent of the containers entering the Port of New York/Newark were opened and inspected, ships would begin to back up in New York harbor.[20] Indeed, by shutting down commercial air traffic and heightening border security after the September 11 attacks, the US in essence did to itself what no enemy has done before: implemented an embargo on trade.[21]

Responding to this dilemma, the US Customs Service (now Customs and Border Protection – CBP) in January 2002 announced the Container Security Initiative (CSI), which is intended to "push out the border" by pre-screening cargo containers at ports of origin or during transit rather than when they reach the US. The logic behind the measure is that detection of a WMD after it has arrived in a US port may be too late if the device can be detonated by remote control, or if the container is booby-trapped to detonate if it is opened for inspection. The initiative is set to establish security criteria to identify high-risk containers, to use technology to pre-screen high-risk containers before they arrive at US ports, and to develop and use smart and secure containers. CSI initially focused on engaging the top 20 ports that ship 66 percent of the cargo containers to the US. Since time was critical and the EU lacked a homeland security counterpart with whom Tom Ridge could negotiate, the US opted for approaching EU member states on a bilateral as well as a multilateral basis. The US quickly signed CSI "statements of principle" with the Netherlands, Belgium, France, Germany, Italy, and Spain.

Smaller ports in the EU were concerned that trade would be diverted to Europe's megaports, and some in the European Commission viewed the propagation of bilateral CSI agreements with individual member states as a policy of "divide and conquer."[22] EU exporters then received a jolt from US Customs' proposed regulation that manifest data be submitted 24 hours before a container has been loaded. Many experts argued that "It is certainly a much bigger issue than the US is making out. This will be a major change."[23] The official EU response to Commission Bonner's proposals, which came in September 2002, argued that they would "seriously disrupt EU transport operations without necessarily giving the US the security assurance it seeks."[24] Partly motivated by the implementation of the 24-hour rule on 2 December 2002, the European Commission initiated a process in

December 2002 that could have brought several member states before the European Court of Justice for engaging the US in bilateral arrangements that affected trade. Before things came to a head, however, the Commission put these proceedings on hold while the Commission and the member states moved toward developing a common European framework for negotiating with the US. In March 2003, the EU's Council of Ministers gave the European Commission permission to negotiate a multilateral agreement on container security with the US.[25]

Despite the dire predictions of European shippers, the 24-hour rule did not lead to major disruptions of transatlantic trade. On 28 January 2003, US Customs also initiated Phase II of CSI, which expanded the program to additional ports based on volume, location, and strategic concerns. In November 2003, the US and EU initialed an agreement that involved the expansion of the 1997 EU–US Customs Cooperation Agreement, and on 22 January 2004 the Commission submitted the draft agreement with the US to the Council of Ministers. The agreement allows existing bilateral agreements to be maintained (provided they do not breach the EU treaty); permits implementation of the 24-hour rule; requires that CSI be extended to all EU ports (as long as they have significant trade with the US and sufficient screening technology); requires risk assessment standards and standards for screening technologies that are set by a group of US Customs and Commission officials; and establishes procedures for EU member states that wish to make additional arrangements with the US.[26] As of April 2004, CSI was operable in Rotterdam, Bremerhaven, Hamburg, Antwerp, Le Havre, Göteborg, La Spezia, Genoa, and Felixstowe, with Algeciras set to become operational in the near future.

CSI agreements are reciprocal, meaning that European customs inspectors could be stationed in US ports, but so far EU member states have not deployed inspectors in the US. In response to CSI, however, the European Commission has proposed its own version of a container security policy. This includes a common risk criteria for shipments, increased use of container scanners and nuclear radiation detection instruments, and a requirement for advanced submission of cargo data 24 hours in advance of arrival in an EU port[27].

Advanced passenger information

The use of fuel-laden commercial airliners as weapons against civilian targets prompted the US Congress to pass the Aviation and Transportation Security Act in the fall of 2001. The act requires that airlines with US-bound international flights submit a passenger manifest electronically and mandates that "the carriers shall make passenger name record information available to the Customs Service upon request."[28] Passenger name record (PNR) data is created each time a passenger books a flight, and is stored in the airlines' reservation systems.

To comply with these regulations, US-based airlines gave access to their (PNR) databases to the US Customs Service. Many opted simply to give database passwords to US Customs, which allowed Customs to "pull" all PNR data rather than select and "push" a subset of that data which met specific Customs requests.

The US Customs Service also requested PNR data from European-based airlines, but several resisted, contending that it would be a violation of EU data protection rules. Essentially, European airlines were presented with the choice of either breaking US laws, facing fines, and potentially losing landing rights, or violating EU and EU member state data protection laws and facing fines.

Discussions between the European Commission and the US Customs Service yielded US compliance extensions for these airlines until 5 March 2003, by which time the EU and the US had arrived at an interim "arrangement."[29] After months of negotiations the European Commission and Customs and Border Protection (CBP) secured an agreement, in the form of a Commission "adequacy decision,"[30] that data will be adequately protected, and corresponding "undertakings" issued by the CBP (2004) promise that data will receive agreed treatment.[31] Key features of the agreement restrict use to preventing and combating terrorism and serious crimes that are transnational (i.e. not domestic crime); limit retention of data for up to three-and-a-half years; and provide redress to passengers through a new DHS Privacy Office, with the possibility of EU data protection authorities representing EU citizens.[32]

Despite this arrangement, the European Parliament called upon the Commission to withdraw the draft decision, arguing that the Commission's decision "Presents the risk that millions of European passengers will be subject to comprehensive surveillance and monitoring by a third country."[33] As long as the European Council continues to support the Commission on this issue, the Parliament cannot stop the transfer of PNR data on its own authority. Persistent parliamentary objections, hearings, and engagement of advocacy groups, however, may undermine support in individual EU member states. Moreover, the European Parliament has now referred the agreement for a challenge in the European Court of Justice.[34]

Interestingly, if EU member states were to demand PNR data from US-based airlines, there is no legal framework for permitting this and the airlines could easily refuse. The CBP "undertakings" state that:

> In the event that the European Union decides to adopt an airline identification system similar to that of the US Government, which requires all carriers to provide European Authorities with access to PNR data for persons whose current travel itinerary includes a flight to, from or through the European Union, CBP would encourage US-based airlines to cooperate.[35]

In the wake of the Madrid bombings, the European Council of 25 March 2004 agreed to expedite a Council directive to require airlines to submit PNR data.[36] It stands to reason that US-based airlines that have already given access to US Customs and Border Protection will not resist giving access to European authorities. Due to their own privacy policies and potential for lawsuits, however, US-based airlines may resist voluntarily giving access to PNR data to European border control authorities unless specifically required to by new US legislation.

Document security, biometrics and the future of visa-free travel between the US and the EU

Responding to the attempt by a UK national, Richard Reid, to detonate a bomb hidden in his shoe while on a transatlantic flight, some US legislators raised the possibility of eliminating the US Visa Waiver Program, which allows nationals of 27 states (including most EU member states) to enter the United States without a visa for a stay of up to 90 days.[37] Instead of abolishing the Visa Waiver Program, Congress passed provisions designed to increase its security. The Enhanced Border Security and Visa Entry Reform Act requires that Visa Waiver Program countries have a program in place by 26 October 2004 to issue machine-readable, tamper-resistant passports containing biometric data, and that all passports issued after that date contain biometrics.[38] Many countries informed the State Department and the DHS that they could not meet this deadline, and Secretaries Tom Ridge and Colin Powell asked Congress for a postponement to December 2006.[39] Congress responded with legislation providing only for a one-year extension, to 26 October 2005.[40] Shortly after the deadline extension request, the DHS announced that nationals of the 27 Visa Waiver countries would be required to enroll in US-VISIT and submit to a digital photograph and finger scanning upon entry, beginning 30 September 2004.[41]

The US Congress deferred to the International Civil Aviation Organization (ICAO) on setting the biometric standard, and it was not until 28 May 2003 that the ICAO announced an agreement – facial recognition plus optional fingerprints and/or iris scans stored on a contactless integrated circuit (IC) chip.[42] The contactless IC chip is central to the vision of the "revolution in border security," and is part of a Radio Frequency Identification (RFID) system in which data on a chip or tag are transmitted via radio waves to a reader. As opposed to machine-readable travel documents, which contain data on magnetic strips, a passport with an RFID chip can be read by the reader at a distance, therefore allowing faster transfer of data from the passport. As envisioned, holders of new biometric passports issued by Visa Waiver countries will give their passports to CBP inspectors, who will simply bring the passport close to the reader. The reader will capture the personal data and the digitized biometric. This information can then be checked against terrorist and law enforcement watch lists. If there are no hits, the inspector can then allow the traveler to continue through passport control and enter the US. Similarly, upon exiting within the 90-day limit of the Visa Waiver Program, the traveler will "check out" of the country with a wave of the passport over a reader, possibly even using a self-service kiosk.

Even if a Visa Waiver Program country had incorporated biometrics on contactless IC chips into its passports in time to comply with the original 26 October 2004 deadline, DHS officers at US ports of entry may not have had the right equipment to read the data from those passports because until recently there was no agreed international standard for guaranteeing interoperability of contactless IC chips and RFID readers. Different radio frequencies are used by different companies that make RFID systems, and if countries in the Visa Waiver Program begin purchasing these systems before a single RF standard is agreed, the IC chips in some passports might not be readable by the machinery at the US port of entry, or the US might have to invest in as many as 27 different readers for all of the different passports.[43] After the 22 March–2 April 2004 meeting of the ICAO Facilitation Division the ICAO revised the standard to address this interoperability problem, and this standard was approved in May 2004. Without the biometric deadline extension, that would have left five months for Visa Waiver countries to deploy new passports with RFID chips, and five months for the US to install RFID readers compatible with those passports at all US air and sea ports of entry. Given this very short timeframe, DHS Secretary Ridge also asked for and received an extension of the Enhanced Border Security and Visa Entry Reform Act deadline for the DHS to install equipment for biometric comparison and authentication of passports.[44]

If the US were to drop a current EU member state from the Visa Waiver program, that could trigger a chain of events that would end visa-free travel between the US and the EU. If, for example, the US were to begin requiring visas of Spanish nationals, Spain might follow the traditional approach to visa policy, which is to reciprocate and require visas from US nationals. As the EU has a common visa policy, Spain might invoke the solidarity clause of this common policy, which would require visas of all US nationals traveling to the EU. Nine of the ten states that entered the EU on 1 May 2004 are not members of the Visa Waiver Program (none except Slovenia). Any one of them could also invoke the solidarity clause of the common visa policy, should the US persist in not granting their nationals visa-free travel.

Reciprocity could take other forms as well. Stuart Verdery, Assistant Secretary for Policy and Planning at the Border and Transportation Security Directorate of the DHS, noted the security benefits of adding fingerprint biometrics to Visa Waiver country passports. This would permit checks against existing law enforcement fingerprint databases, whereas there is as yet little in the way of equivalent facial recognition biometric databases.[45] If the US were to require additional fingerprint biometrics in Visa Waiver country passports, Jonathan Faull, Director General for Justice and Home

Affairs at the European Commission, warned that EU member states would reciprocate and require fingerprints of US nationals.[46]

All EU nationals will have to submit fingerscans when enrolling in US-VISIT upon entering the US, but EU member states have yet to require fingerscans of US nationals upon entry. Nevertheless, Secretary Ridge has noted that:

> "Many VWP (Visa Waiver Program) countries themselves are actively engaged in developing programs like US-VISIT that allow them to collect biometrics through the visa issuance process and match those biometrics upon entry into the country. We are actively working with many of these countries to share information about terrorism, other security threats, and opportunities for improvements in immigration and border management."[47]

Another possible scenario is that a Visa Waiver country that does meet the requirement to issue biometric passports by 26 October 2004 may follow the principle of reciprocity and require the same of US nationals. Secretary Powell admitted that the State Department was not prepared to meet such a requirement, noting that the first US biometric passports would be issued in December 2004.[48] Therefore, the US could not meet the requirements of its own Visa Waiver program because it would still be issuing passports without biometrics after the 26 October 2004 deadline.

If Congress had rejected the biometric deadline extension, most (if not all) EU states would have been dropped from the Visa Waiver Program. Nationals of these states would then have had to apply in person at US embassies and consulates, and have a digital photograph and fingerscan taken that would then be compared with biometrics collected upon arrival at the port of entry. This would have been very costly and problematic for both the US and the EU. If the US had dropped several EU member states that send large numbers of travelers to the US, Maura Hartley, Assistant Secretary of State for Consular Affairs, acknowledged that the State Department could not process these additional visa applications. Not only would the State Department have to hire and train a large contingent of new consular officers; in many European countries acquiring the necessary space and physical infrastructure to interview and process visa applicants would also take over a year – until just about the time when many of these countries would have their new passports enabling them to once again meet the Visa Waiver Program requirements.[49]

Although State Department officials have expressed confidence that European countries can meet an October 2006 deadline, it is not clear that the one-year deadline extension will be enough. The UK has indicated that it expects to begin issuing passports with standardized biometrics in late 2005, and other countries may not begin issuing biometric passports until "well into 2006."[50] The US transition to biometric passports is not expected to be complete until the end of 2005[51] – again, not being able to meet even the extended deadline that Congress has imposed on other countries.

Conclusion

When some EU member states and the US came to loggerheads in the Security Council over military intervention in Iraq, commentators declared that US–EU relations had hit a new low and the prospects for future international cooperation were very bleak. The US–European diplomatic impasse may have rendered multilateralism moribund in the halls of the United Nations, but intensified contacts between US and EU border security officials produced cooperative informal arrangements and more formal agreements.

From a theoretical standpoint, this cooperation on container security, PNR data transfer, and biometric passports is very significant because it requires acceptance of mutual constraints on a broad range of state action in the area of border control – one of the defining aspects of territorial sovereignty. On a practical level, it is very difficult to measure the impact of this cooperation on homeland security.

The CBP has announced that US inspectors working with their European counterparts have intercepted shipments of small arms and military equipment; however, there have been no announcements of seizures of a WMD or WMD materials. During December 2003, the combination of intelligence information and screening of passenger manifests and PNR data led the DHS to conclude that there was a risk that several US-bound flights from London and Paris had been targeted for terrorist attacks, and they were subsequently cancelled. While biometric passports have yet to be implemented, the implementation of national programs to increase travel document security in anticipation of higher international security standards is making it more difficult for smugglers and terrorists to cross borders with fraudulent documents.

While individual cases can be cited, it is impossible to quantify the overall impact. Moreover, border control authorities may not necessarily make every case public in order to protect intelligence sources and methods, and it is impossible to know how many terrorists have been deterred by increased security measures and the transatlantic cooperation that has enabled them. In contrast, businesses have attributed decreased travel and trade to tougher security measures. It has been estimated that travel to the US since 11 September 2001 is down by 30 percent. The Travel Industry Association of America fears that extending US-VISIT to Visa Waiver countries will divert European travelers to other destinations.[52] According to an industry group sponsored report, US companies lost an estimated $30.7 billion due to delays/denials of business visas between July 2002 and March 2004.[53] Policymakers may wish to base their decision on precise cost–benefit analysis, but the incalculable and often intangible benefits of increased security measures are not easily compared to their negative economic impacts. This analytical imbalance plays itself out politically as legislators confront homeland security officials with the economic costs imposed on the legislators' constituents. As the 9/11 Commission hearings demonstrate, however, administrators and legislators will be held accountable for their inaction on homeland security in the aftermath of more attacks.

Transatlantic cooperation on border and transportation security has come a long way in the past few years; however, further cooperation may be interrupted by differing legal regimes governing privacy and personal data protection. From the standpoint of the European Parliament, the European Commission appears to be willing to compromise to an unacceptable degree on data protection standards for the sake of security and increasing transatlantic cooperation. Increasing cooperation on travel document security and entry–exit tracking systems is also inhibited by social norms against fingerprinting. The German and British politics surrounding biometric data collection demonstrate some of the political barriers that European interior ministers may face should fingerprint biometrics be required on passports for maintaining US Visa Waiver status. But at least the German and UK governments have raised the issue of fingerprinting their citizens for the sake of increased security. So far, the Bush Administration and Congress have largely avoided the issue of collecting fingerprint biometrics from US citizens who wish to travel abroad, and have only imposed the requirement on nationals of other states.

US–EU cooperation on transportation and border security provides ample evidence for a rethinking of homeland security to span the transatlantic space. Nevertheless, the bilateral and subsequent US–EU agreements that have thus far structured transatlantic cooperation may be transitory. They may be a just a first step towards global cooperation based in the World Customs Organization and the International Civil Aviation Organization as standards for technology are much more effective if they are agreed to on a global basis and, therefore, globally applicable. Moreover, European popular perceptions and political fallout from US-initiated bilateral agreements could be dissipated by broader multilateral agreements toward the same objectives. While multilateral agreements and global standardization may take much longer to achieve, they may be much more politically sustainable in the long run.

Notes

1 Research for this article was supported by a fellowship from the Woodrow Wilson International Center for Scholars and National Science Foundation Grant IIS-0306838.
2 J. Stevenson, "How Europe and America defend themselves," *Foreign Affairs*, 82(2), 2003.
3 Hart–Rudman Commission. US Commission on National Security/21st Century, co-chaired by Gary Hart and Warren Rudman, *Road Map for National*

Security: Imperative for Change: The Phase III Report of the US Commission on National Security/21st Century, 15 February 2001.

4 INS 2002. *INS Restructuring Plan – Next Steps*, INS Fact Sheet, 17 April 2002

5 The Department of Homeland Security Budget has increased from $31.2 billion in FY 2003, to $35.7 billion in FY 2004, and $37.6 billion in FY 2005 (DHS, 2004: 3, 12). These figures do not include funding for Project Bioshield, the government program to pre-purchase vaccines and medicines, which is authorized by separate legislation, nor does it include the funds from the 2004 Iraq supplemental appropriation.

6 The White House, *National Strategy for Homeland Security*, Washington DC: Office for Homeland Security, 2002, p. 22, available online at: www.whitehouse.gov/homeland/book/ (accesssed 20 September 2004).

7 Response to author's question at "Transatlantic Homeland Security? European Approaches to 'Total Defense,' 'Societal Security' and their Implications for the US" Center for Transatlantic Relations, Paul H. Nitze School of Advanced International Studies Johns Hopkins University, 19 February 2004.

8 Germany's *Bundesgrenzschutz* (Federal Border Police) has 40,000 employees (see Federal Border Police website. Available online at: www.bundesgrenzschutz. de/Aufgaben/index.php, the UK Home Office's Immigration and Nationality Directorate (IND) has over 11,000 employees (Home Office, 2003), and Poland has 16,000 border guards and will hire 5,300 more by 2006 (Kole, 2004). The Bureau of US Customs and Border Protection has approximately 41,000 employees (DHS, 2004: 19), only slightly larger than Germany's *Bundesgrenzschutz*.

9 European Council, "Conclusions and Plan of Action of the Extraordinary European Council Meeting on 21 September 2001."

10 European Commission. "Establishing a European Agency for the Management of the Operational Co-Operation at External Borders," RAPID Press Release IP: 03/1519, 11 November 2003.

11 European Report "Justice and Home Affairs: council moves to add Al-Qaeda members to Schengen Information System," *European Report*, 26 June 2002.

12 "Danish presidency proposes intra-police e-mail system," *European Report*, 24 July 2002.

13 "Commission wants new Schengen data base to store biometrics," *European Report*, 13 December 2003.

14 European Commission, "Communication from the commission to the Council and the European Parliament on a common policy on illegal immigration," Commission of the European Communities, Brussels, 15 November 2001, COM (2001) 672 final.

15 "EU visa database takes shape," *European Report*, 5 June 2002.

16 European Commission, "Commission's proposal on biometric identifiers for visa and residence permit for third country nationals," RAPID Press Release, IP/03/1289, 24 September 2003.

17 "MEPs allow visa data base plan to proceed despite misgivings," *European Report*, 24 April 2004.

18 Office of US Senator Bob Graham, "A landmark bill that will bolster security at America's deepwater ports passed the Senate by voice vote today," press release issued 20 December 2001. Available online at: www.graham.senate.gov/ pr122001.html (accessed 20 March 2002); R. C. Bonner, "US Customs Commissioner Robert C. Bonner Speech before the Center for Strategic and International Studies (CSIS)," Washington, DC, 17 January 2002.

19 D. M. Browning, Statement at hearing on "Combating Terrorism: Improving the Federal Response," House Committee on Government Reform, Subcommittee on National Security, Veterans Affairs and International Relations, 11 June 2002.

20 R. M. Larrabee, Statement at hearings on "Container Security" before the House Transportation and Infrastructure Subcommittee, Subcommittee on Coast Guard and Maritime Transportation, United States House of Representatives, Washington, DC, 13 March 2002.

21 S. E. Flynn, "America the vulnerable," *Foreign Affairs*, 81 (1), 60–74.

22 *Lloyd's List International*, 24 June 2002.

23 *Lloyd's List International* 14 August 2002.

24 "Security – Brussels puts a Brake on US Drive for Ports Clamp," *Lloyd's List*, 12 September 2002.

25 "Commission wants new Schengen data base to store biometrics, *European Report*, 13 December 2003.

26 Delegation of European Commission to US, "EU Welcomes Signature with US of Agreement Expanding Custom Cooperation to Trade Security;" European Commission, "Proposal for a Council Decision on the signature and conclusion of the Agreement between the European Community and the United States of America on intensifying and broadening the Agreement of 28 May 1997 on customs co-operation and mutual assistance in customs matters to include co-operation on Container Security and related matters," European Commission COM (2004) 36 final 2004/0007, Brussels, 22 January 2004.

27 F. Bolkestein, "EU Customs Policy – Boosting Security and Modernizing Procedures," Address at Freight Forwarders Day, Brussels, 1 December 2003, available online at: www.europa.eu.int/comm/taxation_customs/customs/information_notes/containers_en.htm (accessed 13 April 2004).

28 Section 115 of the "Aviation and Transportation Security Act," Public Law 107–71, 19 November, 2001.

29 European Commission. "Establishing a European Agency for the Management of the Operational Co-Operation at External Borders," RAPID Press Release IP: 03/1519, 11 November 2003; CBP, "Results of talks on 4 March 2003 between the European Commission and US Customs and Border Protection (CBP) with regard to Passenger Name Record (PNR) sensitive data," US Department of Homeland Security, Customs and Border Protection, 4 March 2003.

30 European Commission. Draft Decision on the Adequate Protection of Personal Data Contained in the PNR of Air Passengers Transferred to the United States' Bureau of Customs and Border Protection," European Commission (C5–0000/2004).

31 F. Bolkestein, "Frits Bolkestein Member of the European Commission in charge of the Internal Market, Taxation and Customs EU/US talks on transfers of airline passengers' personal data," address to European Parliament Committees on Citizens' Freedoms and Rights, Justice and Home Affairs and Legal Affairs and the Internal Market Strasbourg, 16th December 2003, Commission of the European Communities, RAPID, SPEECH: 03/613, 16 December 2003

32 Bolkestein, ibid; US Department of Homeland Security, *Fact Sheet: Homeland Security and European Commission Reach PNR Agreement*, US Department of Homeland Security, Office of the Press Secretary, 16 December 2003, available online at: www.dhs.gov/dhspublic/display?content=3036 (accessed 20 January 2004).

33 European Parliament, "Motion for a Resolution on the Draft Commission Decision noting the Adequate Protection of Personal Data Contained in the PNR of Air Passengers Transferred to the United States' Bureau of Customs and Border Protection (C5-0000/2004)," Committee on Citizens' Freedoms and Rights, Justice and Home Affairs, 17 February 2004.

34 E-Government News, "European Parliament refers transfer of air passenger data

to the Court of Justice," 22 April 2004. Available online at: www.europa.eu. int/ISPO/ida/jsps/index.jsp?fuseAction=showDocument&documentID=2440& parent=chapter&preChapterID=0–140–194v (accessed 26 April 2004).

35 CBP, "Undertaking of the Department of Homeland Security Bureau of Customs and Border Protection (CBP)", 16, para. 45, annex I to European Commission 2004.

36 European Council, "Declaration on Combating Terrorism," Brussels, 25 March 2004.

37 R. Carr, "Concern Grows over INS Visa Waiver Program," Cox News Service, 28 February 2002.

38 Section 303 of the Enhanced Border Security and Visa Entry Reform Act of 2002, Public Law 107–173, 14 May 2002.

39 Colin Powell and Tom Ridge, Letter to Jim Sensenbrenner Jr, Chairman, Committee on the Judiciary, House of Representatives, 17 March 2004, available online at: www.house.gov/judiciary/ridge031704.pdf (accessed 29 March 2004).

40 See "An Act: To modify certain deadlines pertaining to machine-readable, tamper-resistant entry and exit documents." H.R. 4417.

41 D. Stout, "US Extends Fingerprinting Rule to Millions More Visitors," *The New York Times*, 2 April 2004.

42 ICAO, "Biometric Identification to Provide Enhanced Security and Speedier Border Clearance for the Traveling Public," International Civil Aviation Organization, PIO/2003, 28 May 2003.

43 J. Williams, Response to author's question at presentation at the event "Entering America: Challenges Facing the US-VISIT Program," *Heritage Foundation*, 1 March 2004.

44 T. Ridge, "Testimony of Tom Ridge, Secretary of the Department of Homeland Security, before the House Committee on the Judiciary, 21 April 2004."

45 Response to author's question posed after Mr Verdery's presentation at "Fortress America? The Implications of Homeland Security on Transatlantic Relations," American Enterprise Institute, 4 March 2004, available online at: www.aei.org/events/eventID.758,filter.all/event_detail.asp.

46 Response to author's question posed after Mr Faull's presentation at "Fortress America? The Implications of Homeland Security on Transatlantic Relations," American Enterprise Institute, 4 March 2004, available online at: www.aei. org/events/eventID.758,filter.all/event_detail.asp

47 Ridge, op. cit.

48 C. L. Powell, "Passports and Visas with Embedded Biometrics and the October Deadline," Prepared Testimony of Secretary of State Colin L. Powell, House Judiciary Committee, 21 April 2004.

49 M. Hartly, "Answer to question during testimony of Maura Hartly, Assistant Secretary for Consular Affairs, Department of State at the Seventh public hearing of the National Commission on Terrorist Attacks Upon the United States, 26 January 2004."

50 Catherine Barry, Director Office of Visa Services, Statement at Hearing on Visa Waiver Program and Terrorist Screening, House International Relations Subcommittee on International Terrorism Nonproliferation and Human Rights, 16 June 2004.

51 Ibid.

52 Travel Industry Association of America, "TIA Raises Concerns over Expansion of US-VISIT," Press Release Travel Industry Association of America, 2 April 2004.

53 Santangelo Group, "Do Visa Delays Hurt US Business? – Survey and Analysis," Prepared by the Santangelo Group, 2 June 2004.

6 Cops across borders

The evolution of transatlantic law enforcement and judicial cooperation

Jonathan M. Winer[1]

Spurred by the need to develop new instruments to combat international terrorism, on 25 June 2003 the US and the European Union signed a treaty on legal cooperation. Being the first of its kind entered into between the EU and a third party, it was heralded as ground-breaking.

The visible changes in global security arising out of the September 11 terrorist attacks, however, have tended to obscure larger changes in relationships in the law enforcement sector – changes already well under way when global terrorism took center stage as the great threat to an interconnected world. Traditional forms of cross-border crime had already catalyzed reconfiguration of domestic law enforcement operations in the developed world before dirty bombs, bio-terror, cyber-terrorism, and other threats to the homeland became a mainstream concern.

In the course of enlargement and the development of the weakest of its three post-Maastricht "pillars," that of justice and home affairs, which included law enforcement and asylum policy, the European Union recognized during the 1990s that it needed new intra-EU institutions, as well as intensified cooperation across the Atlantic, to respond to illicit narcotics and narcotics trafficking, trafficking in persons, arms smuggling, major frauds, cross-border rings of motor vehicle theft, looting, hazardous waste dumping, and massive tax cheating. Similarly afflicted, the US began intensive efforts to globalize its own domestic law enforcement agencies, opening US-led international law enforcement training academies in Asia, Africa, and central Europe, while negotiating mutual legal assistance and extradition treaties at an increasingly vigorous pace.

Initially, some viewed these activities as threatening to existing interests on either side of the Atlantic. For instance, when the EU first established Europol in The Hague as the successor intelligence agency to its predecessor, the European Anti-Drugs Unit, its German director had to apologize to representatives of the US for his inability to share information with American law enforcement, given the limits the European Commission had initially imposed on such sharing with "outsiders." Similarly, when the US created its first International Law Enforcement Academy (ILEA) in Budapest in 1996, the EU refused to participate in the institution due to the veto of

France, whose foreign ministry took the position that a US-led police training academy located in Europe was inherently inappropriate. Similar attitudes slowed US–EU cooperation on maritime security in the Caribbean to engage in "hot pursuit" of drug traffickers across US, British, French, and Dutch controlled waters, and EU participation in US efforts against cocaine in the Andes. However, prior to the September 11 attacks each of these disputes had been resolved, as technocrats needing to solve concrete problems found ways around obstacles and concerns such as perceived national interests, sovereignty, power, and prestige that had imposed political barriers to cooperation.

This chapter lays out the history of the political and technical development of the new transatlantic institutions prior to September 11, describes how they are being applied in the current security environment, and projects their likely further near-term evolution in light of that environment. It argues that despite powerful barriers to cooperation and some widening of political and policy differences since the September 11 attacks, the need to solve practical problems will eventually lead to continued progress in pursuing and prosecuting terrorists across borders.

The world before September 11: technocrats pushing for cooperation

To look at the pre-September 11 world of transatlantic law enforcement cooperation at the technocratic level is to see an infrastructure of considerable depth that had remained largely beneath the surface of political visibility. It included, for example, among its major elements:

- *Evidence sharing.* Routine evidence-sharing occurred between EU countries and the US, between central authorities based at the respective justice ministries, and between and among police and customs agencies, through an array of bilateral agreements supplemented by multilateral ones, and incorporating harmonized standards for procedures and standards in obtaining the right to such evidence.
- *Rendition of fugitives.* There were extradition arrangements among all of the countries, with relatively minimal differences in grounds for rejecting an extradition request.
- *Cooperation in law enforcement intelligence gathering.* The was US participation in EUROPOL and other emerging EU-wide law enforcement and judicial institutions, and liaison between Europol based in Washington and the FBI, Customs, and other US law enforcement agencies.
- *Joint training.* There was EU participation in US law enforcement training academies in Europe, Latin America, Asia, and Africa.
- *Harmonized standards.* Major new multilateral instruments, such as the UN Convention Against Transnational Organized Crime of 2000 (the "Palermo Convention") and the Council of Europe's Cybercrime

Convention of 2000 reflected agreement by the US, Canada and the EU, working closely with Japan, integrated ambitious obligations that required changes in laws or practice in all of their jurisdictions. Here again, technocrats negotiated standards designed to meet the new demands of cross-border enforcement activities, with minimal interference by domestic political constraints.

- *Port security.* Working together, Customs officials from both sides of the Atlantic developed new universal standards for use in containers at all ports in a system agreed upon in 2000 at the World Customs Organization.
- *Financial regulation.* The US, EU, and Canada took identical positions in twin "name and shame" initiatives in the Organization for Economic Cooperation and Development (OECD) in 2000. One at the OECD itself forced countries to abandon what were termed "harmful tax practices" involving the use of bank secrecy to protect tax cheats. The other, in the Financial Action Task Force based at the OECD, identified "non-cooperative countries and territories" for sanctions for failure to adopt sufficient regulations to guard against money laundering and all other forms of financial crime. Both initiatives were remarkable for their recognition of the underlying reality that cross-border movements of funds *required* harmonized financial regulation and enforcement. The results of the initiative were to force the universal and global adoption of standards that in the first instance were limited to the most developed countries only.

This growing array of cooperative initiatives was designed to create a platform for law enforcement, customs, and judicial cooperation that would function irrespective of the particular predicated criminal activity to which such initiatives would be applied. Although some of them had arisen in response to a particular problem, such as international drug trafficking, tax evasion, or computer crime, in the main the initiatives were devised for general application regardless of the nature of the problem they would address. Thus when terrorism became the central overriding focus of transatlantic security discussions after 11 September 2001, these pre-existing initiatives provided a robust platform on which counter-terrorism activities could be based.

The very strengths of these recent initiatives, however – their technocratic design, their avoidance of the political, and their use to facilitate efficient sharing of information across political systems – made them politically vulnerable once they were applied to high-visibility political ends, such as fighting terrorists. Across the board, the initiatives had sought to squeeze discretionary judgment (and local judges) out of the question of whether cooperation would occur, and on what terms. When the time came to use these mechanisms against terrorists in highly publicized cases, it was inevitable that in some instances local authorities would begin to question the underlying premise of such cooperation: that the requests, judgments, goals, needs, and demands of foreign enforcement officials are inherently as legitimate as those of one's own.

On 4 March 2004, for example, Germany's Federal Criminal Court overturned the conviction of the one person convicted of helping the group of hijackers involved in the September 11 terrorist attacks.[2] In overturning the conviction, the German judges ruled that the existing mechanisms for the sharing of evidence *required* the US to make available to the defendant a witness – alleged September 11 paymaster Ramzi Binalshibh – held in US custody and not located in Germany. As presented in the media, the problem was that the US chose not to produce sufficient evidence. However, as a legal matter, the possibility that Binalshibh could provide exculpatory evidence that was being withheld from the defense was at the core of the court's decision. Rather than refusing to recognize the new international regime, whereby countries facilitate the provision of evidence and witnesses to one another, the German court in effect insisted that this regime be followed in order to ensure that the accused terrorist conspirator received a fair trial. Thus a regime designed to assist governments in prosecuting criminal cases regardless of the location of the crime, evidence or witnesses was now viewed as creating a right of accused criminals to such evidence and witnesses.

This surprising result, while unintended and counterproductive to the extent that it has assisted a terrorist escape justice, reflects in some sense the rapid integration of the new transatlantic justice system into domestic legal norms and practices.

A history of fragmentation

Internationalization and trans-border cooperation represent a major departure from the post-World War II law-enforcement realities on both sides of the Atlantic, which were more typically characterized by fragmentation.

Europe

In post-World War II Europe the dangers of authoritarian control of law enforcement institutions were obvious, and post-war Europe largely chose not to replace deconstructed fascist authorities on the Continent with significant national, let alone pan-European, law enforcement and judicial institutions. The exceptions, such as the European Court of Justice, focused on the preservation and strengthening of individual human rights and civil liberties against local abuses, rather than on helping local law enforcement deal with cross-border problems.

The relative weight of these two missions was evident in the work of the Council of Europe (COE), whose membership included all of the European countries, with observer status for other states with related interests, such as the US, Canada, and Switzerland. Over the course of five decades lawyers at the COE created numerous new regimes for legal affairs harmonization, including common standards for extradition and mutual legal assistance. However, the COE's enforcement mechanisms themselves focused solely on investigating and trying alleged cases involving human rights abuses. Individuals needed the protection of the COE and its new court. Nations having problems securing witnesses, evidence, and other forms of police and judicial assistance would have to work things out among themselves.

Meanwhile, within the nations of post-war Europe, police institutions were left deliberately weak. In Belgium, policing was divided between two types of law enforcement institutions, one Walloon in orientation and the other Flemish, with neither being considered especially capable, or able to exercise control over all parts of the country. In Germany, law enforcement was administered solely at the provincial level of the *Länder*, with no national police. The United Kingdom had a similar system of local constabularies, none of whom had national jurisdiction, with the result that the UK had to deal with serious cross-border crime either through customs investigations or as an intelligence national security problem to be handled, as applicable, by MI5 (if it involved domestic crime or the Irish Republican Army) or by MI6 (if it was fundamentally continental in nature). Italian law enforcement was notoriously idiosyncratic and untrustworthy, with local police and judicial institutions recurrently infected by Italian organized crime, corrupt labor unions, and corrupt political parties. In France, the relationship between the police, organized crime, and political parties was, if less incestuous than in Italy, still sufficiently self-referential to be not easily penetrated by those outside of France. And French willingness to assist other countries within Europe on major criminal matters, let alone those across the Atlantic, was notoriously dubious, the counter-narcotics operations of the French Connection notwithstanding. Throughout the EU, local law enforcement institutions functioned at least as well as or better than their counterparts anywhere else in the world. However, cross-border cooperation remained inadequate even among neighbors.[3]

One consequence by the mid-1960s was a Europe awash with serious cross-border crime, including heroin trafficking; trafficking in women, stolen art and cultural artifacts; gun-running; cigarette and liquor smuggling to avoid excise taxes, and recurrent corruption and financial scandals. In 1967, the then European Economic Community (EEC) took its first regional steps to respond, creating a multilateral framework for mutual assistance among the customs authorities of the six countries of the EEC with the Naples Convention. This first "toe in the water" was followed eight years later by the creation of the Trevi Group for intergovernmental cooperation on immigration, asylum, police, and judicial cooperation, which included working parties on terrorism and internal security.[4]

The Trevi Group did not accomplish a great deal substantively, but it provided the first forum for EU law enforcement and immigration officials to talk with one another on a multilateral basis. Previously, such discussions had largely been limited to the individuals performing a liaison function for their governments on such issues at Interpol, acting as an exchange to identify instances where other governments had evidence relevant to one another's cases. In 1984, the Trevi Group work was elevated sufficiently to justify twice-yearly meetings of Justice and Home Affairs Ministers to discuss greater cooperation in these areas. These consultations helped prepare the way for a political declaration in 1986 at the time of the enactment of the Single European Act, which created a single market with the free movement of goods, capital, services, and workers in Europe. The political declaration created no new European institutions to deal with law enforcement or judicial issues, but confirmed the intention of all European member states to "co-operate on the entry, movement, and residence of nationals of third countries and in combating terrorism, crime, trafficking in drugs and the illicit trade in works of arts and antiques." European-wide consultative groups came into existence on immigration (1986), narcotics (1989), and mutual legal assistance (1990). A common system for external border checks was established with the Convention Implementing the Schengen Agreement in 1990, which has gradually come to include 15 European countries.

As of 1990, the European Commission assessed that the existing forms of cooperation were uncoordinated, duplicative, and inadequately susceptible to monitoring and oversight. Accordingly, in the Treaty on European Union (Maastricht Treaty) in 1992, the EU added to the structure of the European Community a "Third Pillar" (to accompany the first pillar of economic and customs union and the second pillar of a common security policy) relating to justice and home affairs policies, with cooperation centered on nine areas of common interest. These included drugs and drug addiction, international fraud, judicial cooperation in civil and criminal matters, and police and customs cooperation.

The coming into force of the Maastricht Treaty in late 1993 created an extensive and overlapping set of five tiers of structure to undertake cooperation in these law enforcement and judicial areas, including cascades of working groups, steering committees, coordination committees, and councils. However, Maastricht had yet to create even a single European-wide structure to implement any decisions that these groups might take. As a consequence, EU member states had a growing burden of consultative mechanisms to discuss coordinated law enforcement activity, but no organization anywhere capable of actually carrying such activity out.

The United States

For more than 200 years, the US has struggled within its own federalist system to deal with criminal threats transcending state borders. As in the UK, US Customs officials had long had an investigative function to deal with smuggling and tax offenses; the Internal Revenue Service (IRS) also had a criminal investigative division. However, the bulk of crime had always been local and handled locally. The US had no federal law enforcement capacity prior to 1908, when President Theodore Roosevelt created the antecedents to today's Federal Bureau of Investigation (FBI) to investigate the small number of federal crimes. Over time, the FBI's focus and jurisdiction expanded from investigating trafficking in women pre-World War I, to espionage and sabotage during the war, to gunrunning and bootlegging alcohol during the 1920s and 1930s, before returning to the themes of espionage and sabotage during World War II. In the 1940s and 1950s the Bureau dealt with the perceived domestic threat from Communist agents, which evolved into investigations of the civil rights and anti-war movements in the 1960s. While many of these threats included a perceived foreign element, the FBI's investigations focused on their domestic elements. The need for cooperation from foreign authorities was minimal.

All of this changed radically during the 1970s and 1980s, as the FBI increasingly became called upon to deal with international organized crime and terrorism. In turn, these investigative foci pushed the FBI outward, so that it undertook the creation of liaison offices based overseas at US embassies. This pattern was mirrored in other US law enforcement agencies, including Customs for smuggling; the Immigration and Naturalization Service (INS) for immigration crimes and trafficking in persons; the Treasury Bureau of Alcohol, Tobacco, and Firearms (ATF) for gunrunning and smuggling; the Secret Service for international counterfeiting and financial crimes; and the new Drug Enforcement Administration (DEA).

Prior to the 1970s, the DEA had not even existed. By the early 1980s it had permanent overseas offices and agents engaged in investigations in Europe, Asia, and Africa, as well as in Latin America, reflecting the reality that the US narcotics problem was a subset of a global problem and could not be addressed solely within a domestic context.

As of 1994, the US had a total of approximately 2000 federal law enforcement agents based at US embassies around the world, accountable to no central US authority. They functioned as local representatives of their individual US agencies under a disorganized miscellany of arrangements which varied from formal government-to-government bilateral agreements to *ad hoc* agency-to-agency exchanges operating outside the context of any legal instrument or written agreement.

These decentralized activities were generally undertaken with no central coordination or intra-agency discussion. Accordingly, conflict between and among the law enforcement agencies when they operated internationally was common, as was further tension and conflict between the law enforcement activities and concurrent, but uncoordinated, intelligence and diplomatic activities relating to similar topics, persons, and incidents.

At the same time, the lack of any coherent framework for these activities also resulted in confusion and inefficiency for foreign governments needing assistance from the US. In the absence of formal judicial assistance agreements, most US courts would only recognize foreign legal assistance requests that had been delivered from a foreign judge to that country's foreign ministry for transfer to the US Department of State, which in turn would work with the US Department of Justice to obtain a letter rugatory from a US court to authorize the provision of evidence to the foreign court.

Prior to 1977, the US had negotiated several thousand treaties with foreign countries on a myriad of topics affecting legal relationships, including extradition treaties with most other countries, without ever undertaking negotiation for mutual judicial assistance. The first such treaty, a 1977 MLAT with Switzerland, was followed by dozens of similar instruments negotiated with essentially every European state, as well as most other governments with functional law enforcement capacities and democratic governments. At the same time, the US began to sign up to mutual judicial obligations in a number of multilateral settings, including various conventions issued by the Organization of American States (OAS), and the UN. However, it used such multilateral instruments only *in extremis*, when a bilateral agreement did not exist, strongly preferring to force mutual legal assistance requests to and from the US central authority of the Department of Justice through these bilateral agreements. Meanwhile, even with the existence of the bilateral MLATs, police-to-police and customs-to-customs cooperation often continued to take place for the exchange of lead and investigative information not destined for court use on the basis of agency-to-agency arrangements outside the central authority structure. Often the US Departments of Justice and State were not even aware of such agreements, learning about them only as crisis or circumstance caused them to surface.

As of the early 1990s, US interagency cooperation and communication in the field of international law enforcement remained fragmented. Similarly, US relationships with other countries in these fields were governed by a host of decentralized arrangements, only some of which were memorialized in government-to-government agreements.

In sum, just as the member states of the new EU were concluding that existing arrangements were inadequate, the US undertook work to centralize and integrate its domestic law enforcement capacities so that they could be brought to bear in a more coherent fashion internationally.

Existing models and new institutions for international cooperation

As the dark side of globalization has become increasingly evident, the limits and strengths of the pre-existing international law organizations, primarily Interpol, founded in Vienna in 1923, and the World Customs Organization (WCO), also became increasingly evident, and new models were considered on both sides of the Atlantic. Both of these institutions had evolved to carry out four principal mechanisms:

1   Acting as a central telephone exchange mechanism for queries and responses on particular law enforcement matters through a system of central liaisons.

2   Functioning as a general library for problems in common. In the case of Interpol, this has included maintaining a library of the world's largest collection of counterfeit documents, and technical expertise to help match suspected counterfeits to those in the library.

3   Facilitating the adoption of universal standards and norms to which member states can conform their laws, both to adopt best practices and to ease operating with others.

4   Providing a forum for those involved in enforcement in different countries to meet, share professional concerns, and promote common objectives through adopting resolutions they could then usefully market back home for enhancing their status, resources, or capacities.

Each of these organizations eschewed the risk of undertaking operational activities. They moved information and standards across borders. They did not undertake investigations. This was not the result of any unwillingness of the management of the organizations to investigate, but was inherent in their charters. They had never been granted the legal right by the member states to carry out investigations. These remained, with a few exceptions (generally involving bilateral task forces), a matter for the country in which a particular piece of evidence was located.

Although Interpol and the WCO have each undertaken some ambitious new initiatives in recent years, they have not tried to challenge the prohibition on participating in operational activities. They have, however, offered lessons. For example, in its array of bilateral liaison relationships, the US both exploited and circumvented the Interpol model. Whereas Interpol operated as a single location where police from different countries could meet to address one another's queries, US local liaison offices operated in a similar fashion on a bilateral basis. Where Interpol provided databases for counterfeit documents, currencies, and firearms, the US maintained its own similar databases. Similarly, where the WCO provided basic forms and formats for cross-border movements of goods, the European Union was able to adopt these approaches EU-wide as of the time of the Maastricht treaty, largely obviating any need to rework any of the formulations adopted by the WCO.

Other models were available from the area of international financial regulation and enforcement. The speed of movement of electronic money prompted the rapid acceleration of regulatory measures to harmonize financial transparency standards on a global basis over a relatively brief period.[5] The first of many complementary initiatives began with the inclusion of anti-drug money laundering and law enforcement commitments in the 1988 United Nations Convention to Combat Illicit and Psychotropic Drugs (Vienna Convention), and the creation of the Financial Action Task Force by the G7 in 1989.[6] They have since included the project undertaken by the Organization for Economic Cooperation and Development (OECD) against harmful tax competition in 1998,[7] the G7's creation of the Financial Stability Forum on 22 February 1999,[8] the 2000 UN Convention Against Transnational Organized Crime (Palermo Convention),[9] the Council of Europe's GRECO program to assess and implement corruption prevention and prosecution mechanisms,[10] and the creation of various regional bodies to engage in a process of mutual assessment as a means to greater financial transparency.[11] Further, there have been related but separate initiatives to promote financial transparency undertaken by important sectoral self-regulatory organizations, such as the Basel Group of Bank Supervisors, in connection with its revisions of standards for assessing risk to bank capital,[12] the International Organization of Securities Commissions,[13] and the Offshore Group of Bank Supervisors,[14] among others. Finally, a coalition of private sector financial institutions, denominated the Wolfsberg Group, established their own set of transparency standards, initially aimed in 2000 at preventing their banks and brokerage firms from being used to hide the proceeds of corruption, and extended in late 2001 to prevent terrorist finance.[15]

These initiatives have shared many common elements. They include the need to know one's customers to ensure that they are not engaged in illicit activity; the need for financial institutions to share information pertaining to illicit activity with regulators, law enforcement, and when needed, with one another; the need to trace such funds; and the need for each country to assist all others in enforcing violations of their domestic laws. Principles initially used to combat drug trafficking and later extended to include all serious crimes and recently, terrorist finance and corruption, were extended to include fiscal offenses through a mutual recognition that a beggar-thy-neighbor approach to tax violations threatened to beggar all.

Similarly, even before the EU began creating EU-wide law enforcement institutions, newly developing regions undertook the creation of sub-regional organizations designed to create cross-border investigative and enforcement capacity to deal with threats that transcended a single country. For example, in the mid-1990s the Southeast European Cooperative Initiative (SECI) agreed to create a SECI Center in Bucharest to develop integrated law enforcement capacities in the Balkans.

Created by a legal instrument signed by participating SECI member states, the SECI Center serves as a regional mini-Interpol by which the nine participating countries can exchange law enforcement and customs operation through a single location. In its first year of operation, SECI handled more than 3000 requests for information relating to trans-border crimes. Since then, it has coordinated specialized task forces aimed at combating drug trafficking, trafficking in persons, customs valuation fraud, financial and cyber-crime, small arms violations, and trafficking in radioactive and other dangerous materials, thus providing strategic, tactical and operational capacities.

Europe: between new institutions and old political obstacles

By the mid-1990s the new EU was faced with a significant problem. It had declared with the entry into force of the Maastricht Treaty that there would be cooperation in the areas of justice and home affairs under the EU's Third Pillar. Yet there was no institution to make Third Pillar activities functional. Moreover, in many EU countries, most importantly including Germany, national institutions had yet to develop sufficient capability to carry out a justice and home affairs function adequate in a world where cross-border crime posed a serious threat. Moreover, an increasing number of EU member states had entered the Schengen area, with a single external border, common rules on visas, asylum and external border checks, and free movement of persons. Yet Schengen remained an institution outside formal EU structures, thus creating an artificial bureaucratic division that prevented the EU's administrative body, the European Commission, from directly addressing problems affecting its member states in the Third Pillar area.

At the same time, individual EU member states remained unable to deal with serious cross-border crime. The UK, for example, had created a new National Criminal Intelligence Service in the early 1990s, to provide assistance to local police on a national basis for cases involving serious crime, and had then separately created a National Crime Squad just a few years later to provide a national investigative capacity to complement the intelligence effort. Neither of these initiatives, however, addressed the problem of the UK's difficulties in obtaining the information it needed about transnational organized crime and terrorism from France, Germany or Italy.

To begin to address this problem, the EU created a European Drugs Unit in 1994 to study common narcotics issues and to serve as an incubator of a later Europol, should the EU member states decide to create one. It took the EU five years to grant Europol the requisite authority for it to function as a mechanism for cross-border coordination between EU national law enforcement agencies, including police, immigration, and customs authorities. This took place after the EU had entered into a further drafting exercise that resulted in the signing of the Amsterdam Treaty in October 1997, which came into force in May 1999.

A key goal of the Amsterdam Treaty was to make the EU "an area of freedom, security and justice." It sought to achieve this objective by giving the European Commission the right of initiative – that is, the right to develop proposals for the development of further EU legislation and institutions. It integrated the Schengen agreements into the framework of the EU, and it provided for a series of follow-on steps that included the development of mutual recognition of court decisions in criminal matters, and the development of an overall strategy on migration, asylum, and refugees. In turn, the

Amsterdam Treaty engendered the Tampere Extraordinary European Council of October 1999, devoted exclusively to the building of institutions capable of carrying out these new missions. At Tampere, EU member states agreed to formalize the creation of a European-wide investigative organization, Europol, and a complementary institution, Eurojust, to improve coordination between legal and judicial authorities in the member states in investigating and prosecuting cross-border cases.[16] The EU also moved forward with common training of law enforcement personnel at a European Police College and the creation of a common peacekeeping force, termed the European Rapid Reaction Force. With Tampere, the EU moved to create institutions whose sole goal was to deal with cross-border criminal threats.

Following Tampere, these institutions developed rapidly. For example, Europol began to function as the central police office for the support of member states for the collection, analysis, and dissemination of information regarding illicit drug trafficking, illicit immigration networks, terrorism, illicit vehicle trafficking, trafficking in human beings, including child pornography, forgery and counterfeiting, and money laundering. As of 2003 Europol employed about 450 people, whose functions included the facilitation of the exchange of information between European Liaison Officers); providing operational analysis in support of member state investigations; generating strategy reports, such as threat assessments on major problems; and providing expertise and technical support for investigations being carried out by the individual EU member states. Significantly, Europol also created a vast computer database (TECS) allowing law enforcement agencies throughout the EU to share information on known and suspected criminals and on stolen objects.

The new Europol database complemented a number of other significant new repositories of EU-wide law-enforcement related information. The first of these databases was the Schengen Information System (SIS), which had been in operation since 1995, but only under EU control since its integration into the EU with the Amsterdam Treaty on 1 May 1999. Two more databases, collectively known as the EU Customs Information System, were created to provide EU customs agencies with the ability to exchange and disseminate information on smuggling activities. Yet another database, known as the FIDE (*Fichier d'identification des dossiers d'enquêtes douanières*), enables customs officials to determine whether a person or a business has been the subject of a criminal investigation in any member state. With the creation of these databases the EU entered a new area, where operational law enforcement information was centralized to create a capacity well beyond the capability of any individual EU member state. With the existence of an array of human rights protections built into the EU's constitution, as well as the constitutions of EU member states, these databases also suggest that past anxieties about providing law enforcement with too wide an ability to gather information are no longer preventing the development of centralized EU law enforcement and judicial institutions.

The legal regime governing the cooperation of EU member states with one another kept pace with the rapid growth of these new EU functional institutions. In 1997, the EU completed the negotiation of a convention on Mutual Assistance and Cooperation between Customs Administrations of Member States, which requires them to cooperate with one another in cases of pursuit, cross-border surveillance, controlled deliveries, and covert investigations. In essence, the convention allows EU member states to pre-clear such activities, which otherwise would violate their sovereignty. The EU also adopted provisions criminalizing corruption in the private sector,[17] developing a EU-arrest warrant, and a decision on the execution throughout the EU of orders in any member state freezing property or evidence.[18] The arrest warrant replaced pre-existing bilateral extradition treaties between and among EU member states, providing for faster extradition (rendition within 90 days of arrest) and simplified procedures.[19] Nevertheless, as of May 2004, two other proposed EU-wide provisions – one governing mutual legal assistance, the other governing mutual recognition of criminal judgments – remained stalled. In each case, too few member states had been able to secure ratification of the provisions by their domestic national legislatures. Touching on core areas of state sovereignty, the pace of EU activity on law enforcement integration had outrun the ability of domestic governments to secure acquiescence within their own national political systems.

At the same time, some of those involved in the new institutions have reported informally that substantial deficiencies remain in the practical operation of these institutions. A US liaison officer to Europol, for example, told participants in a May 2004 seminar on terrorism and crime in Washington that many of the EU governments still provided relatively little information to others in the EU through Europol, and that bilateral agreements remained the foundation of information exchange.[20] The pace of institutional development may have temporarily outrun the capacity of the governments involved to absorb and take advantage of the new structures.

US initiatives: before and after September 11

During the eight years of the Clinton Administration (1993–2000), the US developed a number of initiatives designed to address the growing perception at both political and practitioner levels that transnational law enforcement threats, including drugs trafficking, organized crime, and terrorism, needed to be addressed through enhancing the capacity of other nations, as well as the US. These initiatives included unilateral, bilateral, and multilateral law enforcement activity.[21]

The unilateral activities included conceptual elements, such as developing a national global anti-crime strategy in 1996 that for the first time created an integrated approach by all US agencies to deal with trans-border threats. They also included efforts to integrate information that had previously been segregated by different agencies, for instance through creating common databases on specific identified organized crime threats. These included new integrated databases targeting Russian organized crime, Nigerian organized crime, and cars stolen and found in other countries. The US also engaged in bureaucratic reforms to facilitate greater coordination, such as undertaking a memorandum of understanding (MOU) between the US Departments of State, Justice, and Treasury governing the handling of law enforcement information overseas and the conduct of law enforcement liaison officers based in other countries. This MOU resulted in the creation of law enforcement teams in many embassies, whose function was to coordinate and de-conflict the activities of the law enforcement participants.

These US-oriented activities were supplemented by those that looked outward. These included efforts to build counterpart relationships through training, and placing hundreds of additional liaisons overseas from the wide array of US law enforcement agencies (including the FBI, DEA, ATF, INS, Customs, Secret Service, and Coast Guard), while encouraging other countries to send their liaisons to Washington for reciprocal sharing. To build capacity and reliable partners in other countries, the US established international law enforcement academies in Europe, Southeast Asia, Latin America, and Africa for joint training involving US and foreign law enforcement officials. The US also negotiated dozens of additional mutual legal assistance treaties, mostly with countries in transition (such as in the former Soviet Union and Central Europe and in Latin America), to facilitate prompt sharing of evidence; as well as stronger extradition treaties with narrower grounds for exclusion, and elimination of provisions forbidding extradition of nationals.

The US also sought to create international cooperation in areas that had not previously been covered. For example, it developed and then negotiated new instruments governing the return of stolen cars from other countries and the exchange of information on stolen cars, and new arrangements for harmonizing a policy of prevention, protection (of victims), and prosecution (of smugglers) to respond to trafficking in women. Working groups between the US and selected partner countries on issues of particular concern, such as drugs, organized crime, and terrorism, included Canada, China, Italy, Russia, Ukraine, and the UK.

During the 1990s the US also took advantage of multilateral initiatives, undertaking an array of initiatives through the new Lyon Group of the G8, established in 1995, to develop new arrangements to combat migrant trafficking, trafficking in women, cyber-crime, corruption, stolen cars, Nigerian and Russian organized crime, firearms trafficking, credit card crime, and other forms of serious transnational organized crime. Negotiation of significant new anti-crime and terrorism instruments in the OAS, COE, OECD, and UN included such important instruments as the OAS Convention Against Illicit Firearms Trafficking of 1997, the OECD's Anti-Bribery Convention of 1998, the COE's Cyber-crime Convention of 2000, the UN's Convention Against Terrorist Financing of 2000, and the UN's Palermo

Convention. The last of these included three protocols that had been initiated by the US – on trafficking in women, migrant smuggling, and illicit firearms, each of which promoted practices already adopted in the US to commit other signatories to do the same on a global basis. Other major multilateral activities included the US actively promoting the NCCT process in the FATF to threaten countries with sanctions if they did not put greater protections into place against money laundering, and similarly aggressive participation in the OECD unfair tax competition initiative. The US even initiated new multilateral mechanisms and instruments. For example, the US convened the Global Forum Against Corruption in 1999, which in turn facilitated the negotiation of the UN Convention Against Corruption (2003), and undertook a new initiative for maritime cooperation in the Caribbean to facilitate hot pursuit by the US, the UK, and the Netherlands throughout Caribbean waters of drug traffickers.

Notably, this busy array of activities involved relatively little institution building. Other than the development of regional international law enforcement academies for training, the US did not in this period initiate any fundamental new structures affecting its relationship with other countries in the law enforcement or judicial realm during the Clinton years. Existing cooperative efforts were intensified. Internal US efforts were coordinated. New multilateral arrangements were initiated, and the US signed and ratified a number of major new conventions creating broad new responsibilities for the US to cooperate with other signatories. However, unlike the case of the EU, the US during the 1990s found itself consolidating and integrating existing institutions rather than building new ones.

This approach changed radically following the September 11 terrorist attacks. The attacks produced a rapid shift by the US from its traditional international law enforcement operations focused on countering narcotics and organized crime, to those focused on countering international terrorism – a phenomenon previously left largely to the CIA in its international aspects.

As the special Commission created to investigate and review the US government's response to the September 11 terrorist attacks revealed, US intelligence and law enforcement cooperation continued to have huge limitations. Information available in the field, especially at the FBI, was not shared with FBI headquarters in Washington, let alone with other agencies. Warnings from the CIA were not shared with federal law enforcers, let alone with local police. Persons proved to have been in violation of US immigration laws due to being "out of status," that is, overstaying their visas, had been left freely to move about the US without arrest. Moreover, a strategic focus on preventing and detecting terrorism was almost entirely missing.

With the September 11 attacks, the US undertook the largest reorganization of its law enforcement agencies in its history, consolidating Customs and INS into a single agency, and placing all border control functions into a single integrated Department of Homeland Security (DHS), which in turn had responsibility for such other disparate threats as cyber-terrorism, and for seaport, airport and airline security. The new DHS in turn accelerated existing border security initiatives, such as the Container Security Initiative, seeking to ensure its early universal acceptance.[22]

The US undertook aggressive new uses of the economic sanctions programs administered by the Office of Foreign Assets Control (OFAC) of the US Treasury, to freeze terrorist assets and to demand that other countries do so. The OFAC sanctions named hundreds of organizations, entities, and individuals as subject to sanctions, and threatened other countries with having the assets of their financial institutions and businesses subject to sanction in a secondary freezing if they did business with any of the named organizations, entities or individuals. This unilateral effort was swiftly endorsed by the UN in UN Resolution 1373, and thereby became a multilateral effort of supposed universal application, if inconsistent enforcement in practice.[23]

These actions were relatively non-controversial, applying mainly to the financial assets of Middle Eastern foreigners, or goods in transit. More controversial were the unilateral actions taken by the US to protect airline security. Here, the aggressive screening by the US and its demands for passenger information prior to departure for the US began to run foul of the laws of other countries, especially the data protection laws of those in the EU. As a result, the new US regime began to be treated in the EU as threatening rather than implementing harmonized global standards and norms. US efforts to exempt some enforcement operations from legal norms entirely, such as those directed at persons the US termed "enemy combatants," resulted in strong criticism from the EU human rights community, but muted opposition by EU governments themselves.[24] A number of EU governments expressed stronger criticism for the ongoing efforts by the Bush Administration to require other countries to exempt US persons from possible jurisdiction on the part of the International Criminal Court (ICC). Ultimately the EU entered into a mutual pact, requiring each member state to reject entering into any such agreements with the US.[25]

Conclusion: cooperation or conflict in transatlantic law enforcement?

The paths followed by the US and by the EU regarding law enforcement institutions and judicial cooperation in recent years can be viewed as either diverging or converging, and either the EU or the US model as more powerful in shaping the world's development of law enforcement and judicial assistance institutions.

Those who believe the EU represents the future might describe the situation as follows. Driven by the need to integrate and to enlarge, the EU has created new integrated institutions capable of simultaneously serving the 25 member states of the EU and, in a subsidiary fashion, other invited guests, including the US, so long as the invited guests choose to abide by EU standards. These new institutions are developing growing capacities and over time will be the foundation of cross-border law enforcement and judicial cooperation not only for the EU, but perhaps globally.

An analysis that wished to focus on US power might see a very different universe. In this vision, the US, through its continuing market power in a global economy, and a global infrastructure for financial services, information systems, and transport, continues unilaterally to develop standards and approaches that may or may not fit the needs of other nations, but which are being adopted regardless, because no nation – not even a set of nations such as the 25 now within the EU – is able to disregard standards for cross-border activity set by the US. The EU can develop institutions as it may wish, but the US itself is an institution, and where Goliath walks, others will follow.

On the difficult issue of sharing of airline passenger information, for example, concern about combating terrorism (and the US government's ability to make airline travel difficult for EU passengers) ultimately appeared to trump privacy and liberty concerns, as the European Commission agreed to US demands for the provision of passenger data prior to boarding. In mid-May 2004, the European Commission agreed to a transatlantic deal forcing European airlines to provide personal details of passengers to US authorities in the face of objections by both human rights groups and the European Parliament in Strasbourg.[26]

In practice, however, both US and EU approaches have shaped transatlantic developments since 11 September 2001, and will probably continue to prescribe the future transatlantic law enforcement partnership. It is true that the EU followed the US lead in 2001 in imposing economic sanctions on terrorist targets identified by the US in the days following the attacks. However, by December 2001 the US had signed its first strategic cooperation agreement with Europol, thus enabling the US to share in the EU's growing development of databases and capabilities under EU terms. This agreement was followed a year later by a further agreement governing the handling and transfer of personal data between US and Europol, thus requiring the US to meet the standards for data protection and privacy regarding that data already in place within the EU.

By 25 June 2003, the US and EU had signed legal assistance and extradition agreements that represented a victory for both parties. On the one hand, the EU had secured US agreement to treat the EU as a bilateral partner, capable of negotiating on behalf of all of its member states, despite previous US insistence on negotiating bilateral agreements one-by-one with individual countries. On the other hand, the US secured EU agreement for the formation of joint investigative teams, the use of video-technology for taking testimony, and the provision of information regarding the bank accounts of criminal and terrorist suspects that had previously been protected under EU law. The US also secured agreement by the EU to allow the use of the new agreements to supplement, rather than replace, the existing agreements. Thus each side would have the right to choose which agreement was more helpful to it in securing the assistance it wanted. The result was a win–win situation, and the most recent evidence that even now, reports of the divergence of transatlantic interests may be premature.

Over the past few years cooperation in practice has continued to intensify, even as mutual irritation has been running high on the political level due in significant part to the separate security and human rights issues raised by the US-led war in and reconstruction of Iraq.

However, other practical obstacles remain. Internally, both the US and the EU continue to struggle with creating coherent and effective policies and institutions. The US has yet to digest the implications of its law enforcement reorganization to create an integrated Department of Homeland Security, and its multifaceted approach to combating terrorism. The EU has to deal with a 25-nation common area for human freedom – and the requirements for law enforcement within an immense space inhabited by 456 million people.

In practice, both the EU and the US thus face internal ongoing shortcomings that continue substantially to impair their efforts at effectively coordinating law enforcement within their borders, and therefore also internationally. Internal information-sharing remains uneven. Information systems remain only partially compatible. Cooperation between national law enforcement agencies and local ones remain more *ad hoc* than systemic. The periphery and the center continue to regard one another with skepticism. And these problems have been replicated in substantial part by US liaisons working at the EU and EU liaisons operating in Washington. The principal limitations of transatlantic cooperation are not ideological but pragmatic, just as the principal areas in which cooperation has worked well have arisen from pragmatic bureaucratics.

In sum, as of mid-2004, cooperation, conflict, and efforts to defer having to make decisions about either approach were all ongoing options within the framework of US–EU relationships involving law enforcement. Political and pragmatic hurdles remained despite significant progress. Still, in practice, the US cannot protect itself unilaterally against criminal threats that include EU elements without EU member states choosing to cooperate with the US. In turn, the EU needs the US for particular forms of cooperation, including mutual legal assistance and extradition.

In the end, police officers need to police, customs agents need to stop smuggling, financial regulators need to enforce their regulations, and politicians need to deliver a reasonable degree of security for the citizens to whom they are ultimately responsible. Ideologies and policies may come and go, but these enduring factors are likely to tilt the field towards cooperation in the long run.

Notes

1 Partner, Alston & Bird LLP, US Deputy Assistant Secretary of State International Law Enforcement, 1994–1999.
2 German Federal Appeals Court, Hamburg, in re Mounir Motassadeq, 3 March 2004, ordering Motassadeq to receive a new trial in light of US refusal to provide Ramzi Binalshibh as a witness to the case.
3 Similar problems in the US in the 1920s led to the creation of the FBI, as local police officers had been unable to cooperate across US state borders. To this day, the FBI itself has found that securing the cooperation of individual FBI Bureaus located in different states is still a formidable challenge.
4 For a history of the Trevi Group, see Fact Sheet #2.1 and other documents issued by the Directorate-General of Justice and Home Affairs of the European Commission.
5 See generally "Transnational control of money-laundering," *Strategic Survey 2001/2002*.
6 The member jurisdictions of the FATF currently include Argentina, Australia, Austria, Belgium, Brazil, Canada, Denmark, Finland, France, Germany, Greece, Hong Kong (China), Iceland, Ireland, Italy, Japan, Luxembourg, Mexico, the Netherlands, New Zealand, Norway, Portugal, Singapore, Spain, Sweden, Switzerland, Turkey, the United Kingdom, and the United States, together with the European Commission and the Gulf Co-operation Council. In turn, the FATF has associated regional organizations whose members collectively include more than half the members of the UN.
7 *Harmful Tax Competition: An Emerging Global Issue*, 9 April 1998 report published by the OECD, available online at www.oecd.org/EN/about/0,,EN-about-103-nodirectorate-no-no-no-22,00.html.
8 The Financial Stability Forum (FSF) was convened in April 1999 to promote international financial stability through information exchange and international cooperation in financial supervision and surveillance. The Forum brings together on a regular basis national authorities responsible for financial stability in significant international financial centres, international financial institutions, sector-specific international groupings of regulators and supervisors, and committees of central bank experts. The FSF seeks to coordinate the efforts of these various bodies in order to promote international financial stability, improve the functioning of markets, and reduce systemic risk. It currently includes 25 member authorities. Available online at www.fsforum.org/home/home.html.
9 Resolution adopted by the General Assembly, [*without reference to a Main Committee (A/55/383)*] 55/25. United Nations Convention against Transnational Organized Crime. Available online at: www.undcp.org/pdf/crime/a_res_55/res5525e.pdf.
10 GRECO is responsible, in particular, for monitoring observance of the Guiding Principles for the Fight against Corruption, and implementation of the international legal instruments adopted in pursuit of the Programme of Action against Corruption (PAC). So far three such instruments have been adopted: the Criminal Law Convention on corruption (ETS no. 173), opened for signature on 27 January 1999; the Civil Law Convention on corruption (ETS no. 174), adopted in September 1999, opened for signature on 4 November 1999; and Recommendation R (2000) 10 on codes of conduct for public officials, adopted on 11 May 2000.
11 These include the Caribbean Financial Action Task Force (1990), the Asian-Pacific Group (1997), the Financial Action Task Force on Money Laundering in South America (2000), and the Eastern and Southern Africa Group (1999) to undertake assessments of anti-money laundering vulnerabilities and enforce-

ment capacities. They also include Organization of American States Conventions against Money Laundering (December 1995, amended October 1998), the European Union's first and second Money Laundering Directives (1991 and 2001, respectively), and, to some extent, the work undertaken by the Basel Committee of Bank Supervisors in its current initiative (2000–2003) to revise standards for the treatment of bank capital, which would include certain provisions pertaining to risks associated with non-transparency.

12 "The New Basel Capital Accord: An Explanatory Note," Secretariat of the Basel Committee on Banking Supervision, January 2001, available online at www.bis.org/publ/bcbsca01.pdf.

13 IOSCO's current membership includes the securities regulators and enforcement agencies of approximately 60 countries.

14 "Supervision of Cross-Border Banking," Working Group, members of the Basel Committee on Banking Supervision and the Offshore Group of Banking, Basel Committee on Banking Supervision, October 1996.

15 The Wolfsberg Group consists of the following leading international banks: ABN Amro N.V., Banco Santander Central Hispano, S.A., Bank of Tokyo-Mitsubishi, Ltd, Barclays Bank, Citigroup, Credit Suisse Group, Deutsche Bank AG, Goldman Sachs, HSBC, J.P. Morgan Chase, Société Générale, UBS AG. Available online at www.wolfsberg-principles.com.

16 Eurojust in turn builds on the European judicial network (EJN), created in 1998, a network of contact points in courts or prosecution offices whose function is to facilitate judicial cooperation, and who meet on a regular basis. The EJN is now based in The Hague at the headquarters of Eurojust, which administers the EJN mechanism.

17 OJ/C 192/54 31.7.2003, European Council

18 EU Framework Decision of 13 June 2002 on the European arrest warrant and surrender procedures; EU Framework Decision of 22 July 2003 on the execution in the European Union of orders freezing property or evidence.

19 EU Framework Decision of 13 June 2002, see COM (2001) 522 final/2.

20 Communication to author, former FBI liaison to the EU, George Washington University Conference, "Criminal-Terrorist Nexus," 20 May 2004.

21 This paper does not address the series of police actions the US undertook involving military as well as law enforcement forces over the past two decades, such as those in Panama (1989), Haiti (1994), or the Balkans (1996–present).

22 A detailed discussion of CSI is covered separately in Chapter 5, and hence does not appear here.

23 *Second Report of the Monitoring Group pursuant to resolution 1363 (2001) and as extended by resolutions 1390 (2002) on Sanctions against al-Qaida, the Taliban and their associates and associated entities*, United Nations, December 2003.

24 The new US approach was articulated clearly by US Vice President Richard Cheney.

25 The requested US bilateral agreements under Article 98(2) of the ICC Treaty would require a signatory member state to send any American national sought by the Court to the United States instead of surrendering him or her to the ICC. The EU concluded that ICC States Parties and signatory states have a legal obligation that prevents them from entering into Article 98 agreements with non-State Parties, particularly the United States, the only country to have officially repudiated the Rome Statute. See Council of the EU, 30 September 2002, 12488/1/02 Rev, regarding the ICC.

26 "EC Backs 'Privacy Violation' Deal with US," 18 May 2004, available online at www.expatica.com/source/site_article.asp?subchannel_id=19&story_id=7634.

7 Intelligence and homeland security

Brian M. Jenkins

Unlike traditional foes pursuing specific military objectives or conventional criminals seeking economic gain, terrorists can attack anything, anywhere, any time. They are unbounded by front lines, time constraints or borders, or by distinctions between military and civilian targets, or combatants and non-combatants. In contrast, we cannot protect everything, everywhere, all the time. This basic asymmetry makes homeland security a difficult and costly task. It demonstrates the limits of protection that any government can offer its citizens at home or abroad. It underscores the importance of intelligence.

Good intelligence is crucial, offensively to reduce the terrorist threat by apprehending terrorists, destroying their organizations, and disrupting their attacks, and defensively to allocate security resources effectively and efficiently.

Terrorists increasingly operate globally, but they also frequently draw upon local assistance to carry out their attacks. Therefore, intelligence efforts will have to become at the same time more local and more global. At the global level, dealing with the terrorist threat will require a degree of international collaboration that is yet to be achieved, although great progress has been made in the last few years. At the local level, counterterrorism may blur the lines between domestic security and ordinary law enforcement. It will certainly require greater coordination among traditionally insular intelligence services that tend to regard sharing information as an unnatural act.

To urge greater sharing of intelligence, internationally and locally, by itself is mere exhortation. New organizations, mechanisms, and procedures will be required. Long-time and like-minded allies, like Europe and the United States, along with new partners, will have reason to cooperate, but intelligence operations derived from Cold War models will not work well against elusive and adaptable terrorist foes.

This chapter explores the opportunities, requirements, and obstacles entailed in homeland intelligence and transatlantic cooperation, while addressing some of the basic issues that arise in collecting and analyzing intelligence and communicating the resulting information to the authorities and the public. These include:

Assessing the threat

Terrorists are inherently difficult targets for intelligence. They are led by small groups of conspirators who often have known each other for years, making penetration of the inner decision-making circle more difficult. They are organized into cells, further limiting compromise, or, more recently, into loose networks that defy attempts to discern hierarchy and organization. Traditional order-of-battle intelligence or crime family trees as frameworks for analysis do not work.

Terrorists operate clandestinely. They communicate by such low-tech methods as individual couriers, or by such high-tech means as cell phones and the Internet, in both cases making interception difficult albeit not impossible. Recruiting is often complex, multi-phased and, in the case of the global jihadists we confront today, a decentralized process. Terrorists are motivated by convictions and not easily suborned by offers of money.

Terrorists operate infrequently. They have no requirement to attack specific targets or within specific timeframes. They may lie in wait for months, years. With unlimited targets, they may reconnoiter many, select the easiest, back off if uncertain. When threatened, they go to ground. They are patient. We believe now, for example, that the outlines of the September 11 attack were probably first discussed in the early 1990s, that feasibility studies began in 1996, and actual preparations not later than 1999.[1]

Terrorists plan operations constantly, to explore new avenues for attack but also as an activity that brings its own psychological reward. When not planning, they talk about operations – partly thinking about opportunities, partly fantasizing. Arrests and interrogations often reveal far more plots than officials knew about; knowing about them might have caused even greater alarm. And terrorists use threats as well as attacks to cause alarm and disruption. IRA terrorists set off bombs on British rail and London's underground, and then, with credibility established, compounded the disruption by communicating numerous bomb threats. The initial intelligence and continuing threats indicating that British Airways flight 223 might be a target of al-Qaeda led to disruptive and costly cancellations. Subsequent cancellations reflected new threats of action by persistent terrorists – or had they observed the disruption they produced and were now engaged in pure disruption by means of threat alone? The challenge for intelligence is to separate real plans from fantasies, actual threats from the high volume of noise.

Traditional threat assessments are based upon on an analysis of the enemy's intentions and capabilities. In times of war, even during the years of the Cold War, this was fairly straightforward. The enemy's intentions were easy to discern, the number of potential targets limited and identifiable. Analysis focused on obvious military capabilities, things that could be counted – tank divisions, submarines, missiles, warheads – and more broadly on the country's ability to support a military effort – its economy, industrial production, available manpower, transport, etc.

For terrorism, threat assessment is a far more difficult task. Hostility is manifest, but intentions – the what, where, and how – remain unclear. Capabilities are variable depending on unlimited target selection – terrorists will always find a suitable target within the range of their capabilities. Discerning their intentions requires hard-to-get human intelligence. Penetration takes years; even then there are surprises.

Given the difficulty of traditional threat-based analysis, those with security responsibilities have turned to vulnerability-based analysis, which begins at the other end by identifying obvious vulnerabilities, postulating a terrorist foe, and conjuring up an (almost invariably) worst-case scenario. This style of analysis usually begins with "suppose that terrorists were to ..." This is not a bad way to explore the potential consequences of a terrorist attack and to evaluate preparedness – "what would we do if terrorists were to do this?" However, the hypothetical scenarios are often reified into actual threats. What starts out as a theoretical possibility is interpreted as a probable, then inevitable, and ultimately an imminent event. Vulnerability analysis thus replaces threat assessment, which it is not.

Indeed, the substitution of vulnerability-based analysis for threat-based analysis can be counterproductive. Since vulnerabilities in a modern industrialized society are almost infinite, vulnerability analysis by itself gives us too many targets to protect. This is not to say that the potential consequences of a successful attack should not be an important criterion for allocating security resources – nuclear facilities, for example, must always be well protected. However, thick catalogs of vulnerabilities will exhaust our resources and complicate their allocation.

The nightmare scenarios also end up being discussed in the public domain, which exaggerates the perceived danger and increases public alarm, further distorts resource allocation. And it complicates intelligence. Public discussions of vulnerabilities may or may not tutor terrorists, but they certainly provoke discussion among terrorists, who read and listen to what we write and say. Their discussions – "Could we actually do this?" – picked up through intelligence efforts may then be interpreted as verification that terrorists are contemplating the very attacks we worry about publicly.

A third method, utilizing "red teams," attempts to mimic terrorist thinking and planning. Beginning with a thorough understanding of the terrorists' belief system, worldview, and mindset, a red team, operating from the terrorists' perspective, selects targets and plans attacks. The process is not predictive, but it is informative; for example, it is noteworthy that while a red team may begin with unlimited targets and a vast library of hypothetical nightmare scenarios, actual planning quickly narrows the list. Some things, from the terrorists' point of view, are simply not appealing, while detailed planning reveals others to be far more difficult than we imagine.[2]

Intelligence collection and analysis

The nature of the threat

Arguably, recent events oblige us to alter completely how we view threats. Developments since the end of the Cold War have complicated intelligence requirements. The collapse of the Soviet empire, continuing globalization of the economy, and rapid advances in information technologies – all developments with positive consequences – have at the same time generated new causes, created new vulnerabilities, and provided adversaries with new capabilities. As a result, today we face a far more complex array of threats and adversaries.

Of significant danger is the clandestine exchange of nuclear material and know-how, and the spread of weapons of mass destruction. The recent revelations regarding the clandestine nuclear assistance network centered in Pakistan provide a dramatic example. There is also the threat of escalating terrorism, and the possibility that terrorists may themselves acquire or develop chemical, biological, radiological, and perhaps even nuclear weapons. Then there are wars, chronic conflicts that in some areas have become economic enterprises or sudden outbursts of ethnic, tribal, or religious warfare that, unchecked, may threaten genocidal atrocities and humanitarian disasters. Global organized crime, trading in drugs, human beings, weapons, and strategic materials, along with cyber-crime and potentially cyber-terrorism, large-scale corruption and money-laundering, have also been elevated to the level of international concern. Each of these issues has generated its own list of intelligence collection requirements.

Several of them fall within the domain of homeland defense: certainly large-scale terrorism; threats resulting from weapons of mass destruction in the hands of states or non-state actors; actual or threatened use of chemical, biological, or radiological weapons by terrorists or ordinary criminals, which can result in hazards to health as well as widespread alarm; narcotics, alien, and weapons smuggling, including the clandestine delivery of weapons of mass destruction; and threats to critical infrastructure. It is not enough merely to catalog the old and new threats to homeland security, but to see them as dynamic, ever-evolving forms, not as anomalies but as fundamental changes in the ecology of crime and conflict.

The most immediate threat, however, and the one driving concerns about homeland defense, is the continuing global terrorist campaign waged by al-Qaeda and like-minded jihadists. This is the principal concern of the United States and the conclusion of a recent Europol report.[3] Between 11 September

2001 and August 2005, al-Qaeda and its allies carried out 19 major terrorist attacks, killing nearly 1,000 persons and injuring several thousands.[4] Fortunately, these attacks have been at the pre-September 11 level – primarily vehicle bombs – but they demonstrate that this is an enterprise bent upon causing large-scale death, destruction, and terror as evidenced also in the terrorist plots that have been discovered through intelligence efforts and foiled. These have included plans to sabotage a commercial airliner; hijack an airliner and crash it into a major airport; shoot down a commercial airliner with precision-guided surface-to-air missiles; stage a suicide attack on an ocean liner; launch large-scale bombings at public gathering places; and deploy ricin and other toxins.[5] Had these succeeded, we would be looking at thousands of additional casualties and even greater impacts on travel, commerce, and the economy, to say nothing of the societal and political consequences of the widespread terror they would create. Defense of democracy – our principal shared value – begins with effective intelligence.

Since September 11 we have made considerable progress against the al-Qaeda network and like-minded jihadists. International cooperation has led to numerous arrests. As indicated, many attacks have been foiled and terrorist financing has been impeded. Terrorists must now operate in a more hostile environment. But we have not yet dented the terrorists' determination to impose upon us their version of perpetual war. We face a protracted struggle, and probably never will be able to return to the *status quo* as it existed before September 11. Like combating terrorism, homeland defense will remain an enduring task, one that will engage the domestic and foreign intelligence-gathering services of all nations.

Intelligence bureaucracies

Intelligence is a complex business. For historical, functional, legal, and technical reasons, many countries have multiple intelligence services focusing on domestic and foreign collection activities. Military establishments have their own intelligence corps, which in some countries also assume the role of collecting foreign intelligence. Domestic and foreign intelligence collection efforts are often divided: the FBI and CIA in the United States, the DST and DGSE in France, MI5 (or now the SIS) and MI6 in the United Kingdom, SISDE and SISMI in Italy.

Domestic intelligence collection may be further subdivided. In Germany, the Federal Criminal Police Office (BKA) focuses on issues of direct concern to law enforcement, while the Federal Office for the Protection of the Constitution (BFV) deals with security of the state. Terrorism, of course, falls within the domain of both services.

Additional services may collect intelligence in certain functional areas (finance, customs duties, corruption, drug trafficking, the protection of high-ranking officials), or may be devoted to certain collection technologies such as electronic surveillance or satellites. Again, terrorism cuts across all of these areas, international and domestic, subversion and crime, human and high-tech.

This puts a premium on cooperation, which is not easy. The goals, rules, organizational cultures, and career incentives that govern each of the various entities involved in the collection and analysis of intelligence differ greatly. In some cases, cooperation or the sharing of information is explicitly prohibited to protect privacy, for example, or the integrity of criminal prosecutions, or it cannot be shared because knowledge of a crime requires prosecution, which cannot be deferred in order to gather more intelligence.

A further complication is created by the fact that these services often report through different ministries (Defense, Interior or Home Office, Justice, or Treasury). This not only impedes cooperation internally, but also complicates international cooperation. It is difficult for police, who report to a Home Office in one country, to coordinate directly with Ministry of Defense agencies in another country.

While this makes bureaucratic sense to us – it is the product of our organizational histories – it is meaningless to terrorist foes, who represent a new threat that cuts across these jurisdictions, which can impede the flow of intelligence necessary for homeland defense. The review of US intelligence prior to September 11 reveals a number of systemic problems that prevented authorities from "connecting the dots" and uncovering the September 11 plot.[6] This is not to say that, had all of the information available to the CIA, the FBI, the Immigration and Naturalization Service and others been readily shared, analysts would easily have discovered the planned hijacking–suicide scheme, but institutional barriers denied them even the opportunity. Following the terrorist attack in Madrid on 11 March 2004, Spain's government initiated an investigation as to whether its multiple intelligence entities cooperated effectively.

The September 11 attack prompted governments in both the United States and Europe to review their intelligence collection and analysis. In the United States, it led to the setting of new collection priorities, a number of organizational changes, and exhortations to the various services to improve sharing. Right after September 11, European governments adopted an action plan to increase common security measures, expand the role of Europol, facilitate cooperation in investigations, and share more intelligence on terrorism. Cooperation among European nations indeed increased, but much of the initial plan was not implemented. The bombings in Madrid on 11 March 2004 renewed pledges to improve Europe's intelligence capacity, but differences arose over the creation of a European intelligence agency, an idea proposed by Austria and Belgium but rejected by France and Germany, which suggested instead that the major national intelligence services take the lead. The Europeans did appoint an EU counterterrorism coordinator, but he has little power beyond persuasion.[7]

Thus far, all governments have avoided wholesale reorganization of their intelligence services, which would require major legislation. In creating its new Department of Homeland Security, the most ambitious reorganization by any government to deal with new threats, the United States left its existing intelligence services untouched, except for exhortations to share more information. Apart from the small intelligence components it inherited with the Secret Service, Coast Guard, and a few other bits, the US Department of Homeland Security has no independent collection capabilities. It is a consumer.

Instead, the United States prior to and since September 11 has created new "scaffolds" to bridge the services and improve analysis. These include the Counter Terrorist Center (CTC) in the CIA, to which officers from other agencies may be assigned, the Terrorist Threat Integration Center (T-TIC) which brings together CIA and FBI analysts, and the Department of Homeland Security's Directorate of Information Analysis and Infrastructure Protection. To facilitate coordination between local police (there are more 18,000 local police jurisdictions in the United States), the US Government also has expanded the number of Joint Terrorist Task Forces (JTTF), which combine FBI and other national (or federal level) agencies with local police. Critics argue that the JTTFs remain locked into a tightly controlled hub-and-spokes structure that often produces a one-way flow of information to Washington.

International terror – international intelligence sharing

At the federal level, the US Departments of Homeland Security, Defense, and Justice, and the FBI have expanded their activities abroad to improve international cooperation. The FBI's direct involvement abroad derives from earlier legislation, which asserts the jurisdiction of US courts over terrorist-related crimes committed against US citizens abroad, making the FBI the lead investigator. Historically, the FBI also has bilateral arrangements with foreign counterparts to deal with organized crime. All of these efforts are in addition to the expanding relationships among intelligence services abroad, which for the United States is the responsibility of the CIA.

The proliferation of Americans abroad seeking cooperation from foreign governments has on occasion provoked complaints from some that they are asked the same questions by representatives of various US agencies who apparently fail to talk to one another. There are also not-infrequently heard complaints that the United States regards the "war on terror" as its war, demanding information but providing little in return. Indeed, some willing allies, in efforts to dismantle terrorist organizations, have warned that Americanization of global counterterrorist efforts, even American insistence on a vocabulary of "war" and "terrorism," scoring every local arrest as a victory to be publicized, impedes cooperation in countries where terrorists must be plucked from populations often hostile to American policies.

There are both bilateral and multilateral agreements to allow cooperation among national intelligence services. Cooperation before September 11 was good, and since September 11 it has improved further. Even sharp political differences have not adversely affected cooperation against terrorism at the technical level. All nations have a major stake in the effort. The challenge now is whether and how the existing cooperation can be institutionalized, and thereby improved and streamlined.

Intelligence sharing during the Cold War could be a glacial process. Every intelligence service suspected (in most cases correctly) that everyone else's intelligence service had been infiltrated by the enemy. Intelligence was therefore processed, analyzed, and sanitized carefully to protect sensitive sources and methods before it was passed on. There were exceptions, of course.[8]

While the danger of penetration of national intelligence services by state and non-state adversaries remains a threat, a Cold War mindset, arguably, does not match current circumstances. Inter-penetration of intelligence services during the Cold War took place over many years, and it was essentially a two-sided contest. Compromise at high levels could destroy an entire espionage network that had taken years to build. Penetration of national intelligence services by al-Qaeda spies, to take one example, seems less likely, and the consequences of compromise, if it did occur, are more likely to be tactical than strategic.

Moreover, intelligence about terrorism cannot afford to wait. Information about possible attacks must be passed on quickly to foil terrorist plots. There may be little time for processing and careful analysis; sometimes the intelligence is raw. However, problems arise and tensions grow when there is a requirement to move fast. Normal arrangements may be bypassed. *Diktat* replaces discussion. We saw this in the cancellations of flights from Europe to the United States that occurred at the end of 2003 and beginning of 2004. On the other hand, sharing only the finished intelligence product reduces global effectiveness in combating terrorism, while sharing everything only multiplies the number of haystacks for everybody, without necessarily improving the odds of finding the terrorist needles.

One approach was indicated years ago by the former Chief of French intelligence, Alexandre de Marenches, who in a remarkably prescient book entitled *The Fourth World War* described many of the very threats we face today.[9] He recommended the creation of a transatlantic "club of decent people" that would cooperate even more closely against terrorists, proliferators, and other dangerous villains than the liaison arrangements that existed at the time. What de Marenches had in mind was the coordination of both intelligence and operations, but he did not elaborate exactly how this was to be achieved.

We have come a long way, and de Marenches' vision remains tantalizing, but implementation remains a daunting task. Can we think about a multilateral Terrorist Threat Integration Center (T-TIC) that receives information from all national sources who are members, analyzes it, and dispatches it in a user-friendly form that meets the specific requirements of an investigating magistrate in one country, a homeland defense office in another, an arresting officer in a third, an interrogation center in a fourth, or a government prosecutor somewhere else? Who would be eligible to join? How would it work? What exactly would be shared? Would it accelerate the process, or only add another layer?

Decentralized terror – local intelligence

Pressure on al-Qaeda's transnational network since September 11 has resulted in more decentralized terrorist operations. While the possibility of a centrally-directed strategic terrorist strike cannot be ruled out, future terrorist operations are more likely to comprise already dispersed loyal fanatics, perhaps assisted by itinerant technicians, but relying heavily upon local recruits. Or the threat may emerge from purely local fanatics who may share al-Qaeda's mindset, but who are not connected with al-Qaeda's leaders – which seems to have been the case with the bombings in Casablanca and Madrid. In the former case, recruiting begins locally with promising acolytes passed on to training centers and fighting fronts for indoctrination and "blooding," to return some day as the cadre and cannon fodder for new attacks. In the latter case, the entire recruiting, planning, and execution chain may occur locally. As a consequence, intelligence activities must take place at the local level, where police often have the advantage over national intelligence services. Police are more likely to be locally recruited, and possibly more ethnically diverse; they are from the community and familiar with the community in which they serve, and are not likely to be rotated around the country, as federal officials often are.

They tend to be an overlooked resource in intelligence, but it is the local police department and its network of confidential informants that are in the best position to identify the "hot spots" for recruiting; to talk to local merchants, community leaders, and kids on the street; to respond to citizens' tips; and to discern the departures from pattern, the anomalies that might signal "something is up."

Police officers often have the additional advantage over their intelligence service counterparts in the form of experience in interviewing and interrogating suspects, which they do far more of than most intelligence agents. Few can match the experience and skills of a senior detective with 25 years of criminal investigation under his belt. We may want to figure out how to directly employ such officers not only in their own cities, but also in the interrogation of terrorist suspects detained anywhere.

The effectiveness of local police would be increased by enabling them to network directly with each other rather than solely through the Joint Terrorism Task Force structure operating in the United States. Some argue that the result would be anarchy, but big corporations in the private sector have deliberately developed protocols and corporate cultures that encourage autonomous networking and knowledge-sharing.

To exploit the capability of local law enforcement will require empowering local police to be more active in intelligence-gathering, which in some places may be a legislative matter, and shifting resources to the homeland – something national governments always find hard to do. Local police will require training, and in some cases need technology not now widely available.

The New York Police Department, which for understandable reasons devotes considerable resources to counterterrorism, has 1,000 officers (of a total of 40,000, or about 2.5 percent) devoted to counterterrorism, including intelligence. If major city police departments were able to match this, the United States would have an effective domestic counterterrorist force of 15,000 with a substantial domestic collection capability.

Obviously, there are differences between the United States and Europe, and among the European nations, on this score. The United States has no equivalent to the Gendarmerie, Carabinieri, or Guardia Civil; it has no national police. Law enforcement is a local matter, with the FBI limited to the investigation of federal crimes, counter-intelligence, and counterterrorism. The structures in Europe vary from country to country. All have local frontline cops; not all have the equivalent of America's FBI.

In a few cases, local police departments in the United States have established their own direct liaison with allied police forces outside the country to learn lessons from recent terrorist attacks and facilitate the flow of intelligence. At the same time, major police departments in Europe such as Scotland Yard have sponsored meetings and encouraged the development of networks across national boundaries to share best practices in various aspects of homeland defense. These police-to-police linkages often exist outside the formal treaty relations between national intelligence services, as well as outside the more confined operating space of Interpol or Europol. The ultimate objective is a loose but muscular network, based upon shared goals and values, capable of responding to the terrorists' transnational network.

How these linkages will evolve is unclear. Europe, which has moved toward harmonizing laws, may also move in the direction of even greater coordination among police departments. However, one European police officer, experienced in dealing with terrorism, told this author years ago that to work effectively, police liaison must retain a degree of informality and will always be based upon personal relationships and trust – just like al-Qaeda. Creating too formal a structure, in his view, would produce a bureaucracy that would only complicate and slow the flow of information. So while greater coordination among police departments domestically and internationally is desirable, are formal institutions to achieve this to be avoided?

Developments in Europe

While European countries have re-focused and increased their intelligence efforts to combat terrorism, there has been a corresponding increase in cooperation at the European Union level. Cooperation at the regional level traces its origins to the Trevi (the acronym in French for terrorism, radicalism, extremism, and international violence) arrangement in 1976, which initially provided a forum for European ministers of justice and the interior, as well as senior police officials, to meet regularly and exchange views on common threats. Trevi helped Europeans address the phenomenon of 1980s Euro-terrorism, a set of loose connections between left-wing extremists in Italy, France, Germany, Spain, and Belgium, and to deal effectively with the growing threat of Islamic terrorism, principally Hizbollah, in the late 1980s.

The Treaty of Maastricht replaced Trevi with Europol, the European Police Office, to facilitate cooperation among police throughout the European Union. Since September 11 Europol has become an increasingly important center for counterterrorism, with a special unit devoted to threat analysis. Europol also has become a contact point for American law enforcement officials, with Americans now permanently stationed at Europol's headquarters, although separate bilateral and multilateral arrangements for intelligence continue.

Efforts to combine intelligence collection, analysis, and dissemination efforts (as opposed to merely sharing information among services) are likely to continue within Europe, between the United States and Europe, and in other selected networks. It is not clear whether developments in Europe toward a single counter-terrorist office or a European intelligence office will further or impede transatlantic exchanges.

Certain common themes become evident on exploring possibilities for joint task forces, multi-agency threat information centers, networking police departments within and across national frontiers, autonomous information sharing, clubs of decent people, or multilateral processing of intelligence. Local intelligence collection capabilities should be exploited and linked with one another and to national intelligence services at the same time that global collaboration is increased. New transatlantic and wider international connections are needed, possibly through new organizations, but without creating new bureaucracies. We need more intelligence, and we need to move it faster – but, as argued, powerful institutional barriers remain.

Defining the appropriate limits of domestic intelligence collection and police powers

Every European country that in the past was compelled to deal with an ongoing terrorist campaign modified the rules in some way. New criminal offenses were created. Police powers were expanded. Domestic intelligence gathering was facilitated. In some cases, special courts or tribunals were established. Rules of evidence were changed. Defendant rights were limited.[10] In a few cases there were excesses, but all of these nations – Italy, Germany, France, Spain, the United Kingdom – have clearly remained liberal democracies, heads of the family of free nations.

The United States has recently gone through the same process. Some of this legislation responded to earlier terrorist threats and was in place before 11 September 2001. Since that date, new rules have been established, and these have been modified by judicial decisions.

None of this has occurred without debate, which continues and may be seen as an indication of a healthy democracy. Balancing security with civil liberties is the subject of Chapter 9 in this book. It is discussed here only as it pertains to certain aspects of intelligence and transatlantic cooperation.

Technological advances have permitted the storage and retrieval of huge amounts of data. These are now used in the private sector to monitor the travel and purchasing patterns of credit card holders for marketing and fraud prevention purposes. Automated data systems also record the passage of vehicles on toll roads, bridges, and tunnels, and automatically deduct the correct amount from an "easy-pass." These have been combined and standardized for greater convenience. A driver can now travel from New York to Florida on the same electronic pass. Frequent flyers' numbers record air travel and hotel stays. Financial records monitor deposits and other transactions. ATM and debit cards record cash withdrawals and purchases. Health care records are increasingly automated. Website log-ons are routinely recorded, and an Internet user's site visits can be monitored.

These same databases are powerful tools for intelligence gathering and investigation – even more powerful when data from many sources can be accessed and assembled at a higher level and combined with information already on government databases.

Some of these data are now accessible during a criminal investigation with court approval. Legal restrictions and lack of a single IT architecture, however, make this a tedious and inefficient process which could be improved by creating an information superstructure that would allow single-point access to all. A single query would thereby provide investigators with employment, financial, travel, and purchasing information, along with phone records and Internet usage.

It is theoretically possible to construct an IT system that is able continuously to "observe" all of these databases and is "taught" to recognize patterns and anomalies that arouse suspicion. A recent research program sponsored by the US Department of Defense, initially called "Total Information Awareness," explored such a possibility, until it was shut down by Congress. It is now done on a limited basis to assist in the screening of airline passengers. The Computer Assisted Passenger Profiling System (CAPPS) now in use takes information from an individual passenger's numerical record to identify "selectees" for increased scrutiny by security systems. A more advanced CAPPS II awaits implementation. In a more ambitious application of an all-seeing information system, privacy would be protected by an intervening veil which would identify individuals only as ciphers until such time as they became subjects of investigation.

Critics concerned about civil liberties, who find individual databases in government and the private sector to be tolerable, become quite concerned about the potential for abuse should such databases be connected. At the very least, connected databases impinge on privacy in a way that multiple individual databases, although irksome, do not. And in government hands, the very existence of a super data system linking private and public records represents to many people an unacceptable degree of social control, which, it is argued, destroys privacy and erodes civil liberties by its very existence.

In Europe, where privacy has explicitly been recognized as a right, resistance would be even greater. A recent German court decision, for example, has already banished electronic surveillance from the bedroom.[11]

We are probably going to see continued efforts by government intelligence services to utilize increased computing power to effectively exploit the vast pools of personal data to identify suspicious anomalies and assist in investigations. This will be a continuing source of tension with existing concerns about privacy and civil liberties.

The determination of the US Administration to view the fight against terrorism as a war presents yet another problem. This construct is shared by very few of America's allies, who instead see combating terrorism primarily as a problem for law enforcement. And even though the United States and European partners used military force to remove the Taliban and destroy terrorist training camps in Afghanistan, and have employed irregular methods to apprehend terrorist leaders around the world, the fact is that most arrests are carried out by law enforcement agencies.

Whether to deal with terrorism as war or as crime has significant operational consequences for intelligence. What is the target – specific individuals who may be guilty of a terrorist attack, or the enterprise that is engaged in continuing terrorist activity? What is the goal – justice or destruction of the organization? What is the status and what are the rights of those detained? Is courtroom quality evidence required, or will good intelligence suffice? And what rules will govern its use?

There has been a lot of argument in the United States about the merits of the two approaches. The fact is that terrorism represents a new threat requiring the orchestration of efforts in both domains. Law enforcement may be the main route, but military force may be required at times. Over time, it seems likely that we will have to create new categories of law enforcement and precision warfare to meet the threat effectively.

In a law enforcement approach, terrorism is defined according to the quality of the act, not the identity of the perpetrators or the nature of their cause. Intelligence is aimed at uncovering and thwarting terrorist plots, while law enforcement is aimed at apprehending perpetrators and bringing them to trial. The September 11 attack changed perceptions. Terrorism on this scale made prevention paramount, and obliged governments in Europe and America to become more proactive in their approach. We have seen a similar although less dramatic effect in Europe since the Madrid bombings.

In the United States, after September 11 the FBI was pressured to devote more attention to preventive intelligence rather than conducting investigations solely to support criminal prosecutions. This was a reversal of what the Bureau had been instructed to do over the previous 25 years.

The shift toward prevention requires an ongoing campaign in which we change how we define terrorism in the legal realm, and thus how we govern intelligence gathering. It no longer suffices to define a terrorist act. The law required the designation of a "terrorist organization" – an ongoing enterprise whose otherwise legal actions such as recruiting, raising money or buying arms could also be outlawed.

The addition of a terrorist organization to a terrorist event as a basis for defining terrorism, and thus counterterrorism, in effect put terrorism closer to an ongoing war framework, even while remaining a law enforcement problem. Since almost all of the activities of a designated terrorist organization were now proscribed by law, it opened the investigative space and expanded the legitimate arena for intelligence activities.[12]

The United States, Canada, the governments of the European Union, and other countries have cooperated closely in listing terrorist organizations, although not all lists agree. Generally, Europeans have been more reluctant to list the "political arms" of terrorist organizations, preserving what is often a fictional distinction between the political and armed wings of the same organization.

Arguably, the use of military power will in many circumstances increasingly be viewed internationally as an extension of law enforcement. As a result, we will gradually define new rules for operations, custody, and possible prosecution where law enforcement and armed conflict overlap.

Involving the public in intelligence collection and security

Countries that have been compelled to deal with continuing terrorist campaigns have involved the public in intelligence collection, surveillance, and security. It is appropriate since terrorists recognize no distinction between combatants and non-combatants – everyone is on the front line.

The United Kingdom has led in this area. Through government appeals, signage, and public address announcements, citizens are advised to keep a look-out for suspicious activities and parcels left in airports, train stations, and other public areas, and to notify authorities promptly when they see something suspicions. Special phone boxes have been placed in train and tube stations to facilitate this. As a result, during the IRA terrorist campaign, authorities could be confident that they would be notified within minutes of any suspicious activity or left package. Extensive use of closed-circuit television and deployed security forces then enabled the authorities rapidly to diagnose the situation and take appropriate measures to protect the public while minimizing disruption. Similar measures were adopted in

Israel along with extensive use of military reservists to augment surveillance and security.

Public involvement in civil defense, from plane spotters to coast watchers, and air raid wardens, declined as missiles replaced aircraft and the Cold War receded. The Nordic countries, however, still have "total defense" approaches that envision specific tasks for citizens in the case of major threats or disasters. These are primarily response roles. Nonetheless, total defense offers a concept and organizational structure that can be expanded and adapted to homeland security. This is treated in detail in Chapter 9.

In the United States, "Neighborhood Watch" programs where local communities organize themselves to safeguard their neighbors' families and property have long been a feature of local law enforcement. This is more difficult at a national level, but federal officials, when raising the threat level, have admonished the public to be vigilant, although exactly how is not explained. More specific assistance has been sought from various sectors such as truckers and boaters who have been asked to watch for specific things in their respective domains. Terrorists have been apprehended on the basis of citizen's tips, in the United States and in Europe.

At the local level, police have echoed admonitions to report suspicious activity and have set up hotlines to receive tips. The response has been good, providing numerous reports of possible surveillance and other activity. Although many tips inevitably turn out to be false alarms, follow-through can be an important source of intelligence.

Working from intelligence and scenarios generated by red teams, police have visited specific categories of merchants (uniform suppliers, chemical distributors, etc.) asking them to report purchases consistent with possible attack plans. Police have also visited leaders in certain local communities where terrorists may attempt to recruit operatives, requesting their cooperation in discouraging violence.

All of these efforts appear to be part of a more general trend toward increased public participation in surveillance and apprehension. Urbanization has dissolved notions of community, but technology seems to be reviving them. A modern example of the traditional practice of "hue and cry" is provided by America's "Amber Alert" program, where notices of abductions with accompanying descriptions of persons and vehicles are promptly broadcast on radio and television, and shown on electronic billboards along the highways. The effort has had great success and has resulted in lives being saved, as well as in the apprehension of kidnappers and child molesters.

There is an intriguing proposal to deploy the same kind of web cameras that are now positioned at ski slopes in Europe around critical facilities. Broadcasting continuously on the Internet makes it likely that someone will always be watching, thereby increasing public involvement in continuous surveillance.

Increased direct and indirect involvement of the public in a surveillance role, from first-hand observation to remote monitoring, is likely to increase.

Europe and America may want to identify and share best practices on how to increase public involvement in intelligence and surveillance. The objective is not a "security state" to delight Napoleon's Fouchet, one populated with cameras and an army of informants, monitoring every move, reporting every potentially subversive utterance, denying all privacy. Instead, the goal must be an involved citizenry that is enabled collectively to participate in its own security, for which there are long and noble traditions in both Europe and America.

Notifying the community of the threat

Intelligence must ultimately be communicated to users. Information that is very specific – names, meeting places, operational plans – is communicated to those who can take direct action against the terrorists. More often we are dealing with less specific information which can still be useful to those with security responsibilities, helping them to allocate resources or increase security under heightened threat conditions.

In response to the IRA's terrorist campaign, the British government developed a tiered warning protocol called "vellum." Vellum established four threat levels which could be communicated to law enforcement as well as those with security responsibilities in the private sector. Each threat level prompted the implementation of certain security measures.

The United States adopted a similar system based upon five colors, a red alert being the highest. The color-coded system was merely a shorthand way to communicate a judgment, based upon available intelligence, to federal government agencies, states, local authorities, those with security responsibilities in the private sector, and the public.

The utility of public warnings, however, is debated. When authorities have precise information, action is possible and public warnings are not necessary. Threats communicated to the public will therefore almost always be vague.

To create alarm with vague warnings of threats, which people can do nothing about, looks like nothing more than bureaucratic tail covering. Indeed, failure to issue a public warning when the government had information prior to the bombing of Pan Am Flight 103 in 1988 (information which turned out to be completely spurious but coincidentally correct) caused public outrage – a warning that governments withhold threat information at their peril.[13]

America's pervasive and aggressive news media make it difficult to communicate threat information to thousands of recipients in government and law enforcement, who will then visibly increase security measures, without attracting public attention. Absent a public statement, reporters will seek their own sources of information and hundred different versions will emerge along with the inevitable rumors, causing uncertainty and even greater alarm. It is better sharing with the public what the authorities know. And it is possible, although not demonstrable, that public warnings and increased security have a deterrent effect.

Public warnings have rarely been issued in Europe. There may be cultural differences here. Americans are more demanding, as well as highly litigious. However, if terrorism continues (as seems likely), and especially if terrorists acquire chemical, biological, radiological or nuclear capabilities, then public warnings, even at the risk of false alarms, will become more necessary in both America and Europe. Arguably, some type of public warning system for terrorist threats will remain necessary (as they are for dangerous weather conditions or threats to public health) and, like the United Kingdom and the United States, the governments on the European mainland will develop some type of common alert system.

In the long run, the public will probably become more sophisticated consumers of threat information, realizing that even the heightened probability of a terrorist attack does not translate into significantly increased danger for the individual, unless we find ourselves in the realm of weapons of mass destruction. The terror effect can also be reduced by providing members of the public with more specific actions to take. This may include advance education and public drills. Here again, the Nordic concept of "total defense" may provide an interesting model.

Conclusion

Homeland security is a broad and complicated field. It requires the coordination of security functions from controls at national frontiers with the protection of specific systems and facilities. These include commercial aviation, surface transportation, maritime shipping, energy networks, communications, water supplies, food processing, chemical plants, pipelines, and other components of the infrastructure. The potential vulnerabilities that may be targeted by terrorists or saboteurs vastly exceed the resources available for security, making intelligence crucial in both anticipating terrorist preferences and thwarting specific attacks.

The September 11 attack in the United States and the March 11 attack in Spain underscore the reality of the terrorist threat, and have provided strong incentives to improve intelligence collection and analysis and increase international cooperation in dealing with a global enemy. Indeed, collaboration among the intelligence services within individual countries and between nations has increased, although much remains to be done.

In principle, it would be desirable to institutionalize and expand this cooperation beyond the various intelligence treaties and other sharing agreements already in place. The object is always better intelligence that is shared more quickly so that it may be acted upon to block the plans of a dynamic, flexible, and fast-moving foe. European experience and existing institutions offer a framework, as do existing transatlantic agreements. Further improvement is necessary.

At the same time, we must recognize that intelligence is the most sensitive activity of a government. It is the nature of intelligence to create compartments, and it is tough to breach walls. Inclusion often means dilution. We are many years away from a unified European intelligence service, and progress in this area will be slow and uneven. The evolution of the Schengen agreement provides an instructive model: it has taken years to develop, and many see it as a vulnerability, only as good as its weakest link. Intelligence will be even harder than border controls. The continuing expansion of the European Union far beyond its traditional horizons will further complicate matters.

The fact is that European governments will continue to employ their intelligence services to do things that they will not share with others. European governments run some unilateral intelligence operations in each other's countries. European countries have spied on each other and continue to do so, although perhaps less so now than in the past.

Still, terrorism demands and offers the greatest opportunity for cooperation. It presents a common foe, although even in combating terrorism there have been sharp differences in policy and approach. There are also significant differences in perceptions of the threat.

One way to overcome these differences is to define terrorism precisely and prescribe a common set of crimes that all agree upon, thus removing intelligence and enforcement from politics and policy. This approach fits with Europe's preference to treat terrorism as a law enforcement problem as opposed to the US government's "war" framework. It will help with detention and extradition. It is also consistent with a European tendency toward bureaucratic rule-making. Arguably, however, this kind of formalism will not work well in the more ephemeral area of intelligence.

Neither would institutionalization leading to a highly centralized European intelligence effort be best suited to dealing with decentralized terrorist networks. Both local and global situation awareness is required. This means local police as well as national services must be part of the overall intelligence network. All this suggests continuing complexity rather than consolidation, but networks can be created within complex operating environments. They evolve, they can be encouraged and facilitated; they cannot easily be designed from the top.

For the foreseeable future, whatever intelligence function is created at the European level will coexist with national intelligence services, who will share information with it while maintaining their existing sharing arrangements with other European and non-European countries. Gradually a European intelligence entity may become the more efficient fusion point, but this will be by accomplishment, not by fiat.

The creation of a European-level intelligence structure will not supplant existing transatlantic agreements. The United States will maintain its existing networks, which include both European and non-European countries, while establishing liaison with any new European structures. Actual pieces of intelligence may move more rapidly through existing bilateral and multi-lateral channels, while the European-level structure may add a useful, more global layer of analysis if it can perform in a timely fashion.

Progress toward multilateral intelligence structures will depend on perceptions of threat, which, in turn, will be driven by events. Right now, perceptions of the terrorist threat vary enormously despite recent attacks. They vary sharply between the United States and Europe, but also among Europeans. Many in Europe and not a few in the United States see September 11 as a one-time anomaly. Some in Europe also see terrorism as principally America's problem, one which Washington has exacerbated through its own actions. Although European governments promptly rejected Osama bin Laden's offer of immunity to those countries that pulled their troops out of the Middle East, despite the rhetoric of solidarity in dealing with terrorism there is still appeal in policies that seek immunity by demonstrating distance from Washington. Accelerated progress in intelligence cooperation, sadly, will depend on further large-scale terrorist attacks.

Notes

1 Al-Qaeda and its jihadist allies are typical of this looser global network structure. See B. M. Jenkins, *Countering al Qaeda: An Appreciation of the Situation and Suggestions for Strategy*, Santa Monica: Rand, 2002.

2 For a brief discussion of the "red team" approach, see B. M. Jenkins, *Looking at al Qaeda from the Inside Out: An Annotated Briefing*, Arlington: Hicks and Associates, Inc., 2003.

3 J. van Buuren, "Europol: Islamic terrorism main threat against the European Union," *Telepolis*, 2 December 2002; and Europol, *Terrorist Activity in the European Union: Situation and Trends Report October 2002–15 October 2003*, The Hague: Europol, 2003.

4 The major attacks include:
11 April 2002 – a truck bomb explodes near a synagogue in Djerba, Tunisia, killing 20, mainly German tourists.
8 May 2002 – a car bomb kills 14, including 11 French technicians, in Karachi.
14 June 2002 – a car bomb outside the US Consulate kills 11 and wounds 45.
7 October 2002 – a boat filled with explosives damages the French tanker *Limberg* off the coast of Yemen.
12 October 2002 – bombs explode in Bali, Indonesia, killing 202 and wounding hundreds.
28 November 2002 – a car bomb attack on a hotel in Mombasa, Kenya, frequented by Israeli tourists kills 15, while two surface-to-air missiles are fired at an Israeli airliner.
12 May 2003 – suicide bombers attack foreign housing compounds in Riyadh, killing 51.
16 May 2003 – suicide bombers set off five bombs in Casa Blanca, killing 45 and wounding more than 60.

5 August 2003 – a suicide bomber attacks a Western hotel in Jakarta, Indonesia, killing ten and wounding 150.
9 November 2003 – a suicide car bombing in Riyadh, Saudi Arabia, kills 17 and wounds 117.

15 November 2003 – two car bombs explode near synagogues in Istanbul, Turkey, killing 29.

20 November 2003 – two more bombs detonate at the British consulate and HSBC bank in Istanbul, Turkey, killing 32 and injuring more than 400.

11 March 2004 – ten bombs explode on commuter trains in Madrid, Spain, killing 190 and wounding hundreds.

22 April 2004 – a suicide bomb attack on the security forces headquarters in Riyadh, Saudi Arabia, kills 4 and injures 148.

4 May 2004 – armed assault kills seven in Yanbu, Saudi Arabia.

1 June 2004 – armed assault kills 22 in Khobar, Saudi Arabia.

9 September 2004 – a suicide bomber kills 11 at the Australian embassy in Jakarta.

7 October 2004 – bombs at a resort in Taba, Egypt kill 34.

7 July 2005 – four suicide bombers kill 56 in London.

22 July 2005 – suicide bombers kill 62 in Sharm el-Sheikh, Egypt.

5 In January 2003, British police arrested a number of terrorists believed to be planning attacks involving ricin (J. Bennetto and K. Sengupta, "Alarm over terror suspects with deadly toxin," *The Independent*, 8 January 2003). Further arrests were made in April 2004, of terrorists plotting to use osmium tetroxide (BBC News, "Chemical 'bomb plot' in UK foiled," 6 April 2004). According to reports, terrorists arrested in Jordan in April 2004 planned to carry out bombings and poison gas attacks (see J. Halaby, "Jordan Airs al-Qaida Suspects' Confessions," Associated Press, 26 April 2004).

6 Several national commissions before September 11 addressed the shortcomings of the US intelligence community in dealing with terrorism. See Advisory Panel to Assess Domestic Response Capabilities for Terrorism Involving Weapons of Mass Destruction (known as the Gilmore Commission); National Commission on Terrorism (known as the Bremer Commission), *Countering the Changing Threat of International Terrorism*. Washington DC: NCT, 2000; The United States Commission on National Security/21st Century (known as the Hart–Rudman Commission), *Road Map for National Security: Imperative for Change*, 2001.

The failures of intelligence to anticipate the September 11 attacks have been explored by the US Congress, see *Report of the House and Senate Intelligence Committees on the Events of September 11, 2001*. Washington, DC: Government Printing Office, 2002. The report of the National Commission on Terrorist Attacks upon the United States (also known as the 9/11 Commission), due to be completed in July 2004, will provide the most detailed account.

7 See "Europe Steps Up Fight Against Terrorism," European Union News Release 67/01, 20 September 2001. See also an excellent review of Europe's response to September 11 in T. Delpech, *International Terrorism and Europe: Chaillot Papers No. 56*, Paris: Institute for Security Studies, 2002.

8 The challenges to US intelligence in general in the post-Cold War era are discussed in G. F. Treverton, *Reshaping National Intelligence for an Age of Information*, New York: Cambridge University Press, 2001.

9 A. de Marenches and D. A. Andelman, *The Fourth World War: Diplomacy and Espionage in the Age of Terrorism*, New York: William Morrow and Company, Inc., 1992.

10 There is an extensive literature describing the terrorist campaigns in Europe from the late 1960s into the 1990s, and the government responses. For general overviews and discussions of countermeasures, see various chapters in W. Gutteridge (ed.), *The New Terrorism*, London: Mansell Publishing Company, 1986; P. Wilkinson and A. M. Stewart (eds), *Contemporary Research on Terrorism*, Aberdeen: Aberdeen University Press, 1987; and P. Wilkinson (ed.), *Terrorism:*

British Perspectives, Aldershot: Dartmouth Publishing Company, 1993. After September 11, US officials became more interested in seeing what lessons could be learned from foreign experiences in dealing with terrorism. See P. Chalk and W. Rosenau, *Confronting the Enemy Within: Security Intelligence, the Police, and counterterrorism in Four Democracies*, Santa Monica: Rand, 2004.

11 See "German Eavesdropping Law Unconstitutional," in *Deutches Welle* DW-WORLD-DE, 3 March 2004.

12 Under the US Antiterrorism and Effective Death Penalty Act of 1996, the Secretary of State is required to designate groups that threaten US interest and security as Foreign Terrorist Organizations (FTO). The FTO designation makes it a crime for a person to provide funds or other material support (including equipment, weapons, lodging, training, etc.) to such a group. There is no requirement that the contributor knows that the specific resources provided will be used for terrorism.

13 This incident is described in S. Emerson and B. Duffy, *The Fall of PanAm 103*, New York: G. P. Putnam's Sons, 1990, pp. 53–56.

8   Safeguarding civil liberties in an era of in-security

A transatlantic challenge

Esther Brimmer

In the wake of the September 11 terrorist attacks, the United States embarked on a major anti-terrorism campaign abroad and at home. International elements included the war in Afghanistan, to root out al-Qaeda and the Taliban; increased law enforcement cooperation; and new measures to monitor the movement of goods and people across borders. At home the Department of Justice, its Federal Bureau of Investigation, and later the new Department of Homeland Security, led domestic efforts to find people connected with the September 11 attacks and to prevent future terrorist activity in the US.

In Europe, most national governments and the European Union also enacted measures to constrain international terrorism, and suspected al-Qaeda members were prosecuted in court for connections to the September 11 attack. Building on an already existing net of transatlantic agreements, the US and Europe moved towards an unprecedented level of law enforcement and judicial cooperation. Moreover, efforts to prevent terrorist activity through increased information sharing and surveillance within and between countries took center stage.

In an age of potentially catastrophic attacks, US leaders believed that anti-terrorism law enforcement efforts had to focus on not only finding and prosecuting terrorists, but also on identifying and forestalling potential terrorists. United States Attorney General John Ashcroft, for example, asserted "At the Department of Justice, we are dedicated to detecting, disrupting, and dismantling the networks of terror before they can strike at our nation."[1]

However, identifying potential terrorists and anticipating their actions requires close surveillance of people, where they go, and what they do, but surveillance automatically raises civil liberties concerns. Leaders on both sides of the Atlantic realize that they face a common threat from massive international terrorism and from groups affiliated or sympathizing with al-Qaeda. As democracies, these countries also face a similar challenge of finding ways to safeguard civil liberties in an era dominated by the search for greater security from international terrorism.

Anti-terrorism security measures are intended to safeguard societies, but civil liberties are part of what makes our societies worth defending. This chapter argues that a number of the measures introduced in order to combat terrorism raise serious civil liberties concerns. However, it also argues that liberal democracies like the US and the countries of the European Union (EU) could learn from each other's experiences of finding ways to enhance security while upholding liberty. This chapter will begin to explore this issue by comparing and contrasting experiences on the two sides of the Atlantic.

Liberty and security – a trade-off?

At first glance, enhancing security and protecting civil liberties seem to conflict. Whereas law enforcement officials want to be able to search property and track people, civil liberties advocates want to protect liberty and privacy from unwarranted government intrusions. As this chapter will show, liberal democracies in Europe and North America are finding that security and civil liberties are connected – that security presupposes liberty. Indeed, one of the reasons our societies merit preservation is that they protect certain individual and human rights.

In times of crisis, leaders may be tempted to adopt stringent security measures at the expense of civil liberties. Officials and critics too easily use the language of balance as if there were clear trade-offs between these two concepts. The language of security has been used to curtail civil rights. The temptation is clear. Officials believe that they need to prosecute perpetrators of terrorist acts and to prevent future disasters, and gathering evidence of a crime and information about perpetrators is a key component of their work. Yet many terrorists endeavor to melt into the societies around them, trying to avoid attention until they attack. Law enforcement officials want ways to uncover suspects and to track aberrant behavior that may signal a conspiracy to strike. Gathering information can mean searching homes and businesses, listening to conversations, and monitoring meetings to ascertain if suspects are plotting an attack. Such surveillance immediately raises questions about government invasion of privacy, monitoring of free speech, and undermining freedom of association.

In extreme cases, governments have imprisoned or deported groups of people to prevent suspected individuals from acting against the state. Governments are more likely to take such action if many of the suspects come from a particular ethnic or cultural group seen as being outside the mainstream population. Even in the United States, officials have at times been willing to curtail the rights of certain people suspected of siding with an external enemy.

The most egregious cases in modern American history were the 1919 Palmer raids against suspected communists that led to deportations of immigrants from Eastern Europe, and the internment of over 110,000 Americans of Japanese descent during World War II. In each case, the Federal Government thought it needed to act to confront criminals that had infiltrated immigrant communities.[2] Easy scapegoats on the margins of society, many people – including citizens – were swept up in mass measures.

The case of the Japanese-Americans is particularly resonant in the post-September 11 period. After the 1941 Japanese attack on Pearl Harbor, US authorities feared an invasion of the West Coast of the United States and considered people of Japanese ancestry to be possible collaborators. On 19 February 1942, the President of the United States, Franklin Delano Roosevelt, signed Executive Order 9066, which permitted the Secretary of War to designate areas from which people could be excluded for security reasons. However, it was only the Japanese-Americans, not all residents, who were relocated. The combination of wartime and the fear of another devastating attack made officials ready to countenance denial of the right to liberty. The Federal Government created a War Relocation Authority that managed the relocation and housing of Japanese-Americans, even though the Authority acknowledged at the time that most of the people in relocation camps were loyal American citizens.[3] These episodes scarred American political memory, and arguably added little to the security of the United States. Expensive dragnet efforts, targeting thousands of people, most of whom were assumed to be innocent, diverted resources that should instead have been deployed in a much more targeted way against real spies.

The September 11 attack – a strike at the very symbols of American economic and military power – was a psychological blow that killed more people than did the assault on Pearl Harbor.[4] In response, President George W. Bush declared that the United States was at war against al-Qaeda, which launched the attack, and against terrorism itself. In a major televised address given only nine days after the September 11 attack, the President declared;

> Our enemy is a radical network of terrorists, and every government that supports them. Our war begins with al Qaeda, but does not end there. It will not end until every terrorist group of global reach has been found, stopped and defeated.[5]

The nation had suffered mass casualties on its own soil at the hands of an enemy whose agents had lived mostly invisibly in the United States and in Europe. Moreover, the specter of additional attacks hung in the air. The nation felt vulnerable, but the President swore to uphold freedom:

> And in our grief and anger we have found our mission and our moment. Freedom and fear are at war. The advance of human freedom – the great achievement of our time, and the great hope of every time – now depends on us.[6]

The President called the country to support the "advance of freedom." Yet freedom rests on a respect for civil liberties. In the years immediately after September 11, how well did the United States do?

The US experience after September 11

September 11 brought an end to the Americans' feeling of relative invulner-
ability at home. The attacks killed nearly 3,000, destroyed the twin towers
of the World Trade Center, and badly damaged the Pentagon. Americans
were acutely aware that the horror could have been even worse. A fourth airliner crashed in Pennsylvania, and many Americans believe that the plane
was being diverted to Washington, DC to wreak havoc in heart of the
nation's capital. The country was gripped by fear. Were more attacks imminent? On the East Coast the sense of foreboding was heightened by probably
unrelated terrorist attacks with cutaneous anthrax spores in letters to then
US Senate Majority Leader Tom Daschle. Two postal workers in the Brent-
wood sorting office died, and many people who worked in Congress were
prescribed antibiotics as a precaution. Leaders in the White House and Congress felt that they were under siege. Politicians and publics wanted strong
action taken to address the threat and salve the feelings of vulnerability.

In this charged atmosphere, the Bush Administration pushed for and
Congress passed significant legislation to empower agencies and others to
combat terrorism. The most important new law was the USA Patriot Act,
which was passed by Congress and signed by President George W. Bush on
26 October 2001. The Act was designed to enable the Department of
Justice to target and constrain actual and potential terrorists, and people
who support them. The administration has defended the USA Patriot Act as
an important tool in the war against terrorism. When he signed the Patriot
Act, President Bush asserted, "But one thing is for certain: These terrorists
must be pursued, they must be defeated, and they must be brought to
justice. And that is the purpose of this legislation." He went on to say, "This
legislation is essential not only to pursuing and punishing terrorists, but
also preventing more atrocities in the hands of the evil ones. The government will enforce this law with all the urgency of a nation at war."[7] Over
the years, Attorney General John Ashcroft repeatedly hailed the new law.[8] In
2003, Ashcroft defended the legislation, arguing that it gave

> each branch a role in ensuring both the lives and liberties of our citizens
> are protected. The Patriot Act grants the executive branch critical tools
> in the war on terrorism. It provides the legislative branch extensive
> oversight. It honors the judicial branch with court supervision over the
> Act's most important powers.[9]

Yet from the start civil rights groups were alarmed. The American Civil
Liberties Union (ACLU) charged that the "legislation gives the Executive
Branch sweeping new powers that undermine the Bill of Rights and are
unnecessary to keep us safe."[10]

The Administration continues to see the legislation as central to its
domestic anti-terrorism campaign. Although the Patriot Act does not expire

until the end of 2005, the President has called on Congress to extend the law. In his 20 January 2004, State of the Union speech, President Bush explained ". . . one of those essential tools is the Patriot Act, which allows federal law enforcement to better share information, to track terrorists, to disrupt their cells, and to seize their assets." He continued his appeal to Congress, saying, "Our law enforcement needs this vital legislation to protect our citizens. You need to renew the Patriot Act. America is on the offensive against terrorists who started this war."[11]

The debate on civil liberties is a key feature of the debate about the USA Patriot Act. The central provisions of the Patriot Act expand the Federal Government's ability to investigate, detain, and try suspected terrorists and the people who support them. The law was passed hastily in both the Senate and House of Representatives only six weeks after the attacks, as part of multiple efforts by law enforcement agencies to respond to the assault. The Patriot Act is the most prominent, but not the only, anti-terrorism measure passed after September 11 that raises civil liberties concerns. The Department of the Treasury, for example, requires financial institutions to report on certain activities of their customers. While these measures are intended to halt money laundering and curb terrorism financing, they require that private companies report on actions by their customers who have not yet been charged with any crime.

This new body of legislation has caused concern. In the United States, civil libertarians are particularly uneasy about three areas of the anti-terrorism campaign:

1 Infringements on the First Amendment, which protects freedom of speech, freedom of thought, and the right to assembly
2 Invasions of privacy and increased surveillance
3 Incarceration without charge as a form of preventive detention.

Infringing on the First Amendment?

American civil liberties are based on the first ten amendments of the United States Constitution, known as the Bill of Rights. The First Amendment states "Congress shall make no law . . . abridging the freedom of speech, or of the press; or the right of the people peaceably to assemble, and to petition the government for a redress of grievances."

New federal anti-terrorism measures try to track people and groups suspected of supporting terrorism directly, and third parties that may have information about suspected groups. Authorities want to know a suspect's range of contacts, funding sources for certain groups, and other patterns of interaction that could indicate a plan to commit a terrorist act. However, monitoring who says what to whom and who meets whom could infringe upon rights to free speech and assembly. For example, the September 11 hijackers were Muslim men from the Middle East.[12] Since then, US law enforcement has intensified its focus on Muslim men from Arab countries and South Asia, and on American citizens with connections to these regions. Does this provision become a pretext to investigate any group that supports Muslims?

The Patriot Act banned assistance to known terrorist groups. Yet the scope of "assistance" is not clear. Are lawyers or accountants who advise civic groups providing "assistance" if some members of the group use the organization as cover to plan a terrorist act? A federal judge has criticized the Patriot Act on this point. On 26 January 2004, Federal District Court Judge Audrey B. Collins struck down part of the Patriot Act saying, "The USA Patriot Act . . . bans the provision of all expert advice and assistance regardless of its nature." The breadth of the law could include "unequivocally pure speech and advocacy protected by the First Amendment."[13]

Invasion of privacy?

The Patriot Act raises concerns because it attempts to cast a wide net to gather as much information as possible in the hunt for potential terrorists. The Patriot Act permits the Federal Government not only to investigate suspects, but also to demand information from third parties who have had contact with suspects. Thus, the Federal Government could ask libraries, Internet service providers and others to divulge what types of information a person reads. The American Libraries Association (ALA) has warned that the Federal Government could ask to see what books a person has read at a public library. In its strongly worded statement, the ALA resolved that "the American Library Association considers sections of the USA Patriot Act are a present danger to the constitutional rights and privacy rights of library users . . ." The ALA was alarmed by the infringement of privacy noting that "[p]rivacy is essential to the exercise of free speech, free thought, and free association; and, in a library, the subject of users' interests should not be examined or scrutinized by others. . ."[14]

In addition, the Patriot Act loosens the requirements for obtaining suspect's records. Previously, prosecutors would have to demonstrate "probable cause" that a suspect was involved in a crime. Under the Patriot Act, officials just need to inform a judge that a suspect is implicated in an ongoing anti-terrorism or foreign intelligence investigation in order to review the person's books, letters, and other expression of speech and thought.[15] The subject cannot talk to other people about the records under review, making it difficult to seek advice from a lawyer. In addition, under the Act the FBI is allowed to conduct a search and only notify the targeted person afterwards. If the subject happens not to be present when the search occurs, it will be hard for that person to check whether the FBI has exceeded its warrant. Civil libertarians are particularly concerned that this measure, intended for anti-terrorism investigations, may be used in any criminal case, even if there is no connection to terrorism.

The American Civil Liberties Union has raised a similar concern about wiretaps on US citizens.[16] Prior to the passing of the Patriot Act, US law required a high standard of justification before the authorities could listen in on suspects' telephone calls. The FBI had to show probable cause before a judge allowed a wiretap. In 1978 the Foreign Intelligence Surveillance Act made an exception, permitting US citizens' telephones to be tapped without showing probable cause in cases where the purpose was to gain information relating to foreign intelligence and the information would not be used to prosecute the person being tapped. The person being tapped was incidental; the target was the third party to the communication. The information obtained would be used in a foreign policy context, but not a criminal trial. The Patriot Act expanded the exception to allow wiretaps on US citizens without showing probable cause even in regular criminal cases. Thus, as the line between internal and external security has become blurred by terrorists that operate transnationally; measures originally intended to advance foreign policy objectives have led to loosening domestic protections in criminal cases.

Detention

In the charged atmosphere immediately after September 11, the Department of Justice and other authorities rounded up mostly Arab, South Asian, and Muslim men, and held them pending investigations of any possible connections to the terrorist attacks. Most observers estimate that over 1,200 people were put behind bars in these sweeps.[17] In jurisdictions across America, police collected people who were deemed suspicious. Many people turned in Arab and Muslim neighbors and coworkers. Nearly 28 per cent of the people arrested after September 11 were turned in by private citizens.[18] In the 11 months after September 11, 762 were eventually charged with immigration violations, but none was charged with terrorism related activities.[19]

The Federal Government has yet to release full information about the number of people detained, released or deported in these sweeps. Many were held without charges for months or years. In the first several weeks, many were unable to contact family members or legal counsel. Civil liberties advocates charged that immigration laws were used because these allowed the government to hold people without charges for an extended period of time while investigating them for connections with other crimes, thereby circumventing constitutional protections. Human Rights Watch considers this practice "a form of preventive detention not permissible under US criminal law."[20]

People who overstay their visas are usually not detained before their deportation unless there is a risk of flight or the person is deemed dangerous. However, these detainees were held until the FBI cleared them, even if a judge had ordered them released or deported. Many of the complaints about mistreatment of detainees concerned people held in the Federal Bureau of

Prison's Metropolitan Detention Center in New York City and the Passaic County Jail in Paterson, New Jersey, which was under contract to the federal Immigration and Naturalization Service.[21] Even the Department of Justice's Office of the Inspector General (OIG) admitted that its investigation found "significant problems in the way the Department [of Justice] handled the September 11 detainees."[22] Among his findings, the Inspector General Glenn A. Fine noted:[23]

- The FBI did not adequately distinguish between foreigners suspected of direct connections to the September 11 attacks and those who were not suspected but happened to be questioned during the investigations.
- Some detainees were not charged for weeks or over a month, which "affected detainees' ability to understand why they were being held, obtain legal counsel, and request a bond hearing."

Arguably, conducting thousands of interviews has sowed distrust of the government among law abiding people in Muslim communities in the United States and discouraged many who might have useful information from bringing it forward to authorities, and has thus compromised rather than enhanced US security. These interviews are examples of large-scale profiling, categorizing and treating people differently according to demographic features such as race, religion, and age.

Detention and deportation

Americans tend to differentiate between their government's actions abroad and those conducted at home. Generally, higher standards and greater protection of rights is expected to apply within the US borders. Yet, according to civil liberties advocates, even a person captured in the United States seems not to have civil liberties protections expected under the Constitution if that person is deemed valuable in the anti-terrorist effort.

One of the most dramatic examples is that of US-born José Padilla, who was arrested in Chicago in June 2002 and has been held ever since. Here is a case of a US citizen captured on US soil who has been held despite the US Constitution's Fourth Amendment prohibition against "unreasonable searches and seizures." The unusual nature of the situation was evinced by a comment by the US Secretary of Defense, who does not normally comment on domestic legal proceedings. He asserted "we are not interested in trying and punishing him at the moment. We are interested in finding out what he knows."[24] Padilla's case is in the court system. Acting on a technical point, in June 2004 the United States Supreme Court told Padilla's lawyers to press his case in at a lower level before coming to the nation's highest court.[25] Therefore, his lawyers pursued the case in federal district court. On 28, February 2005, US District Judge Henry Floyd ordered the Bush Administration to charge or release Padilla, stating that "The court finds that the president has no power, neither express nor implied, neither constitutional nor statutory, to hold the petitioner as an enemy combatant,"[26] and gave the Administration 45 days to act. The Administration immediately appealed. In April 2005, Padilla's lawyers asked the Supreme Court to act.

The case illustrates how the anti-terrorism campaign has changed the tenor of law enforcement in the US. The FBI has shifted from investigating past crimes to trying to prevent future attacks. This policy shift changes the nature of the organization, and raises civil liberties questions. The traditional safeguards built into the US law enforcement system were designed to protect suspects and the innocent during an investigation, not to shield people from prospective efforts to forestall terrorism.

In addition, safeguards need to be improved to cover situations in which domestic agencies undertake international activity that affects Americans. The FBI works internationally in ways that it did not before. The US Government has created some constraints on federal agencies that gather foreign intelligence, which govern how information on US persons may be used and shared. Policymakers should consider crafting similar restraints for the FBI, traditionally a domestic agency, when it works on what are really intelligence issues.

The Padilla case is special because the detainee is a US citizen. In the anti-terrorism campaign there has been the deepening of legal differentiation between citizens and non-citizens in the United States. While citizens have always enjoyed unique rights (such as the right to vote or run for office), in court, non-citizens had similar legal standing to citizens. Both citizens and non-citizens enjoyed the presumption of innocence, the right to a fair trial, and freedom from unwarranted search and seizure.

Yet critics charge that the government, in the name of security, has sought to circumvent these protections in the anti-terrorism campaign by using immigration rules. Relying on immigration legislation, US authorities can deport suspicious non-citizens without having to attain the higher standard of evidence required for conviction. Moreover, if a law enforcement officer finds an illegal alien in the course of an investigation, that official cannot ignore the person's legal status. The officer will have to turn over the person to border control authorities, who will invoke immigration rules. However, by definition, immigration rules apply to non-residents. The use of immigration rules means that in the post September 11 sweeps, non-citizens have been more likely to be rounded up and then held without contact with a lawyer.

Currently, the United States is holding thousands of people without trial because they may have information relevant to the anti-terrorism campaign. What they may know is what is important. The Secretary of Defense's comment is indicative; the government is less concerned with trying detainees like José Padilla; instead it is "interested in finding out what he knows." This is a fundamental change in outlook. For the most part, many government authorities are trying to obtain information to prevent future terrorist attacks rather than to prosecute suspects for crimes. If officials are planning a prosecution, they want to be sure that the evidence they have can be admitted in court. If they want information on other possible conspirators, officials may be inclined to push for answers rather than admissible evidence. This tendency could create an atmosphere in which unacceptable – even illegal – tactics are used on suspects.

Guantanamo Bay

The issue of how to extract information from detainees in US custody was acute for those the Defense Department considered beyond the reach of US law. The detention of prisoners at Guantanamo Bay was a festering sore in the anti-terrorism campaign, but in the spring of 2004 the problem of illegal treatment of detainees burst on to the international scene. Revulsion was widespread. The tragedy of abuses by US personnel at Abu Ghraib prison in Iraq called into question the administration's policy of saying that the anti-terrorism campaign was beyond the rule of law or judicial review. Historic, June 2004 decisions by the United States Supreme Court confirmed that the rule of law had to be observed even when detaining terrorism suspects. Yet the issue was not new. As early as 2002 human rights advocates had raised concerns about US detention practices, not in the Middle East but barely 100 miles from Florida, in Guantanamo Bay, Cuba.

Not only has the United States held thousands of people without trial on the US mainland; it also holds hundreds more at a US naval base in Guantanamo. Nearly 600 people captured in the war in Afghanistan have been held at the base under the authority of the Department of Defense, some for over two years. The Administration argued that these prisoners were not on US territory, and therefore had no right to challenge their detention in US courts. In effect, they had no way to protest; the US considered them neither prisoners of war under the Geneva Conventions, nor captives subject to US courts. As images of shackled prisoners held outside the law appeared on televisions around the world, the United States was soundly and repeatedly criticized by human rights groups, and even by some national governments.

In a landmark decision on 28 June 2004, the United States Supreme Court ruled that prisoners at Guantanamo did have the right to have their cases heard by a US court. Writing the Court's Opinion, Justice John Paul Stevens stated, "Aliens held at the base, no less than American citizens, are entitled to invoke the federal courts' authority . . . "[27] After the decision, the administration scrambled to respond to this direct judicial rejection of the administration's policy. On the one hand, the Pentagon said that a military tribunal would be set up to try three suspects at Guantanamo. On the other, Pentagon spokesman Larry DiRita implied that some detainees would be released to avoid having them lodge cases in civilian courts. He noted that some prisoners "need not necessarily be part of a judicial process."[28] In less than a week after the Court decisions, the United States Senate passed a measure demanding that the President abide by the Geneva Conventions.[29]

A related case confirms the Court's point that people detained in the anti-terrorism campaign have legal rights even if the Administration contends that respecting rights restrains the exercise of executive power. Also on 28 June 2004, the Supreme Court ruled that US-born Yaser Esam Hamdi, who was caught in Afghanistan and initially held in Guanatnamo, had a right to challenge his detention in US courts. The Supreme Court ruled in favor of Mr Hamdi and against the Administration.

Writing for the majority, Justice Sandra Day O'Connor noted;

> Moreover, as critical as the Government's interest may be in detaining those who actually pose an immediate threat to the national security of the United States during ongoing international conflict, history and common sense teach us that an unchecked system of detention carries the potential to become a means for oppression and abuse of others who do not present that sort of threat.[30]

The Court understood that the conduct of the fight against terrorism affects American society and its foreign relation:

> It is during our most challenging and uncertain moments that our Nation's commitment to due process is most severely tested; and it is in those times that we must preserve our commitment at home to the principles for which we fight abroad.[31]

There was a real need for legal redress. As confirmed by documents released by the Defense Department, on 2 December 2002, Secretary Rumsfeld himself approved interrogation techniques at Guantanamo that included "removal of clothing," "forced grooming (shaving of facial hair etc . . .)," and "using detainees individual phobias (such as fear of dogs) to induce stress."[32] The Secretary of Defense even wrote a handwritten note questioning leniency, "I stand for 8–10 hours a day. Why is standing limited to four hours?"[33]

Amid the unfolding tragedy of abuse of prisoners in US custody in Guantanamo and Abu Ghraib, an even more sinister issue emerged. Some prisoners were not even documented. In some cases, their very existence had been hidden from the International Committee of the Red Cross (ICRC), the organization entrusted to defend the Geneva Convention. The ICRC is the most respected international monitor of prison conditions in conflict. Yet at a 17 June 2004 press conference, the Secretary of Defense admitted in reference to an Iraqi prisoner that the Central Intelligence Agency had asked that the Defense Department "not immediately register the individual. And we did that." He continued, "And we're in the process of registering him with the ICRC at the present time." The press conference was held over seven months after the person was arrested. In response to additional press questioning about why the Department did not tell the Red Cross about the prisoner, Secretary Rumsfeld said "The decision was made that it would be appropriate not to for a period. And he wasn't lost in the system. They've known where he was, and that he was in Iraq for this period of time."[34] These statements mean that senior US officials actively obstructed the work of the ICRC. The implications are disastrous for the United States and the anti-terrorism campaign.

Prisoner abuse and sliding standards of human rights protection

The conditions of detention suffered by prisoners in US custody in the anti-terrorism campaign have become a major international issue with wide and negative implications for US security. In addition to people held in the United States in the post September 11 sweeps, the United States holds detainees in Guantanamo, Afghanistan, and Iraq. The horrific abuses committed by US personnel at the Abu Ghraib prison in Baghdad have not only exposed specific crimes, but also raised questions about the nature of US conduct towards those in custody. The US Government asserts that fighting terrorism precludes permitting access to usual protections and procedures, particularly for those labeled "enemy combatants", and that they can be held without formal charges, a lawyer, or a trial, even if they are American citizens.

Although the level of abuse is dramatically different, there are disturbing similarities among the conditions in which prisoners are held in detention in the anti-terrorism campaign. In all four situations, whether in the United States, Guantanamo, Afghanistan, or Iraq, officials' willingness to relax prisoner protection rules in an anti-terrorism campaign arguably opened the door to abuse. Members of Congress, officials, the media, and the public are all trying to learn more about what practices have been condoned in the various places of detention.

In Abu Ghraib, the abuse was particularly inhumane. In contrast, prisoners held in the US after September 11 were not subject to such degrading treatment, yet they were held for extended periods without access to lawyers or family, which is not the norm in the American criminal justice system. Meanwhile, as early as 2002 the Department of Defense argued that it was not obliged to follow the Geneva Conventions on prisoners of war with respect to detainees from the war in Afghanistan who were transported to Guantanamo.[35] Indeed, practices in Guantanamo may have been explicitly transferred to Iraq. Clearly in at least one section of Abu Ghraib the Geneva Conventions were not followed. One of the reasons responsible militaries have strict codes of conduct is that – especially in wartime – power over an imprisoned enemy can easily lead to abuse. Not abiding by the Geneva Conventions in an explicit manner led to an overall relaxation in the respect for law.

The abuses have undermined domestic confidence in the government and international support for the anti-terrorism campaign. The American public cannot understand how such inhuman acts were conducted in its name. In the eyes of many people around the world, the United States has lost its moral authority. Even before the Iraq prison scandal, perceptions of poor treatment of prisoners at Guantanamo affected some countries' and individuals' willingness to work with the United States. In such cases, inadequate attention to human rights has undermined the anti-terrorism campaign. This problem is even greater following the revelations of Abu Ghraib. The US will have to work hard to regain international respect. Investigating and punishing those responsible for the atrocities at Abu Ghraib is an important step; improving respect for civil liberties at home is another.

In sum, managing the government's need for knowledge to prevent terrorism while maintaining the presumption of innocence and upholding international standards for treatment of prisoners and detainees is difficult, as illustrated by recent experience. Arguably, the United States will need to consider seriously how to ensure respect for civil rights, a subset of human rights, in the conduct of the anti-terrorism campaign.

The European experience after September 11 and March 11

After September 11, Europeans also intensified anti-terrorism measures, though with less of a sense of urgency than US policymakers. Not only were United States citizens angry and energized because their country was the victim; many Europeans also remained of convinced that what was mainly required was an extension of their existing legislation and experience stemming from their long fight against domestic terrorism. Still, European leaders understand that fighting a decentralized international threat like al-Qaeda requires new levels of cooperation across borders. The 11 March 2004 bombings in Madrid reinforced the point that Europe is also vulnerable to large-scale terrorism.

In Europe the anti-terrorist campaign runs on three tracks; not only national and global, as in the US, but also European. Intra-European measures are particularly relevant for members of the European Union, which have a framework for cooperation in Justice and Home Affairs that provides not only collaborative tools, but also legal obligations. The additional overlay of the European Union both challenges civil liberties and offers ways to mitigate concerns.

After September 11, national governments passed or enhanced their own legislation and acted to implement European measures. On 21 September 2001, the European Council adopted a Plan of Action to Combat Terrorism. Yet implementation depends on member states. At the first European Council summit after 11 March 2004, the Council urged member states to implement the policies already agreed, including the Framework Decision on the European Arrest Warrant, the Framework Decision on Combating Terrorism, the Framework Decision on Money Laundering, and "the identification, tracing, freezing, and confiscation of instrumentalities and proceeds of crime."[36] The Council also created a new post of Counter-Terrorism Coordinator, who would report to High Representative Javier Solana.[37]

The EU-wide anti-terrorism legislation raised distinct civil liberties concerns, to which the European Parliament responded by supporting the creation of an EU Network of Independent Experts in Fundamental Rights (CFR-CDF). The CFR-CDF and other human rights organizations have highlighted basic concerns, including:[38]

- Imprecision in the definition of terrorism
- Increased surveillance and detention
- Reduced privacy and relaxed management of private data
- Extension of law enforcement powers
- Changed context for judicial proceedings, including restrictions on the defense and encroachments on the presumption of innocence.

Vague definition of terrorism

Leaders on both sides of the Atlantic have charged that the potentially devastating consequences of terrorism justify enacting harsher measures than those used for tackling regular crime. Yet, as CFR-CDF noted, vague descriptions of terrorism could mean that a person may unwittingly become subject to stricter anti-terrorism prosecution for what might have seemed to be regular criminal activity, or even lawful action. For example, an official might think that financial connections to certain groups should be prosecuted as terrorist activity. Without clear definitions, there is a chance that people will inadvertently commit a crime or that lawful activity will not be undertaken to avoid the risk. As the CFR-CDF experts noted, a person should be able to understand when "he/she can be held liable."[39]

This situation is similar to the freedom of association issue in the United States. Certain associations or actions could be defined as supporting terrorism. The right of association heralded in both the US Constitution and the EU Charter of Fundamental Rights is especially vulnerable to anti-terrorism measures. The organized nature of terrorism makes prosecution of membership in certain groups an attractive and practical approach.[40] Germany, for example, already had a law against anti-democratic associations on which additional anti-terrorism legislation could be built.

However, the definitional vagueness is not surprising. For years there was little international agreement on defining who was a terrorist. The conventional wisdom was that one person's "terrorist" was another's "freedom fighter." After September 11, in national governments and international organizations including the UN, political leaders agreed that certain acts constituted terrorism, and to regard the attacks of September 11, "like any act of international terrorism, as a threat to international peace and security."[41] Thus, rather than be caught in the stale theoretical debate about defining terrorism in political terms, leaders focused on the methods used. The notion was to place certain behavior beyond the bounds of acceptability, irrespective of the political motives.

Surveillance and detention

The debate about surveillance occasioned heated debate among Europeans. Member states of the EU have very different traditions concerning what information the government can hold, and how closely citizens' movements may be watched. These differences are fundamental to the nature of political organization, but they make establishing a European standard harder. Most continental European countries have identity cards; many require people to register their names and addresses with the police, making monitoring of movement easier. In contrast, traditionally the United Kingdom has not collected such information from citizens (although it does so for foreign students.) After September 11 the UK went further, taking an exemption from the European Convention on Human Rights to expand the conditions under which the UK could detain foreign suspects. The derogation prompted an Opinion by the Council of Europe's Commissioner for Human Rights, who criticized the UK derogation to permit detention without charge with limited review, saying:

> The indefinite detention represents a severe limitation on the enjoyment of the right to liberty and security and gravely prejudices both the presumption of innocence and the right to a fair trial in the determination of one's rights and obligations or of any criminal charge brought against one. It should be recalled that an ill-founded deprivation of liberty is difficult, indeed impossible, to repair adequately.[42]

The idea of restrictions on movement runs against the flow of the European project. The Schengen Agreement was intended to facilitate the free flow of people between signatory countries. Thus, anti-terrorism measures designed to reduce contacts among people runs counter to the EU ideal of an ever closer union based on increasing connections among Europeans. Yet these links are valued as part of creating secure societies and a zone of peace and freedom within the EU. The challenge for EU leaders is how to safeguard security in an age of potentially catastrophic terrorism without undermining the ideals of the European project.

Privacy, intelligence, and data-sharing

Surveillance is a problem because it infringes on privacy, another area of concern. While the CFR-CDF experts were concerned about an overall erosion of privacy, they were especially troubled about the danger of sharing private data. The underlying concern is whether to share data about people who have not been charged with a crime. Again, as part of their efforts to find information to prevent or investigate terrorism, officials want to gather large amounts of data. However, the subjects of the data are innocent until proven guilty. Should personal details about people be shared among officials just because their names are similar to those of suspects, or because these people take a certain flight, or bank at a particular financial institution?

Data-sharing raises several questions. Are the data regarding one country being sent by another country to a third country without the knowledge of the subject? What guarantees does the sending country have that the recipient will respect the privacy of the information once it had been transmitted? Many European human rights advocates do not consider US data privacy protection to be adequate. In this realm, the civil liberties concerns mirror long-standing commercial disputes about sending electronic and other information across the Atlantic.

This issue came to the surface in the debate over whether European air carriers would have to supply the names for the new Passenger Name Record system in advance of landing in the United States. Observers ranging from members of the European Parliament to American civil rights advocates are concerned that private data are being shared beyond the level needed for law enforcement.[43] The problems are real. Airlines, including American Airlines and Jetblue Airways, have admitted that information about passengers was passed to private contractors instead of going directly to the US Transportation Security Administration.[44]

Information-sharing in the transatlantic context is highly sensitive. In addition to the questions regarding providing personal data on Europeans to American authorities, there is also a concern about releasing sensitive US intelligence to be used as evidence in trials in Europe.

Many of the September 11 hijackers had lived in Europe, and prosecutions of possible al-Qaeda accomplices in Europe could be bolstered by information gathered through American intelligence channels. However, US authorities are very reluctant to reveal information that could expose sources and methods used for intelligence gathering. At least two cases in Germany have been affected by this reticence. On 7 April 2004, a German court released Mounir al-Motassadeq, who had been convicted in February 2003 of helping to organize the 2001 terrorist attacks by assisting September 11 terrorist Mohammed Atta, whom al-Motassadeq had known when Atta had lived in Germany. On appeal, a German court ordered a retrial because evidence that might have helped al-Motassadeq's defense was not available in his first trial because it was not possible to gain a statement from a key witness held by US authorities. In related proceedings, Abdelghani Mzouri was acquitted in a German court because evidence could not be obtained from the al-Qaeda operative, Ramzi Binalshibh, who was held by the US.[45]

Law enforcement powers

The EU's cooperation on justice and home affairs means that EU measures play a role in anti-terrorism law enforcement. The EU has tasked Europol with assisting national authorities in cross-border anti-terrorism cases, though only on the request of the member states concerned. Europol has no operational powers, though the role of the EU in the area of justice and home affairs is expanding with, among others, the newly agreed common European arrest warrant.

The more immediate concern for human rights advocates, are the actions of national governments, which have also widened the scope of their anti-terrorism legislation. For example, the French Law of 15 November 2001 permitted waivers of the Code of Criminal Procedure to enable searches and seizures on the decision of a judge in anti-terrorism cases.[46] In Germany, the Federal Criminal Police (BKA) gained new powers, allowing it, in certain circumstances, to obtain information directly from banks, airlines, telecommunications companies, and others.[47] Civil liberties supporters are particularly concerned about "profiling," using gender, ethnic, religious, and other categories to characterize suspects considered likely to be terrorists. Such profiling , it is feared, could contribute to xenophobia, affecting immigration and asylum policy, and having a negative impact on security similar to the case discussed above on the US side.

Judicial proceedings

The legal changes in the anti-terrorism campaign raise concerns about how trials are conducted. In some countries, the use of anonymous witnesses in anti-terrorism trials can undermine the defendant's right to know his or her accuser. In addition, some advocates charge that freezing assets and placing people on watch lists erodes the presumption of innocence. Moreover, there are few channels of recourse for actions taken at the diplomatic level. EU members have passed two Common Positions against terrorism, yet what recourse does a person have against an EU-level diplomatic agreement? These Positions are not subject to the normal national democratic channels. It is harder to contest an EU Common Position than a national law.

Comparing the reaction to terrorism on the two sides of the Atlantic

On both sides of the Atlantic leaders have passed new legislation to advance the anti-terrorism campaign. Having been the victims of the September 11 attacks, Americans were willing to accept greater restrictions on their liberties based on their government's promise of greater security. The post-attack sense of national outrage and shock, the existence of a strong Federal Government structure, and the determination of an Administration that faced little opposition in Congress, meant that laws could be passed quickly with very little review. Rapid action in such circumstances can lead to hasty measures that infringe on civil liberties. In contrast, the EU's cumbersome decision-making process, which reflects its balance of inter-governmental and communitarian elements, means that it is harder to pass dramatic anti-terrorism legislation for the EU as a whole without review. For example, European governments have to reconsider the legislation when enacting EU laws at the national level. National governments could be subject to the same pressures to act quickly without review, as in the US, if there were the same sense of urgency. However, the EU's Charter of Fundamental Rights provides political support for civil liberties, while the Council of Europe's European Court of Human Rights provides legal recourse. Navigating societal security in democracies in an era of catastrophic terrorism raises concerns of legitimacy, but also offers mechanisms that could mitigate the worst abuses.

Liberties and legitimacy

Maintaining civil liberties while enhancing security is crucial for the well-being of our societies. To undermine our principles in the name of a narrow version of security would mean losing the reason the society should be defended in the first place. Moreover, as argued above, curtailing rights does not lead to security. Protecting societies against terrorism requires the cooperation of people within the country. Not only do people need to be vigilant observers to spot anomalies that may indicate a plot, they are also the wellspring of political support for anti-terrorism measures. Our societies are still democracies. Voters' and taxpayers' support is needed to sustain the government campaigns.

The anti-terrorism campaign needs to respect civil liberties in order to be seen as legitimate; if perceived as illegitimate, it will not be effective. This is true both domestically and internationally. If people in North America and Europe think that their own government is pursuing the wrong course, they will respond at the ballot box. (Yet civil libertarians are rightly concerned that majority populations do not respond when only the rights of minorities or immigrants are threatened.) Similarly, international cooperation, and especially transatlantic cooperation, in law enforcement will erode if the governments are seen to be violating human rights. That is why the treatment of prisoners in US custody in Guantanamo affects the anti-terrorism campaign. For over two years the treatment of prisoners at Guantanamo has been an irritant in transatlantic and international relations. The torture at Abu Ghraib prison is even more serious.

If poor conduct in the anti-terrorism campaign strains transatlantic relations, it is devastating for perceptions of the West in the Arab world. It is hard for the US to be a credible defender of democratic values if it is seen to be ignoring the Geneva Conventions and basic principles of human rights. Even if governments adhere to the letter of the national law on civil liberties, they still need to be mindful of the precepts of universal human rights. Human rights to life, liberty, and security of person are enshrined in the Universal Declaration on Human Rights, and are held by all people irrespective of nationality. Thus, even non-citizens have human rights. It is problematic that many anti-terrorism measures on preventive detention and the authorization of surveillance differentiate between citizens and non-citizens.

The Council of Europe Commissioner for Human Rights' comments in reference to a UK case could be applied more widely " . . . since these measures are applicable only to foreigners who cannot be deported, they might appear to be ushering in a two-track system of justice, where different human rights standards respectively apply to foreigners and nationals."[48] While these differences are grounded in practicality and the principles of the rights of citizens, the cleavages risk stripping non-citizens of protection due to them as holders of human rights. Anti-terrorism measures have accelerated changing attitudes towards relationships between citizens and non-citizens that were already sensitive after years of illegal immigration. If the Western world is to begin regaining a measure of credibility in the Arab world and make advances in "the war on ideas," adherence to notions of universal rights needs to become more prominent.

Mitigating mechanisms

Despite the serious concerns raised by the anti-terrorism campaign in the United States and Europe, there are mechanisms available to safeguard civil liberties and mitigate the effects of excessive authority.[49] These include parliamentary and judicial oversight, internal mechanisms for preventing abuse (such as Inspectors General or Ombudsmen), a vigilant civil society, and innovative use of technology. All of the countries in the EU are liberal democracies governed by the rule of law, as is the United States. Each country has its own laws and safeguards to constrain executive authority. The issue is how to ensure that these safeguards are preserved and not challenged by subtle assaults on fundamental civil liberties.

The United States Constitution provides for a separation of powers in which the judicial, executive, and legislative branches are separate and equal. The system of checks and balances provides for each branch of government to have some control over the other. For example, courts can overturn legislative measures. The most important judicial decisions to date in the anti-terrorism campaign are the June 2004 Supreme Court decisions. In addition, civil rights advocates have brought lawsuits against the USA Patriot Act with some success. For example, in January 2004 Federal

District Judge Audrey B. Collins struck down part of the USA Patriot Act, saying that it violated the First Amendment.[50] On the legislative side, one of the most useful measures is the "sunset clause," which authorizes a law for a certain period of time. The legislature must explicitly extend the law in order for it to remain valid. This enables legislation to terminate without a formal repeal. Therefore, the balance of proof is on those who wish to extend the given law rather than on those who wish to end it. This mechanism allows for review of legislation that may have been passed in the heat of a crisis, which is particularly relevant for anti-terrorism measures. The Patriot Act was passed with a four-year life; it is set to expire in 2005. Enacting anti-terrorism laws for limited periods requiring renewal creates a need to re-examine legislation and debate its relevance, and should be considered by European countries as well.[51]

The US executive branch also has internal measures to protect civil liberties. Although Attorney General Ashcroft was an outspoken advocate of the USA Patriot Act, some of the clearest analysis and critique of the government's detention of suspects after September 11 came from the Justice Department's own Office of the Inspector General (OIG). The OIG is an independent office that reports directly to Congress as well as to the Attorney General. The very fact that there is an Inspector General to investigate and report to Congress demonstrates that there is a senior official dedicated to protecting civil liberties.

Outside government, an active civil society energized by numerous nongovernmental organizations and independent media provide perspectives on the state of civil liberties in the United States. Immediately after September 11, there was little outcry about civil liberties. In the subsequent years, however, preventive detention and other encroachments on civil liberties have raised legitimate concerns.

In Europe, too, normal democratic structures provide recourse for perceived abuses. There is also an additional layer of protection. Most European countries, EU and non-EU members alike, are signatories of the European Convention on Human Rights. The Convention was created within the Council of Europe, but has been adopted into EU law. The European Convention on Human Rights provides a foundation for the defense of rights. From its inception in 1950, the document has contained an innovative procedure enabling individuals to take their own country to court for human rights violations.

Within the EU, the European Parliament has been active in focusing some MEP's existing interest in international human rights on civil liberties in the Union. The European Council also weighed in at its December 2003 summit meeting, extending the mandate of the existing European Monitoring Centre against Racism and Xenophobia to create a EU Human Rights Agency. Moreover, the process of adopting EU measures into national law provides an opportunity for national legislatures to discuss civil liberties.

Thus in both the United States and Europe there are judicial mechanisms that can help mitigate or overturn egregious abuses of civil liberties. These are democratic countries based on the rule of law; judicial action is effective because it is obeyed. With a somewhat more widespread use of sunset clauses, the US has useful tools that can be used to revisit or terminate legislation after it has been passed. The EU has more hurdles to enacting and implementing anti-terrorism laws, usually requiring action on EU and national levels. These procedural steps can provide time for consideration of new measures and evaluation of the impact on civil liberties. The EU could look at whether a greater use of sunset clauses might be appropriate. Whereas Americans may find that in addition to using their own judicial channels, appealing to US commitments to international standards beyond national law (such as the Geneva Conventions) or perhaps the International Covenant on Civil and Political Rights (of which the US is a signatory) could provide additional tools for defending civil liberties.

Finally, innovative use of technology may also help. Information technology experts are endeavoring to find ways to depersonalize data and develop tools for tracking who accesses government databases, in order to ensure that data are only accessed on a need-to-know basis and handled in a responsible manner.[52]

Conclusion: Europe and the US, different systems, similar problems

Although the members of the transatlantic community are liberal democracies facing similar challenges in safeguarding civil liberties amid the anti-terrorism campaign, their approaches are colored by their distinctive histories, which influence how laws are used and who uses them. For example, there are differences between countries shaped by Napoleonic law versus those molded by customary law. While many European countries have long had a Ministry of the Interior that manages internal security and special internal intelligence agencies, the United States has not. Even the United Kingdom has a single internal security agency, MI5.

After intense debate, the United States, in the wake of September 11, has chosen another model, merging a number of existing agencies that managed issues ranging from border control to customs, immigration, and eventually airport safety, into a Department of Homeland Security, but leaving the new department without an intelligence collection capability. Thus, despite the wide scope of the work of the Department of Homeland Security, the US does not have a single internal security agency. For example, judicial action, investigation, and prevention of terrorism remain with the Department of Justice and the Federal Bureau of Investigation.[53]

Still, the countries in the transatlantic area can learn from each other. They are liberal democracies facing similar challenges in the anti-terrorism campaign. They need to begin by recognizing that protecting civil liberty and national security is not a trade-off. The anti-terrorism campaign cannot be fully effective if is not seen to be legitimate, domestically and internationally. Moreover, as argued above, mitigating mechanisms such as legislative oversight, judicial review, and sunset clauses can help a country advance both liberty and security.

Governments on both sides of the Atlantic should look closely at how they handle freedom of speech and of association, preventive detention, and the use of profiling in the anti-terrorism campaign. Moreover, parliaments, and civil liberties and human rights groups need to remain vigilant.

Not only can the US and Europe help each other live up to their own standards, they also can help set human rights standards for the international anti-terrorism campaign. They can begin by close scrutiny of the terms of law enforcement cooperation with countries with weak safeguards for the rights of the accused. North America and Europe can be proud of their tradition of defending civil liberties. They should not depart from their values. Respecting civil liberties can strengthen societies and help deepen the values that enable them to withstand the challenges of the threat of mass terrorism.

Notes

1 Attorney General John Ashcroft, "Prepared Remarks of Attorney General John Ashcroft, Federalist Society National Convention," 15 November 2003, p. 2, available online at: www.usdoj.gov/ag/speeches/2003/111503ag.htm.

2 A. C. Muzaffer, D. Meissner, D. G. Papadenetriou *et al.*, "America's challenge: domestic security, civil liberties, and national unity after September 11," Washington, DC: Migration Policy Institute, 2003, p. 8, available online at: www.migrationpolicy.org.

3 The War Relocation Authority noted, "The residents of the relocation centers, however, have never been found guilty – either individually or collectively – of any such acts or intentions. They are merely a group of American residents who happen to have Japanese ancestors and who happened to be living in a potential combat zone shortly after the outbreak of war. All evidence available to the War Relocation Authority indicates that the great majority of them are completely loyal to the United States." War Relocation Authority, "Relocation of Japanese Americans," Washington, DC: War Relocation Authority, May 1943. Online, available at: www.sfmuseum.org/hist10/relocbook.html.

4 "September 11, 2001," The White House, available online at: www.whitehouse.gov/march11/timeline/oneb.html.

5 George W. Bush, "Address to a Joint Session of Congress and the American People," 20 September 2001, available online at: www.whitehouse.gov/news/releases/2001/09/print/20010920–8.html.

6 Ibid.

7 George W. Bush, "Remarks by President George W. Bush at Signing of the Patriot Act, Anti-Terrorism Legislation," 26 October 2001, available online at: www.lifeandliberty.gov/subs/speeches/p_bush_102601.htm.

8 See John Ashcroft, "Statement of John Ashcroft Attorney General of the United States before the Committee on Appropriation, Subcommittee on Departments of Commerce, Justice, State, the Judiciary and Related Agencies," 26 February 2002, available online at: www.usdoj.gov/ag/testimony/2002/FY2003AG_WrittenStatement-Senate.htm, and John Ashcroft, "Prepared Remarks of Attor-

ney General John Ashcroft, Federalist Society National Convention," 15 November 2003, available online at: www.usdoj/ag/speeches/2003/111503ag.htm.

9 John Ashroft, "Prepared Remarks of Attorney General John Ashcroft to the Federalist Society National Convention," 15 November 2003, p. 2.

10 The American Civil Liberties Union, "The USA Patriot Act and Government Actions that Threaten our Civil Liberties," available online at www.aclu.org.

11 George W. Bush, "State of the Union Address," 20 January 2004, available online at: www.whitehouse.gov.

12 Of the 19 hijackers, 15 were from Saudi Arabia, 2 from the United Arab Emirates, and one each from Egypt and Lebanon. See G. J. Tenet, "Unclassified Version of Director of Central Intelligence George J. Tenet's Testimony before the Joint Inquiry into Terrorist Attacks Against the United States," 18 June 2002, available online at: www.odci.gov/cia/public_affairs/speeches/2002/dci_testimony_06182002.html.

13 Judge Audrey B. Collins, quoted in E. Lichtblau, "Citing Free Speech, Judge Voids Part of Antiterror Act," *The New York Times*, 27 January 2004, p. A16.

14 American Library Association, "Resolution on the USA Patriot Act and Related Measures that Infringe on the Rights of Library Users," Adopted by the ALA Council, 29 January 2003, available online at: www.ala.org/Template.cfm?Section=ifresolutions&Template=/ContentManagement/ContentDisplay.cfm&ContentID=11891.

15 American Civil Liberties Union (ACLU), "Surveillance Under the USA Patriot Act," p. 1, and American Civil Liberties Union (ACLU), "Section 215: Frequently Asked Questions," 24 October 2002, p. 1. Both available online at www.aclu.org/news (both accessed 4 December 2003).

16 ACLU, op. cit., p. 2.

17 Amnesty International, "United States of America: Amnesty International's concerns regarding post September 11 detentions in the USA," p. 1, available online at web.amnesty.org (accessed 4 December 2003) and Migration Policy Institute, "America's Challenge," p. 9.

18 Migration Policy Institute, "America's Challenge," p. 9.

19 US Department of Justice, Office of the Inspector General, "Report to Congress on Implementation of Section 1001 of the USA Patriot Act," 17 July 2003, p. 12, available online at: www.usdoj.gov/oig.

20 Human Rights Watch, "Presumption of Guilt: Human Rights Abuses of Post-September 11 Detainees," Vol. 14(4), August 2002, p. 4, available online at: www.hrw.org.

21 US Department of Justice, Office of the Inspector General, 17 July 2003, p. 12.

22 US Department of Justice, Office of the Inspector General, 17 July 2003, p. 13.

23 US Department of Justice, Office of the Inspector General, 17 July 2003, p. 13.

24 "For Whom the Liberty Bell Tolls – Civil Liberties," *The Economist*, Special Report, 31 August 2003.

25 "A mixed verdict on the terror war: Detainees have right to US courts, justices rule," CNN.com, (accessed 29 June 2004).

26 The Associated Press, "Judge: Charge or Release Padilla," 28 February 2005, available online at: www.cbsnews.com/stories/2005/02/28/terror/printable677099.shtml.

27 Supreme Court of the United States, "Rasul *et al.*, v. Bush, President of the United States, et al." No. 03–334, 28 June 2004, part IV, pp. 12–13.

28 Associated Press, "Pentagon Might Release Some Detainees," 2 July 2004, available online at: www.nytimes.com/aponline/national/AP-Pentagon-Guantanamo.html?pagewanted=print&position (accessed 2 July 2004).

29 Editorial, "A Vote for Control," *The New York Times*, 2 July 2004, available online at: www.nytimes.com/2004/07/02/opinion/02FRI1.html?pagewanted= print&position.

30 Supreme Court of the United States, Opinion of O'Connor, J., "Yaser Esam Hamdi and Esam Fouad Hamdi, as next friend of Yaser Esam Hamdi, Petitioners v. Donald H. Rumsfeld, Secretary of Defense, et al." No. 03–6696, 28 June 2004, p. 23 (Initial draft available online before formal publication in United States Reports.)

31 Ibid, p. 25.

32 Department of Defense, Joint Task Force 170, Guantanamo Bay Cuba, "Memo for Commander, United States Southern Command, Section 2b (10), 2b (11) and 2b (12). This document lists the specific types of methods approved in Secretary Rumsfeld's 2 December 2002 memo, which is available as William J. Haynes II, General Counsel, "Counter-Resistance Techniques," Action Memo to Secretary of Defense, approved 2 December 2002. These and related Defense Department materials were declassified and released on 22 June 2004, and are available at US Department of Defense. "DOD Provides Details on Interrogation Process," News Release, No. 596–04, 22 June 2004, available online at: www.defenselink.mil/releases/2004/nr20040622–0930.html.

33 US Department of Defense, "DOD Provides Details on Interrogation Process," and Human Rights Watch, "The Logic of Torture," 28 June 2004, available online at hrw.org/english/docs/2004/06/28/usint8967_txt.htm. The Secretary's handwritten note is visible on the Defense Department's pdf document.

34 Donald Rumsfeld, "Defense Department Regular Briefing," 21 June 2004, available online at: www.defenselink.mil/transcripts/2004/tr20040617secdefe 0881.html.

35 "The United States has determined that Al Qaida and Taliban individuals under the control of the Department of Defense are not entitled to prisoner of war status for purposes of the Geneva Conventions of 1949." In Secretary of Defense, "Status of Taliban and Al Qaida," Memorandum for the Chairman of the Joint Chiefs of Staff, 19 January 2002, § 1, available at "DOD Provides Details on Interrogation Process," News Release, No. 596–04, 22 June 2004, op cit.

36 European Council, "Declaration Combating Terrorism," 25 March 2004, Brussels, § 5.

37 Ibid, § 14.

38 See the EU Network of Independent Experts in Fundamental Rights (CFR-CDF), "The Balance Between Freedom and Security in the Response by the European Union and Its Member States to the Terrorist Threats," Thematic Comment submitted to the European Commission Directorate General Justice and Home Affairs, 31 March 2003. CFR-CDR stands for "Collection of Fundamental Rights–Collection Droits Fondamentaux." Amnesty International, "Amnesty International's assessment of EU human rights policy: Recommendations to the Irish EU Presidency."

39 EU Network of Independent Experts in Fundamental Rights (CFR-CDF), p. 16.

40 Ibid, p. 8.

41 United Nations Security Council, Resolution 1368, S/res/1368 (2001), adopted on 12 September 2001, available online at: www.ods-dds-ny.un.org/doc/ UNDOC/GEN/N01/533/82/PDF/N0153382.pdf.

42 Council of Europe, "Derogation under Article 15 ECHR exercised by the United Kingdom/Public Danger After 11 September 2001," cited in EU Network of Independent Experts in Fundamental Rights, p. 35.

43 European Parliament, "First Report on the Implementation of the Data Protection Directive (95/46/EC), Committee on Citizens' Freedoms and Rights,

Justice and Home Affairs," 24 February 2004, Marco Cappato, Rapporteur, A5–0104/2004. See also Article 29: Data Protection Working Party, "Opinion 2/2004 on the Adequate Protection of Personal Data Contained in the PNR of Air Passengers to be Transferred to the United States' Bureau of Customs and Border Protection," 29 January 2004, available online at: europa.eu.int/comm/ internal_market/privacy/docs/wpdocs/2004/wp87_en.pdf.

44 D. Roberts, "American admits air data breach," *The Financial Times*, 12 April 2004, p. 15.

45 Issues of intelligence and judicial cooperation are covered in detail in Chapters 6 and 7 of this book; B. Benoit, "Court frees man jailed over 9/11 attacks," *The Financial Times*, 8 April 2004, p. 4.

46 CFR-CDF, p. 32.

47 Ibid, p. 29.

48 Council of Europe Commissioner, cited in CDF-CFR, p. 35.

49 The author wishes to thank Anja Dalgaard-Nielsen for her comments on these issues.

50 E. Lichtblau, "Citing Free Speech, Judge Voids Part of Antiterror Act," *The New York Times*, 27 January 2004, p. A16.

51 A. Dalgaard-Nielsen, *Civil Liberties and Counter-Terrorism: A European Point of View*, Center for Transatlantic Relations, School of Advanced International Studies, Johns Hopkins University, Opinions, February 2004.

52 Markle Foundation, The Task Force on National Security in the Information Age, "Protecting America's Freedom in the Information Age," 7 December 2002, and "Creating a Trusted Network for Homeland Security," 2 December 2003. Both available online at www.markletaskforce.org.

53 For further discussion of the US reorganization, see Chapter 1 of this book.

9 Transatlantic societal security
A new paradigm for a new era

Daniel S. Hamilton

This volume has examined efforts to protect North American and European societies in the wake of horrific terrorist attacks on both continents since 11 September 2001. While there has been no effort to force consensus among the authors in this volume, a basic theme does emerge: effective homeland security may begin at home, but in an age of catastrophic terrorism no nation is home alone. If Europeans and Americans are to be safer than they are today, individual national efforts must be aligned with more effective transatlantic cooperation. Such efforts, in turn, can serve as the core of more effective global measures.

Just because the Cold War is over does not mean that Europeans and North Americans are less dependent on one another. Without systematic trans-European and transatlantic coordination, each side of the Atlantic is at greater risk of attack. Uneven "homeland security" efforts within Europe leave North America more vulnerable, particularly since North America's security is organically linked to Europe's vulnerability to terrorist infiltration. Similarly, if US and Canadian efforts render the North American homeland less vulnerable to attack, terrorists may turn more readily to "softer" targets in Europe.[1]

Neither the framework for the transatlantic relationship nor the way European or North American governments are currently organized adequately address the challenge of catastrophic terrorism. There have been some promising beginnings, but they have been *ad hoc* achievements rather than integrated elements of a more comprehensive approach. Individual efforts must now be complemented by a systematic, high-profile effort to advance "transatlantic societal security" in areas ranging from intelligence, counterterrorism, financial coordination, and law enforcement, to customs, air and seaport security, bio-defense, critical infrastructure protection, and other activities.

Three hurdles to effective cooperation

Throughout the preceding chapters our authors have highlighted three issues that have consistently plagued transatlantic cooperation in this area.

1 *Neither the United States nor Europe is yet organized to advance an effective homeland security effort*

The primary focus of American and European efforts following the September 11 and March 11 attacks, understandably, has been on the domestic aspects of the fight against terrorism. It is essential to ensure that both sides of the Atlantic have the right mechanisms in place both to prevent such attacks and to deal with the consequences if prevention efforts fall short, but the different ways each has chosen to do so have complicated transatlantic cooperation.

The US has yet to digest the implications of either its domestic reorganization or its multifaceted approach to combating terrorism. The Bush Administration's immediate homeland security response – a scattershot burst of urgent domestic initiatives, with little effort at prioritization or consideration of their international impact – has given way to the most extensive reorganization of federal agencies since the end of World War II. The Department of Homeland Security is a huge, multifunction entity encompassing 22 different agencies, with more than 100 bureaus or other subsidiary elements, each with its own distinct culture. The new Department has the potential to bolster the operational capacity of key agencies; improve the way the Federal Government gathers and dispenses sensitive information about possible terrorist threats; enhance US capacity to respond to terrorist attacks; and ensure better oversight of federal security efforts. Unfortunately, these goals have not yet been achieved. Much effort has been consumed by bureaucratic turf wars. The major challenge will be to weld these disparate agencies together without losing sight of the main mission – to prevent, protect, and respond to future terrorist attacks on US soil.[2]

The Department of Homeland Security lacks the type of authority over US intelligence agencies that would enable it to help shape intelligence collection priorities, the international dimension of its activities continues to be weak, and its relationship with the Defense Department remains murky. Moreover, Congress – not the Executive Branch – is pushing through the most far-reaching reorganization of the intelligence services in 50 years. The creation of a US National Intelligence Director and other initiatives stemming from the recommendations of the Commission investigating the September 11 attacks will further complicate matters in the short term, even as they may lead to more effective US intelligence operations over the medium term.

US efforts are matched by a Byzantine collection of efforts on the other side of the Atlantic. The European Union, having just expanded to 25 nations, must now address the domestic security needs of 456 million people, with more to come in the next few years. But as Anja Dalgaard-Nielsen has explained, the EU is not a federal state and its powers cannot be compared directly to those of the United States. Responsibilities are scattered among a confusing array of actors at the local, national, and EU levels. Civil protection remains primarily the preserve of member states, and there are major turf wars between the European Commission and the European Council. Some competencies and most capabilities needed for an effective European effort are still lagging. There is no European "Minister for Homeland Security" available to the US Secretary of Homeland Security. The EU Coordinator for Counterterrorism, appointed for the first time in the spring of 2004, has neither line authority over Commission bureaucrats or member state agencies, nor a significant budget to promote harmonization of policies, procedures, standards, or equipment, which varies widely across member states. He cannot prescribe; he can only persuade. He reports to the High Representative for Foreign and Security Policy in the European Council, and thus is of a lower level than the US Secretary, and works out of the European Council rather than the European Commission, and so only has a small staff at his disposal.

In the meantime, the EU suffers gaps in intelligence-sharing, and interoperability between the police, judicial and intelligence services is questionable. SitCen, the center for intelligence in the Council Secretariat, analyzes information, but operational work remains the exclusive competence of the national security and intelligence services. There is neither a European FBI nor a European CIA. The new European Network and Information Security Agency created in early 2004 cannot tread on member state authority over issues concerning public security or criminal law.

In short, both sides face serious organizational challenges. The Bush Administration's approach to homeland security has represented more an aggregation of discrete elements, ranging from counterterrorist intelligence, border security, risk management and cargo screening to health and other issues. It remains mired in the bureaucratics of its own reorganization, and has failed to integrate homeland security into the mainstream of national security thinking. The sum is less than the parts, and many parts are still moving to their own beat. The European reaction, in turn, has been concentrated mainly within the areas of intelligence, justice, and law enforcement. Preventive and protective efforts still consist of a patchwork of contributions by the European Union, its member states, and individual ministries, agencies, and services within those states. Links to non-EU members are uneven. And the interaction between these unwieldy, multi-jurisdictional approaches on each side of the Atlantic has complicated efforts to boost transatlantic cooperation.

2 Whereas US efforts represent a radical break with traditional American approaches to security and reflect a tendency to characterize the issue as one of war and peace, initial European efforts represented an extension of previous efforts to combat terrorism and reflect a tendency to characterize the issue as one of crime and justice

The attacks of 11 September 2001 changed the United States in many ways, but particularly in the way Americans think about their security. For a century Americans thought of "national" security as something to be advanced far from American shores. The United States invested massively to project power quickly and decisively to any point on the globe, and invested meagerly to protect Americans at home. September 11 shattered that perspective. On September 11, Americans learned that their greatest strength – their open society – could be used against them. The September 11 attacks were not only an attack on freedom; they were, as *The Economist* noted, "an attack through freedom." Al-Qaeda used the very instruments of a free society to achieve its murderous aims.[3]

Now, Americans share a strange sense that they are both uniquely powerful and uniquely vulnerable. Partisan divisions within the United States are fierce, but they obscure a deeper consensus that the threat of WMD terrorism warrants a reframing of US foreign and domestic policies. Americans disagree intensely over whether the US should have invaded Iraq. They disagree over the degree to which public security efforts may intrude on personal liberties. But most agree that America is engaged in a global war on terrorism, and most are willing to project American power abroad to "win" that war.[4] They are far more receptive to radical breaks with traditional thinking, far more inclined to support crash efforts to protect the homeland, and far less concerned with breaking diplomatic crockery along the way.

Just as Americans have sought to understand the consequences of September 11 within the context of their own national experience, European views have been colored by the kind of domestic terrorism that has confronted them for the past three decades. During that period, more than 5,000 lives have been lost to terrorism in Britain, Ireland, and Spain alone.

European experience with a particular brand of domestic terrorism explains in part the nature of the European response to the terrorist attacks of September 11 and March 11. In each case, solidarity was immediately declared with the victims[5] and the domestic response was concentrated in the areas of justice and law enforcement. Overall, however, reduction of vulnerability and protection against catastrophic terrorism were accorded relatively low priority. Most Europeans view terrorism itself as a tactic rather than an enemy.

Whereas the homeland security effort in the US has been waged with the rhetoric of war, such efforts in Europe have been viewed largely through the perspective of crime. Whereas US officials are suddenly haunted by the prospect of further – and perhaps even more catastrophic – attacks, European officials have long been taunted by domestic terrorists, who have argued that a government's own zeal to apprehend terrorists would lead it to subvert the very rules of the open society it sought to protect.

These perspectives influence the way in which each side has addressed the threat. By and large, American attitudes toward terrorism have been driven by potential consequences, and thus oriented to augmenting and integrating efforts at threat assessment, proactive law enforcement, and robust medical and public health capacities, as well as "taking the fight to the enemy," so as to eliminate as many vulnerabilities as possible. European approaches tend to turn on probabilities, and thus most European governments view terrorism as a problem that can be assessed and dealt with on an emergent basis, after particular threats have arisen. These differing perspectives complicate transatlantic cooperation, as American critics charge Europeans with complacency and European critics accuse Americans of extremism.

3 These difficulties, in turn, have been exacerbated by the negative spillover from a host of other transatlantic disagreements

Transatlantic cooperation in areas related to homeland security has been rendered particularly difficult due to policy differences over a host of other issues, including but not limited to the Iraq war. It is not an exaggeration to say that differences over Iraq produced the gravest crisis in transatlantic relations since the birth of the Atlantic Alliance. In a matter of only 18 months, each side squandered the political capital it had amassed following the September 11 attacks. The US-led war in Iraq triggered a virulent wave of anti-Americanism across Europe, not seen in decades. Similarly, in the United States, opposition and resentment towards Europe – notably the French – swelled along with European resistance to war in Iraq. The huge resentments generated by the US-led pre-emptive war, including in such allied countries as Britain, Spain, and Italy, affected all other aspects of US–European cooperation.

Differences over Iraq, however, were but the most prominent of transatlantic squabbles, which included European criticism of the Bush Administration's treatment of suspected individuals in the United States and suspected terrorist fighters being held at Guantanamo Bay naval station in Cuba, and of its refusal to participate in international agreements ranging from the International Criminal Court and the Kyoto Protocol on climate change to a worldwide ban on antipersonnel land mines, a global treaty to protect biodiversity, a verification mechanism for the Biological Weapons, Control Treaty, and the Comprehensive Test Ban Treaty. The administration's supporters retorted that Europeans seemed eager to lecture Americans about US failings but appeared less willing to spend the money necessary to make European troops effective, were too absorbed with the details of deeper and wider European integration to recognize the dangers posed by terrorists wielding weapons of mass destruction, were eager to trumpet "noble" multilateralist instincts in contrast to America's "retrograde" unilateralism (except when it came to international rules that did not support EU preferences), and failed to advance economic reforms that could sustain European prosperity or anchor world growth in the New Economy. These quarrels, in turn, were exacerbated by a series of transatlantic spats over such traditionally domestic issues as food safety, corporate governance, and the death penalty. Taken together, these disputes sucked the political oxygen out of any possible high-profile transatlantic initiatives to enhance societal security.

Resilience in the face of difficulties

Despite these hurdles, a good deal has been done on both sides of the Atlantic to make life safer for ordinary citizens. Our authors have outlined a considerable number of cooperative intra-European and transatlantic efforts, ranging from border security, air transport, and container traffic to judicial, law enforcement, intelligence and even wider foreign policy issues.

Within Europe, the EU has created an European Arrest Warrant and started joint investigation teams for criminal investigation. It created Eurojust to improve the coordination of member states' law enforcement activities to help with assistance and extradition requests, and to support investigations. The EU has adopted new legislation on terrorist financing and beefed up laws against money laundering. Europol is collecting, sharing, and analyzing information about international terrorism, and assessing EU member state performance. National legislation was tightened by key EU member states. Following the March 11 attacks the EU adopted a solidarity clause that commits member states to help each other to prevent and protect against terrorist attacks and to assist each other in case an attack happens. Moreover, European nations have agreed to develop an integrated threat analysis capability at the EU level.

The US and the EU have stepped up their cooperation. Mutual legal assistance and extradition agreements have been signed. Intelligence-sharing has improved, especially information about specific individuals suspected of ties to terrorism. In 2004 the US and EU signed agreements to improve container security, expand customs cooperation, improve public–private partnerships to ensure transportation security, and transfer passenger name record (PNR) data. They agreed to enhance information exchange to target and interdict maritime threats, work more closely through Interpol to deal with lost and stolen passports and other border issues, incorporate interoperable biometric identifiers into travel documentation, continue a policy dialogue on border and transport security, and start a dialogue on improving capabilities to respond to terrorist attacks involving chemical, biological, radiological or nuclear weapons.

In fact, transatlantic solidarity in this area has continued despite tensions over Iraq. The European Union's Security Strategy, approved in December 2003, echoes the US National Security Strategy's view of terrorism and the proliferation of weapons of mass destruction as two top threats. In April 2004, EU members rejected Osama bin Laden's offer of peace and a truce if they would withdraw their forces from Muslim countries. The June 2004 US–EU Summit Declaration on Terrorism set out on paper, at least, an ambitious agenda for further collaboration.

A number of these initiatives are also interesting for broader reasons. First, transatlantic efforts have helped to advance deeper European integration. The creation of the European arrest warrant and the formation of Eurojust, for example, would scarcely have come about without intense US pressure.

Second, the US is gradually accepting the EU as a bilateral partner in issues of societal protection. As Winer notes, the US–EU mutual extradition and legal assistance treaties represent a significant expansion of traditional bilateral cooperation in law enforcement, and modify transatlantic legal assistance in combating transnational crime in 26 countries. They are the first of their kind to be successfully negotiated between the EU and a third party. Given the divergences in European and US legal systems concerning the death penalty, as well as standards in sentencing and for the protection of personal data, these agreements would have been a political impossibility before September 11.

Third, the US is grudgingly accepting EU standards on issues of vital national importance. US cooperation with Europol, for instance, enables the US to share in the EU's growing development of databases and capabilities, based on the EU's own standards for data protection and privacy.

Fourth, as Koslowski points out, transatlantic cooperation on container security, PNR data transfer, and biometric passports is very significant because it requires acceptance of mutual constraints on a broad range of state action in the area of border control – one of the defining aspects of territorial sovereignty. The Container Security Initiative, for instance, is reciprocal, meaning not only that US customs officials can operate in such ports as Rotterdam, Le Havre, Hamburg, and Algeciras, but also that European inspectors could be stationed in Boston, Houston, Long Beach or Shreveport. Such a program is perhaps but the harbinger of a coming revolution in border affairs that creates "virtual" borders far from a nation's territory.

Moreover, such efforts are not starting from scratch. As both Winer and Lewis demonstrate, when terrorism became the overriding focus of transatlantic security discussions after 11 September 2001, a growing substructure of cooperative efforts to combat criminal and financial threats had already developed among the US and the EU, the G7, the OECD countries, and related interests through the 1990s. These initiatives provided a solid platform on which additional counterterrorism activities could be based.

In short, despite practical, conceptual, and political obstacles to deeper transatlantic cooperation in the area of homeland security, both sides have recognized that deeper collaboration is essential if either side of the Atlantic is to be more secure, and are breaking new ground in their efforts to advance their common security. Taken together, the growing array of US–European cooperative ventures provides ample evidence for a rethinking of homeland security to span the transatlantic space. These agreements underscore the resilience of the transatlantic partnership even in the face of serious disagreements.

This is an important conclusion, because much, much more needs to be done. Borders on both sides of the Atlantic are still relatively unprotected. Public health systems and first responders lack basic equipment and expertise to respond to chemical or biological attack. Most cities lack basic detection equipment regarding hazardous materials. Critical infrastructure remains largely unprotected against sabotage. Airline passengers are screened rigorously, while airline cargo screening is a token effort. Of the 16 million cargo containers that reach American shores each year, 95 percent enter the United States without any sort of physical inspection whatsoever, and the figures are similar for Europe. The agreements on extradition and mutual legal assistance signed at the 2003 US–EU Summit have yet to be ratified on either side of the Atlantic. This lag is hampering the possibility for enhanced joint investigative undertakings and enhanced tools to identify terrorist bank accounts. Difficulties continue over passports, visas, and aviation security. And while EU and US negotiators have been able to surmount difficulties associated with differing legal regimes governing privacy and personal data protection, information-sharing remains a thorny issue.

Moreover, many of the above steps reflect a response to the past tactics of al-Qaeda and do not anticipate possible future means by which that organization or other terrorist groups might try to harm North Americans or Europeans. Some important strides have been made, but with hundreds of thousands of miles of unprotected coastline, tens of thousands of chemical plants and small airports, and hundreds of nuclear power plants – among other things – North America and Europe each still offer a rich target list for terrorists.

While various initiatives have been interesting and useful, they remain isolated successes, rather than integrated elements of more comprehensive strategies. More effective cooperation is needed in areas ranging from law enforcement and financial coordination to information- and intelligence-sharing, customs, air and seaport security, and protection against bio-terrorism. If Americans and Europeans are to engage successfully in a more systematic effort, they need to do three things. First, each must close a conceptual gap they have when thinking about security. Second, greater transatlantic consensus must be generated around some core propositions that integrate homeland security and national security. Finally, these propositions must be applied to practical efforts to advance what might be called "transatlantic societal security."

Thinking about transatlantic societal security

If Americans and Europeans are to be effective in protecting their societies in the age of catastrophic terrorism, each has to close a gap in the way they think about security.

Despite September 11's brutal message that domestic and national security are deeply intertwined, Washington continues to maintain false distinctions between the two. The result: the Executive Office of the President houses a Homeland Security Council and a National Security Council, and the United States has a Homeland Security Strategy and a National Security Strategy. This duality not only reflects a compartmentalized view of security, it also has important implications for resource distribution. Despite almost daily warnings about possible terrorist attacks, for instance, federal funding for homeland security in the two years following September 11 represents only 4 percent of the Pentagon's annual budget.[6] Even though the Department of Homeland Security embodies a large reorganization of many agencies, it represents little more than an incremental, *ad hoc* adjustment to a national security system designed generations ago for a world that no longer exists, to win a war that no longer needs to be fought. The Cold War legacy maintains its grip on Washington's national security culture, which continues to be based on a forward defense mentality in which the US military is primarily based and trained to fight far from America's shores, rather than to protect the territory of the United States at or within its borders.[7] In a nation bounded by two oceans, the natural instinct is still to fight enemies abroad so they don't need to be fought at home. But in this age of catastrophic terrorism, oceans can provide a false sense of security – a point driven home brutally on September 11.[8]

There are some positive signs. The FBI, for example, which has long favored its criminal justice mission over its national security mission, is turning to prevention rather than after-the-fact investigation. Slowly and sporadically, public health considerations are being incorporated into national security thinking. However, overall the disconnects continue.

During the 1950s and early 1960s efforts were made at civil defense, but these were largely abandoned because of their perceived futility in the face of nuclear Armageddon. Today, however, Americans face the prospect of a catastrophic attack that could kill millions. In such a situation, civil defense efforts could save thousands of lives, and adequate preparations could ensure that critical functions of society continue after such an attack. These are very different factors to consider – and they require a rethink of civilian defense programs.

Europe's major powers have faced a different yet equally important disconnect in their security thinking. During the Cold War, "territorial security" was linked to a potential Soviet assault across the plains of Central Europe, and was thus primarily an issue for the military, whereas defense against terror was considered primarily within a domestic context of emergency response and law enforcement. Yet terrorism rooted in internal struggles cannot compare to the geographical scope and transnational dimensions of al-Qaeda, which has been operating in scores of countries worldwide. And when facing the potential for catastrophic terrorism, the concept of "territorial integrity" is inadequate, since the aim of such terrorism is not to acquire territory but to destroy or disrupt society.

In short, compartmentalized approaches to security remain powerful on both sides of the Atlantic at a time when the major challenge may not be that of projecting massive force abroad, saving one's territory or responding to emergencies, but rather ensuring the functioning of society in the face of a potentially catastrophic attack. A systematic approach to *societal* security – an integrated effort to develop the capacity to prevent, protect, and respond to a catastrophic attack so that society can continue to function – is an urgent addition to the transatlantic agenda.

What might "societal security" entail, and how could it be advanced on both sides of the Atlantic? For a start, it may be useful to look at Nordic and Swiss concepts of "total defense" and the British concept of "societal resilience," and particularly how these concepts are being adapted to the security challenges of the day.

Switzerland and Nordic nations have long operated with concepts of "total defense" that may offer some guidance for the integrated system of prevention, protection, and response that the US and major European nations are currently struggling to create. While the small size and unique traditions of these countries may limit the full applicability of their approaches to others, and while each of these countries faces significant challenges of its own as it adapts to new challenges, the thrust of their efforts offers relevant points of departure for homeland security. Not only have traditional Nordic/Swiss concepts entailed integrated plans and common exercises for central and local authorities, first responders, the military, and the private sector in order to promote a coordinated approach; in light of today's threats total defense itself is also getting a facelift in ways that are of surprising relevance to the US and its allies.

Traditional approaches to total defense focused on mobilizing a society's resources to support the military in case of a traditional conflict with a foreign enemy.[9] Today this relationship is being reversed: instead of mobilizing civil society to come to the aid of the military in the face of external attack, the military is now one element to be mobilized as part of an overall response to major societal disruptions, including terrorism. Today the main focus is on preparing society for peacetime crises, but in ways that may also benefit preparedness for catastrophic attack by a thinking enemy. In this context, deterrence takes on a different cast than during the Cold War. Rather than basing deterrence on the threat to impose costs on the opponent, in the context of societal security the focus is on denying terrorists their objectives. Deterrence is based on the terrorists' perception of the robustness of preventive measures designed to detect and respond to threats prior to an incident or to protect/harden potential targets against attack – in short, to convince terrorists that it just isn't worth the effort.

After the Soviet Union collapsed, security planning in a number of these countries shifted to societal security as the central focus for the national mobilization of resources. There has been a paradigmatic shift from Cold War total defense systems, which focused on the security of the territory, to post-Cold War societal security systems, which focus on the security of critical functions of society. In the age of catastrophic terrorism it is not the territory of Western nations *per se* that is at stake, but the ability of democratic governments and free societies to function.[10]

The United Kingdom has responded in somewhat similar fashion, operating under the somewhat different but analogous concept of societal "resilience." The British Government established a Civil Contingencies Secretariat in the Cabinet Office shortly before the September 11 attacks to improve the UK's resilience against disruptive challenges. "Resilience" is defined as the ability at national, regional, and local levels to detect, prevent, and if necessary handle disruptive challenges. These could range from floods, through outbreaks of human or animal disease, to terrorist attacks.[11]

The advantage of these approaches is that they are capacity-based rather than threat-based, and they align efforts to improve internal security with those to promote external security. The disadvantage is that for the most part these efforts have been advanced on a national basis and yet, given both the interdependence of complex systems and the nature of contagious disease, effective societal security must also include an international dimension.

A systematic, high-profile effort on societal security could help frame and spark more effective transatlantic cooperation in a range of interrelated areas. Such an effort is unlikely, however, unless there is greater consensus around two basic points.

1 The threat is real – and common. Europe and North America are both base and targets for catastrophic terrorism

Unfortunately, as Jenkins notes, many in Europe and not a few in the United States view the attacks of September 11 and March 11 as isolated incidents. Some in Europe also see terrorism as principally America's problem – one they believe Washington has exacerbated through its own actions, particularly the war in Iraq. Even though European governments promptly rejected Osama bin Laden's offer of immunity to those countries that pulled their troops out of the Middle East, and even though Europe and the United States are working closely to deal with terrorism, there is still appeal in policies that demonstrate distance from Washington.

These political squabbles, however, cannot be allowed to distract from a basic fact: Europe is both a base for and a target of international terrorism. It would be foolhardy to assume that Europe will not be a target of future terrorist attacks. Al-Qaeda has directly attacked three European members of NATO – the UK, Turkey, and Spain – and has tried to launch attacks in other parts of Europe as well. Al-Qaeda cells have killed European tourists in North Africa. Terrorist cells have been discovered in London, Rotterdam, Milan, Hamburg, and Frankfurt, as have active recruitment efforts by Europe-based radicals in various parts of the world. Plots have been uncovered against the Strasbourg Christmas market, planes using Heathrow Airport, the French tourist island La Reunion, the Russian and US embassies in Paris, the US embassies in Rome and Sarajevo, a US military base in Belgium, and US military facilities in Great Britain. Switzerland and other nations are major hubs for financial transactions by letterbox companies linked to al-Qaeda. Moreover, radicals based in London and Lyon have managed to manufacture and test toxins like ricin and botulism, presumably for attacks across Europe, before being arrested by the authorities. France, Germany, Turkey, Italy, Bosnia, and the UK have all uncovered terrorist activity linked to al-Qaeda. One of the terrorists who crashed into the World Trade Center once flew a precise flight plan over unprotected nuclear installations and key political and economic institutions along the Rhine and Ruhr. Moreover, at least two of Europe's "old" terrorist groupings – the ETA in Spain and offshoots of the IRA in Northern Ireland – remain active, and the horrific school massacre in Beslan emphatically underscored the potential for spillover of terrorism related to the situation in Chechnya. There is simply no question that international terrorism constitutes an active threat to both Europe and North America.[12]

2 *Transatlantic efforts can be the motor of effective multilateral efforts*

Given the nature and scope of the threat, many solutions will ultimately have to be global. There is some recognition of this on both sides of the Atlantic. The 9/11 Commission reports that America's homeland is, in fact, "the planet." Javier Solana speaks of "global homeland security."[13] Yet any "global" solution must be built by a coalition of nations committed to the effort, and the core to any effective global coalition is most often the transatlantic community. Close transatlantic cooperation is thus likely to provide the backbone to any effective multilateral action.[14] Winer provides a good example of how the Financial Action Task Force has advanced universal and global adoption of standards that were derived from cooperation between Europe and North America. There are many other such examples in many different fields. More often than not, transatlantic cooperation is a stepping stone, not an alternative, to broader global cooperation, not only in the UN Security Council but also in such specialized fora as the World Customs Organization or the International Civil Aviation Organization. Moreover, multilateral agreements and global standardization may take considerable time to achieve. Deeper transatlantic cooperation allows for quicker action while providing an important means to set the stage for broader global cooperation.

Five propositions

A more systematic approach to "transatlantic" societal security could be guided by five basic propositions.

1 *Integrate security into everyday life*

Societal security seeks to manage risk by integrating security as an organic, dynamic part of the normal course of business and the everyday elements of life, rather than compartmentalizing security, reacting to events, or being driven by piecemeal approaches. Societal security transcends governmental action to engage broader civil society and the private sector. Stephen Flynn makes a good analogy with the way modern societies have dealt with safety concerns over the past century:

> When the safety agenda first got underway, it was met with the same kind of public ambivalence as is the security agenda today. While most do not question the value of incorporating safety measures into the workplace, home and recreation elements of our lives, many of our fore-bears felt differently.[15]

Today, our challenge is to integrate standards for security, as we have with standards for safety, health and the environment.

Here there is room for exchange of good practice. As Jenkins notes, European countries compelled to deal with continuing terrorist campaigns have involved the public in intelligence collection, surveillance, and security. Similarly, "total defense" approaches typically envision specific tasks for citizens in the case of major threats or disasters. The goal is not a security state but an involved citizenry enabled to participate collectively in its own security, something for which there is tradition in both Europe and America. Jenkins highlights US Neighborhood Watch programs as an example, and offers a variety of suggestions in this field.

Antagonists wishing to inflict harm upon a society are interested in finding the key nodes where critical infrastructures connect. A focus on protecting the functions of society would seek to integrate security considerations into the design and daily operations of such systems – from oversight of food production to the guarding of airport perimeters, to the tracking and checking of ships. A societal security approach would identify potential vulnerabilities linked to the technological complexity of the modern world and seek to transform them into high-reliability systems.[16] This cannot be achieved without the active participation of the private sector, which actually owns and controls most of these networks. Some corporate leaders may resist, but safety makes sense for the bottom line and does not necessarily mean a decrease in productivity. The 24-hour rule in the cargo industry, for instance, has actually increased productivity.[17]

In short, societal security requires constructing dynamic layers of measures – identifying workable, cost-effective, and relatively unobtrusive measures, and then tying them together in such a way that each serves to reinforce the deterrent value of the other. Each of these layers may be imperfect, but collectively they increase the odds of prevention, protection, and response.[18]

2 Pay attention to pace as well as space

As many authors note, such efforts will remain a work in progress, for we are in a dynamic situation. Defense efforts oriented to "territorial integrity" are focused on protecting geographic space. Increasingly, however, it is pace, not just space, that must be at the core of planning for societal security.[19] Given rapid changes in technology and the growth of even more complex interdependent networks, our vulnerabilities will change over time. Anthony Cordesman describes the problem with respect to biological warfare, but in a manner that can be generalized to apply to other potential dangers:

> The most important single message that anyone can communicate in regard to biological weapons is that we face a very uncertain mix of existing threats, politics, commercial development and technology that will change constantly as far into the future as we will look. The issue is not what we know, but how little we know and how little we can predict.[20]

3 *Focus on reducing risk rather than perfecting security*

Efforts to advance societal security at home and abroad must proceed from the recognition that in an age of catastrophic terrorism there is no such thing as perfect security. It is impossible to stop every potential type of terrorist violence. We cannot protect every possible target, all the time, from every conceivable type of attack. The campaign will never entirely be "won." Terrorism is a threat that we must constantly combat if we are to reduce it to manageable levels so that we can live normal lives free of fear.[21] Cordesman again sums it up:

> Victory cannot be defined in terms of eradicating terrorism or eliminating risk. This war must be defined in much more limited terms. It will consist of reducing the threat of terrorism to acceptable levels – levels that allow us to go on with our lives in spite of the fact that new attacks are possible and that we may well see further and more serious tragedies.[22]

By focusing on preventing attacks that can cause large casualties, major economic or societal disruption, or severe political damage, nations can approach issues of societal security systematically and with a better chance of preventing future attacks on the scale of the September 11 or March 11 tragedies.

4 *Don't destroy what you are trying to protect*

Thirty years ago, the Baader-Meinhoff terrorist gang goaded German authorities to hit back at them in ways they believed would break the law and undermine Germany's hard-won democracy. They reasoned that the quickest way to wound the German Government would be to force it to break its own rules, corrupt its own nature, and generate mistrust between the government and the governed. This challenge is perhaps of even more relevance to democratic governments fighting international terrorism today.[23]

Brimmer illustrates how a number of the measures introduced to combat terrorism raise serious civil liberties concerns. In addition, abuses at Abu Ghraib and Guantanamo have undermined confidence in the US Administration and international support for the anti-terrorism campaign. If the campaign is not perceived to be legitimate, it is unlikely to be effective. If efforts to protect our societies from catastrophic disruption are not aligned with the freedoms of those societies, we endanger that which we are trying to protect.

The US and Europe can each learn from each other's experience with mechanisms that seek to advance security and liberty, such as sunset clauses and provisions for legislative oversight and judicial review. As Brimmer notes, if the US and Europe can help each other live up to their own standards, together they can help set human rights standards for the broader anti-terrorist campaign. But if concerns about civil liberties are widespread even in the West's most sophisticated and oldest democracies, how much worse are they likely be in countries without such strong traditions who are also cracking down on suspects? Failure to advance security with liberty has the potential to subvert other key priorities, such as transformation of the broader Middle East, where the overall trend throughout the Arab world has been a decline in social, political, and cultural freedoms in the name of greater security against terrorism.[24]

5   *Recognize that crime and war are merging*

The tendency in Europe to cast the challenge as one of crime and justice and the tendency in America to treat it as one of war and peace are each dangerously myopic. As Jenkins notes, catastrophic terrorism has blurred the lines between crime and war, and poses a new threat that requires the orchestration of efforts in both domains. A decade before September 11, military historian Martin van Creveld anticipated these developments:

> Terrorist organizations and operations will be profoundly affected by information age technologies, which will provide these non-state actors with global reach. Modern communications and transportation technologies will have a profound impact on this new battlefront. There will be no fronts and no distinctions between civilian and military targets. Laws and conventions of war will not constrain terrorists and their state sponsors from seeking innovative means, to include WMD, to attack non-military targets and inflict terrible carnage . . . Once the legal monopoly of armed force, long claimed by the state, is wrested out of its hands, existing distinctions between war and crime will break down.[25]

Most of the crucial battles in the campaign against terror around the world are not being fought by the military, but by police, judges, border officers, intelligence officers, and financial and banking officials. However, military force may be required at times, and in many circumstances military power may indeed need to be considered as an extension of law enforcement. Jenkins suggests that this is likely to lead to new categories of law enforcement and precision warfare, and new rules for operations, custody, and possible prosecution where law enforcement and armed conflict overlap.

Organizing for transatlantic societal security

During the late 1940s and early 1950s, Europeans and Americans responded together to the challenges facing their generation. The potential of catastrophic terrorism now challenges a new generation of Europeans and North Americans to reshape and reposition existing structures, and to devise new approaches that can help us respond more effectively to current threats. We should not settle for incremental, *ad hoc* adjustments to a system designed generations ago for a world that no longer exists. Instead we should supplement traditional efforts, which focused either on territorial security or emergency response, with a third layer of "societal" security as an integral component of our relationship. In the first instance, of course, each nation must look to improve its own capabilities; however, cooperation for societal security has become an urgent addition to the wider transatlantic agenda, and can be advanced on multiple tracks.

National efforts

Nationally, the US has yet to overcome the artificial distinctions between domestic and national security that continue to plague efforts in this area. The 9/11 Commission has made various proposals in this regard, such as merging the Homeland Security Council in the White House into the National Security Council; unifying strategic intelligence and operational planning against terrorism in a National Counterterrorism Center; and unifying the intelligence community under a National Intelligence Director.

Within Europe, national efforts are uneven, given differing traditions. European countries have yet to ratify and implement all UN counterterrorism conventions and protocols. Not all have criminalized material and logistical support for terrorism (and in some cases, terrorism itself). Laws against document fraud need to be strengthened. Not all have the ability to freeze terrorist assets. Legal or technical impediments to closer cooperation among countries on intelligence and information exchanges must be removed. Some countries have legal impediments to taking firm judicial action against suspected terrorists, often stemming from asylum laws that afford loopholes, inadequate counterterrorism legislation, or standards of evidence that lack flexibility in permitting law enforcement authorities to rely on classified-source information in holding terrorist suspects. The US is concerned that some European states have at times demonstrated an inability to prosecute successfully or hold terrorists brought before their courts. Moreover, new EU and NATO members have quite uneven capabilities when it comes to societal security. Many need assistance to strengthen their legal framework and develop their capabilities to counter terrorism.[26]

Finally, nations on both sides of the Atlantic need to mainstream societal security and counterterrorism into foreign policy, including through better coordination of development assistance to address root causes of terrorism; pursuing terrorists and those that sponsor them wherever they may be; and cooperating on various efforts at non-proliferation along the lines Morten Bremer or Brad Smith and I charted in earlier chapters, including significant "internationalization" and expansion of Nunn–Lugar programs.

Bilateral cooperation

Bilateral efforts between the US and individual European nations remain important even after EU enlargement, not only because such key partners as Turkey, Norway, Switzerland and others are not EU members, but also because even within the EU most of the instruments and competences in the fight against terrorism remain in the hands of member states. Although the EU can do a lot to help national authorities work together internationally, the hard work of tracking down potential terrorists, preventing attacks, and bringing suspects to justice remains the preserve of national authorities. Operational decisions are still national decisions. Moreover, even a shift of competences to the EU level is unlikely to lead the US to abandon its important bilateral relationships. In the intelligence field, for example, Jenkins notes that whatever intelligence function is created at the European level will coexist with national intelligence services, and while the US may bolster more direct and active cooperation with any new European structures, it will certainly maintain its existing networks.

The European Union

Better coordination among EU member states, however, could bring considerable dividends. European societies are inextricably intertwined in mutually dependent networks of information and finance, transportation and power generation, food production and health. These networks can only be protected successfully on a transnational basis. EU nations have made some modest improvements in their collective ability to cope with threats to those networks or direct attacks on European societies, but they still remain woefully unprepared. Various suggestions have been made to improve the situation, such as creation of an EU Homeland Security Agency to coordinate the homeland security activities of all member states, or an EU Joint Intelligence Committee to enhance the sharing of intelligence and the dissemination of classified information within the EU.[27] Many of these proposals may have merit, but institutional tinkering is unlikely to improve on-the-ground effectiveness absent a greater sense of urgency within EU nations about the danger and greater political will among EU leaders to unite their often disparate efforts.

NATO and the Partnership for Peace/Euro-Atlantic Partnership Council

In past years NATO reforms have focused on projecting force and coping with threats beyond the NATO area. But NATO's nations – and their partners – must be prepared not only to project power beyond Europe but also to prevent, deter, and if necessary cope with the consequences of WMD attacks on their societies – from any source. Territorial defense in the Cold War sense of protecting sealanes from Soviet submarines or guarding the Fulda Gap from Soviet tanks must give way to a new common conception of societal protection from WMD attacks from any source. If alliance governments fail to defend their societies from a major terrorist attack, potentially involving weapons of mass destruction, the Alliance will have failed in its most fundamental task. It will be marginalized, and the security of Europe and North America will be further diminished.[28]

In most countries these issues are primarily civilian, national, and local priorities. However, NATO has a role to play, particularly in civil–military planning capabilities and in consideration of missile defense. NATO's civilian disaster response efforts are still largely geared to natural disasters rather than intentional attacks, and remain very low priority. It is time to ramp up these efforts to address intentional WMD attacks on NATO territory, to develop more serious transatlantic efforts to protect critical infrastructure, to work with partners such as Russia to develop new capabilities and procedures for collaboration with civilian authorities, and to tap the expertise of partners who have had decades of experience with "total defense."

In fact, the area of "transatlantic societal security" could be an attractive new mission for a rejuvenated Partnership for Peace and its political umbrella, the Euro-Atlantic Partnership Council, since a bio-terrorist attack of contagious disease will not distinguish between "allies" and "partners," and a number of partners have more experience mobilizing for societal security than do many allies. Following the last round of NATO enlargement the Partnership for Peace is a strange mix of prosperous, non-aligned Western countries such as Sweden, Finland, Austria, Ireland, and Switzerland, and a number of Central Asian nations. It is precisely some of these non-aligned countries, however, which have decades of experience with approaches to societal defense, and it is precisely the area of Central Asia in which forward defense and preventive efforts against WMD threats are critical. NATO's special partnerships with Russia and Ukraine could also be utilized to good effect in this area.

Joint work on societal security could also infuse NATO–EU relations with a new sense of common purpose and lend substance to the "strategic partnership" each has declared yet neither has achieved. While both organizations are exploring how to strengthen their cooperation, they have little to show for it except for some successes in the Balkans. A joint focus on societal security, including consequence management, could inject new energy into their efforts, and both organizations have tools to offer.

US–EU cooperation

As has been noted repeatedly, key questions for a transatlantic approach to homeland security depend on the evolving dynamics of European integration. US–EU cooperative mechanisms are likely to evolve as the EU itself evolves. As various authors have suggested, it will be necessary to find new ways to combine or coordinate transatlantic efforts in law enforcement, intelligence, and other areas that operate at the member state level with efforts at infrastructure protection, health security, and other areas that are gradually beginning to be coordinated at the community level. Information-sharing will remain a critical yet difficult issue, given different legal regimes and political perspectives. As in so many other fields of policy, the key is to keep each other informed at an early stage of new policy proposals which might have an impact on the other, so that potential differences can be resolved before legislation is enacted.[29] A good example is the enhanced dialogue now in place on terrorism-related issues, such as the new Policy Dialogue on Border and Transport Security.

More can be done, however, not only to protect European and American societies directly, but also in joint or complementary efforts to help third countries in their fight against terrorism. Both sides could better coordinate their external assistance to relieve the endemic poverty, illiteracy, unemployment, and human misery that foster the resentment in which the support for terrorism can grow. Both sides could work harder on terrorist financing. Both could work more effectively to help third countries implement the UN Security Council Resolutions against terrorism. And, as Bremer argues, both sides could engage in "supply-side security" by working together to deny terrorists the means to carry out their acts of violence by securing highly enriched uranium and plutonium, as well as ensuring implementation of the Security Council resolution on weapons of mass destruction, seeking a successful outcome of the NPT 2005 Review Conference, rendering the Additional Protocol to the IAEA Safeguards system universal, and working to criminalize proliferation activities.[30]

It takes a network to beat a network

Repositioning existing structures will be important, but reliance on traditional alliance mechanisms or government-to-government relationships is likely to prove inadequate to the challenge of globally networked terrorism. It will take a network to beat a network. A key premise of effective societal security is layered defense, which suggests that traditional structures be supplemented by an overlay of informal networks including private as well as public actors and offering a denser web of preventive efforts. Traditional alliance mechanisms may be the densest weave in the web, but other connections will be needed to make the overall effort more effective.

Globalization is causing a shift from state-centric, territorial-based notions to stateless, network-based notions of power and vulnerability.[31] Al-Qaeda and related terrorist groupings are lethal networks, often with global reach. Such networks can be flexible and agile, constantly able to reconfigure themselves to address new challenges and seize new opportunities. They are networks that prey on other networks – the interconnected arteries and nodes of vulnerability that accompany the free flow of people, ideas, goods, and services, and the complex interdependent systems on which free societies depend. These range from global electronic financial networks, networked information systems, "just-in-time" supply chains and air, sea and land transportation to flows of fossil fuels or nuclear energy. It is our complete reliance on such networks, matched with their susceptibility to catastrophic disruption, that make them such tempting targets for terrorists.[32]

When al-Qaeda destroyed the World Trade Center towers, it engaged simultaneously in attacks on the global securities markets through simultaneous market manipulation, demonstrating that terrorists understand how interconnected, and vulnerable, the world's collective infrastructures are to attack.[33] Similar attacks would generate serious repercussions across many sectors and many borders. Accordingly, effective efforts at prevention and response need to cross borders, involve many players, and reach everywhere, leaving no area as a sanctuary. The US may not have needed military support from all countries to attack Osama bin Laden and his terrorist cronies in their Afghan sanctuary, but it does need law enforcement support from all countries to take down terrorist networks that are able to operate across the globe.

The new challenges are stateless and network-centric. However, government responses remain largely state-centric, are often caught in organizational stovepipes, and are conducted with inadequate processes and instruments. Since most of the critical infrastructures that terrorists might want to destroy or disrupt are linked to global networks, it is vital to include citizens and companies in any new societal security regime.[34] This will require governments to define national security more in societal than statist terms, and to move beyond traditional "public diplomacy" and "outreach" activities for NGOs toward more effective public–private networks.

In short, governments on both sides of the Atlantic should consider networking more seriously as a tool of foreign policy. During the 1980s and 1990s, military planners moved defense establishments into network-centric warfare, while business executives moved away from vertical hierarchies to flat structures and networked operations. Foreign ministries and other agencies of government need to undergo the same transformative process, and the need for more effective societal security can both frame and spark such new thinking.

Of course, governments are not starting from scratch. In a number of areas relevant to societal security the rigid trappings of state-to-state diplomacy have been giving way, gradually and unevenly, to new forms of interaction among state and non-state actors. Beyond the media glare on transatlantic squabbles the United States and its European allies have been forming their own complex, almost invisible and somewhat unconventional networks of cooperation that have become the foundation of joint efforts to freeze terrorist funds, toughen financial transparency measures, and bring aggressive threats of sanctions to those not cooperating. National governments are linking with their regulatory counterparts and the private sector across the globe to tackle thorny transnational issues such as money laundering, securities fraud, and drug trafficking. Governments are finding that such networks can be fast, flexible, cheap, and effective. They can lower the cost of collective action, and enable large and disparate groups to organize and influence events faster and better than before. They can build capacities without building bureaucracies.

Both Lewis and Winer underscore that solutions for transatlantic societal security will depend increasingly upon these new forms of cooperation among state and non-state actors. Such efforts have been led almost entirely by institutions that are neither nation states, regional unions, multilateral organizations, or international organizations, but rather informal networks of law enforcement agencies, regulators, and the private sector. Winer describes how "international non-organizations" such as the Financial Action Task Force (FATF), the Egmont group or the Lyon Group can make a difference by setting standards and attacking nodes of terrorist or criminal activity. These structures developed in response to particular crises in the global financial system, as stakeholders came to realize from painful experience that transborder financial crime, including money laundering, terrorist finance, the theft and sequestration of national patrimonies by corrupt officials, and stock market and investment fraud, contributed to such serious domestic problems as drug trafficking, immigrant smuggling, insurance crime, and terrorism. By naming and shaming miscreants and threatening to block their access to the world's two most important markets, the Europeans and North Americans at the core of such networks began to produce practical results.

Such groups might offer models for similar networked cooperation in related fields. For instance, a Chemical Action Task Force was created at the same time as the FATF, but it collapsed because the governments involved did not then consider the issue to be urgent. It may be useful now to revisit this initiative. It may be equally worthwhile to create transatlantic biosecurity networks linking public health authorities, medical laboratories, and emergency responders to those charged with national security. The 9/11 Commission has proposed unifying the many participants in the US domestic counterterrorism effort and their knowledge in a network-based information-sharing system that transcends traditional bureaucratic boundaries. An international dimension to such an effort would also be essential, and if it were to be launched it would most likely begin with America's closest allies. Partnerships exist between US state National Guards and various European nations, but they have focused on traditional emergency response. Such partnerships could be extended and focused on best-practice exchange on prevention, response to, and recovery from catastrophic attack.

Other networks are emerging as well. Local police departments in the United States, for example, have established their own direct liaison with allied police forces outside the country to learn lessons from recent terrorist attacks and facilitate the flow of intelligence. Major police departments in Europe, such as Scotland Yard, have also encouraged the development of networks across national boundaries to share best practices in various aspects of homeland security. These police-to-police linkages often exist outside the formal treaty relations between national intelligence services, as well as outside the more confined operating space of Interpol or Europol.

Such networks aim to protect the critical nodes of activity that connect modern societies while attacking the critical nodes of those networks that would do us harm. Nodal strategies give higher priority to creating an environment hostile to all antagonists than to investing inordinate resources in chasing any particular offender. The "war" on drugs, for instance, has proven to be less effective against drug dealers themselves than against the nodes where drugs are being laundered. Similarly, freezing the assets of any particular terrorist grouping may be less important than sectoral regulation and enforcement that eliminate the very nodes that finance terror. Nodal strategies must be nimble and able to change tactics to match those of their opponents. For instance, while cooperative efforts have successfully driven al-Qaeda away from banks, the amount of funds raised by al-Qaeda and related groups has actually increased, as their funding base expands from other unconventional sources. Having squeezed the banking node, enforcement efforts now need to turn to these other sources. In each relevant sector the ultimate objective must be to create a loose, agile but muscular public–private network capable of responding to the terrorists' own transnational networks.

Conclusion

The early years of the twenty-first century have been rough on transatlantic relations, yet despite some rather spectacular squalls there have been significant, if highly uneven, efforts to protect European and North American societies in ways that span the transatlantic space.

Europeans and Americans again face a new era. The open question is

194 *Daniel S. Hamilton*

whether we are prepared to face it together. Our economies and our societies are too deeply intertwined to allow transatlantic divorce, but we do face the very real possibility of transatlantic dysfunction in the face of dangers that blur the lines between domestic and international security and between crime and war, and that neither Europeans nor Americans will be able to tackle alone.

This volume has provided considerable evidence that separate or competitive approaches are likely to prove inadequate to the common challenge of catastrophic terrorism. A broad transatlantic campaign to confront this threat will require comprehensive cooperation among intelligence officials, police, diplomats, the military, medical doctors, public health authorities and first responders, customs and financial institutions, the private sector, and individual citizens. It will force us to understand more clearly where and why we agree, and where – due to different national experiences and perspectives – our approaches may need to be reconciled. It will mean aligning Europe's grand yet difficult experiment of integration with a reorientation and strategic transformation of transatlantic relations to create new models of Atlantic partnership. Victory will be piecemeal and incremental. In President Bush's words, it will require a "patient accumulation of success." The alternative could be tragedy on a scale exceeding even the horrors of the bloody century we have left behind.

Notes

1 See J. Stevenson, "How Europe and America defend themselves," *Foreign Affairs*, March/April 2003.
2 For critiques of the US national effort, with additional proposals, see S. Flynn, *America the Vulnerable: How Our Government is Failing to Protect Us from Terrorism*, New York: HarperCollins, 2004; and a report by Brookings Institution writers, *Protecting the American Homeland*, Washington, DC: Brookings Institution Press, 2002.
3 See D. Hamilton, *Die Zukunft ist nicht mehr, was sie war: Europa, Amerika und die neue weltpolitische Lage*, Stuttgart: Robert Bosch Stiftung, 2001.
4 See "One nation after all," *The Economist*, 11 September 2004, p. 32.
5 After September 11 the mutual defense clause of the North Atlantic Treaty was invoked for the first time, on behalf of the United States.
6 Flynn, op. cit., pp. 50–54.
7 There are legal constraints reinforcing this dichotomy. The Posse Comitatus Act, passed in the aftermath of the Civil War, sets legal limits on the role of the military within the United States. See the Legal Information Institute, Cornell Law School. Available online at: www4.law.cornell.edu/uscode/18/1385.html; Flynn, op. cit., p. 38.
8 Flynn, op. cit., pp. 50–51.
9 I am indebted to Bengt Sundelius and Jan Metzger for insights into these approaches. See, for example, B. Sundelius, "From National Total Defence to Embedded Societal Security," pre-publication draft presented to the Center for Transatlantic Relations, February, 2004, in the possession of the author; J. Metzger and J.-P. Kessler, "Homeland Security Country Profile Switzerland," (forthcoming publication, in the possession of the author); B. Buzan, *People,*

States and Fear: The National Security Problem in International Relations, Brighton: Wheatsheaf, 1983. For further information on these evolving efforts, see the reports of the various Nordic Vulnerability Commissions: the Danish Vulnerability Commission (National Sårbarhedsudredning), January 2004, Beredskabsstyrelsen. Available online at: www.im.dk//imagesupload/dokument/ Sårbarhedsudredning.pdf; the Finnish Vulnerability Commission (Strategi för Tryggandet av Samhällets Livsviktiga Funktioner), Ministry of Defence, Finland, 2003, available online at: www.defmin.fi/chapter_images/1688_ Strategi_fOr_tryggande_av_samhAllets_livsviktiga_funktioner.pdf; the Norwegian Commission on the Vulnerable Society, The Directorate for Civil Protection and Emergency Planning; and the Swedish Vulnerability Commission, Säkerhet i ny tid – SOU 2001:41. Available online at: www.regeringen.se/ content/1/c4/39/05/244fe2ba.pdf.

10 Sundelius, op. cit.

11 For basic information, see the CCS website. Available online at: www.ukresilience.info/home.htm.

12 For other assessments and reports, see the *Non-confidential Report on the Terrorism Situation and Trends in Europe*, EU TE-SAT 14280/2/02, pp. 19–27; J. Wright, "Terrorism in Europe Since 9/11: Responses and Challenges," available online at www.cdu.edu.au/cdss2003/papers/Sym3papers/joannewright.pdf; D. Butler, "3 arrested over ties to Muslim Militants," *International Herald Tribune*, 29 November 2003; "Die Saudi-Connection," *Der Spiegel*, 14/2003, pp. 70–72; J. Henley, "Al-Qaida terror plot foiled, say French police," *Guardian*, 12 January 2004.

13 On 4 November 2002, during a visit to Brussels, DHS Secretary Ridge stated "[o]ne of the conclusions we drew early on – and I think it's one that our friends in Europe concluded, perhaps before much of the world – was that the reach of terrorism is global, that targets are global in nature, and that at the end of the day the 21st century world needs to find global solutions to global vulnerabilities." "Homeland Security Advisor Ridge in Brussels for EU, NATO meetings – 4 November 2002," available online at www.useu.be/Terrorism/EUResponse/.

14 See D. Hamilton, *Renewing Transatlantic Partnership: Why and How?* Testimony to the House Committee on International Relations, 11 June 2003.

15 See Flynn, op. cit., pp. 61–64.

16 Sundelius, op. cit.

17 Remarks by Eugene Pendimonti, Vice President of Maersk Sealand, to the Center for Transatlantic Relations, 13 September 2004.

18 Flynn, op. cit., pp. 69–70.

19 Sundelius, op. cit., p. 3.

20 A. Cordesman, *Biological Warfare and the "Buffy Paradigm,"* Washington, DC: Center for Strategic and International Studies, 2001, p. 1.

21 Flynn, op. cit.; Bruce Hoffman, Presentation to Open Road 2002, Atlantic Command Transformation, Norfolk, VA, January 2002.

22 Cordesman, op. cit., p. 4.

23 Alyson Bailes recalls this challenge in "Have the Terrorists Already Won?" Speaking Notes, Scanbus Conference, Riga, 14 September 2004. For a review of German efforts to confront terrorism then and now, see O. Lepsius, *The Relationship between Security and Civil Liberties in the Federal Republic of Germany After September 11*, Washington, DC: American Institute for Contemporary German Studies, 2001, available online at: www.aicgs.org/Publications/PDF/lepsius english.pdf.

24 Bailes, op. cit., p. 2.

25 M. van Creveld, *The Transformation of War*, New York: The Free Press, 1991.

26 The EU has earmarked more than 1 billion euros to continue assisting the new

member states in the field of internal security during the period 2004–2006. See Gijs DeVries, European Union Counter-Terrorism Coordinator, to the hearing by the Subcommittee on Europe of the House Committee on International Relations, 15 September 2004. For an official US view of European shortcomings, see the testimony by William Pope, Principal Deputy Coordinator for Counterterrorism, US Department of State, at the same hearing.

27 See, for example, the report of the Venusberg Group: J. Lindley-French and F. Algieri, *A European Defense Strategy*, Gütersloh: Bertelsmann Foundation, 2004, p. 42.

28 See D. S. Hamilton, "Renewing Transatlantic Partnership: Why and How," Testimony to the House Committee on International Relations, European Subcommittee, 11 June 2003; "Our Transatlantic Homeland," available online at www.raeson.dk/indexenglish.htm; and "What is Transformation and What Does It Mean for NATO?," in D. S. Hamilton (ed), *Transatlantic Transformations: Equipping NATO for the 21st Century*, Washington, DC: Center for Transatlantic Relations, 2004.

29 de Vrijs, op. cit.

30 For a European perspective, see the address by Gijs de Vries to the CSIS European Dialogue, 13 May 2004.

31 See J.-M. Guehenno, *The End of the Nation-State*, Minneapolis: University of Minnesota Press, 2000.

32 Flynn, op. cit., p. 86.

33 See J. Winer, *The Role of Economic Sanctions in Combating International Terrorism (and its Place in the Trans-Atlantic Alliance)*, Washington, DC: American Institute for Contemporary German Studies, 2001, available online at: www.aicgs.org/Publications/PDF/Winer.pdf.

34 Flynn provides a variety of proposals, op. cit., p. 166.

Index

References to tables and figures are in *italics*.